THE GRANGEGORMAN MURDERS

Dean Lyons, Mark Nash and the Story behind the Grangegorman Murders

ALAN BAILEY

Gill & Macmillan

Gill & Macmillan
Hume Avenue, Park West, Dublin 12
www.gillmacmillanbooks.ie

© Alan Bailey 2015
978 07171 5433 3

Typography design by Make Communication
Print origination by Síofra Murphy
Printed and bound by ScandBook AB, Sweden

This book is typeset in Minion 12/14.5 pt.

The paper used in this book comes from the wood pulp
of managed forests. For every tree felled, at least one
tree is planted, thereby renewing natural resources.

A CIP catalogue record for this book is available from
the British Library.

5 4 3 2 1

CONTENTS

| LOCUS IN QUO

Number 1 Orchard View is a two-storey four-bedroom end-of-terrace house on Upper Grangegorman, Dublin, at the junction with Marne Villas and Rathdown Road, almost directly opposite the main entrance to St Brendan's Psychiatric Hospital. The terrace itself comprises five similar houses, all of which were owned in 1997 by the Eastern Health Board as part of its community housing scheme. At that time the board owned and operated 106 houses under the scheme, 36 of which were in the vicinity of Orchard View. A total of 930 people lived in the houses.

The residents were for the most part former long-term psychiatric patients, a large number of whom had at one time or other been in-patients in St Brendan's. The aim of the community housing scheme was that through living in the community, in conditions as near to normal as possible, former long-term patients could be assisted towards normalisation and eventual full reintegration in society. Ultimately, except in extreme cases, it was hoped that the scheme would replace institutional care.

Numbers 1 and 2 Orchard View catered for residents who lived independently, while numbers 3 to 5, which were connected internally, had a nurse on duty in them at all times to provide professional support for the twelve residents, none of whom were considered to be as stable as the seven former patients who lived in numbers 1 and 2.

To the front of number 1 was a three-foot wall, while the side and rear gardens were enclosed behind a six-foot wall, with a wicket gate allowing access between the front and rear gardens. Internally, the downstairs comprised two separate reception rooms together with a fully fitted kitchen in the return. A staircase led from the front hallway to a short landing, with three further steps leading to a bedroom and a communal bathroom, both of them in the return. A sharp left turn off the same short corridor led to a further three bedrooms, two with windows facing the front and a third with its window looking out onto the side and rear of the house.

The hospital itself is laid out on an enclosed 75-acre site, with controlled access through the main entrance and further access through its emergency admissions ward. The site comprises a large number of separate granite-fronted buildings. Grangegorman Road Lower bisects the site, with the two sections connected by a tunnel running under the road.

Over the years the number of in-patients in St Brendan's has fallen off considerably, as a result of the community housing scheme and other ventures, and as the wards emptied they were closed down. By 1997 the section of the hospital on the Orchard View side of the road had been fully emptied and had fallen into disrepair.

Chapter 2

LAYOUT AND OCCUPANCY OF THE HOUSE ON 6 MARCH 1997

On the night of Thursday 6 March 1997 only three of the four bedrooms at number 1 Orchard View were occupied. The occupant of the fourth bedroom, a box room to the front of the house, had been asked to leave by the hospital authorities on 16 January 1997, following a number of complaints by the other residents. The only male in the house, he had been in the habit of allowing callers, including women, to visit and stay late in his room. When he moved out he left most of his personal belongings in the room.

Mary Callinan slept in the large bedroom to the front of the house. She was sixty-one years old, having celebrated her birthday three days earlier. A single woman, she had been an in-patient in St Brendan's since 1966, a victim of paranoid schizophrenia. In 1986 she had transferred from the hospital to a local high-support hostel and from there had graduated to a low-support hostel and eventually to independent living. She had lived at Orchard View since 1988. She was described by the hospital staff as 'high-functioning'.

Mary was an only child, both of whose parents had died in the early 1960s, which had precipitated her breakdown. She had left school at sixteen and until being committed to the hospital had worked in a number of factories. By all accounts both her parents had been loving and caring and her upbringing had been, for the most part, uneventful. At the time of her death she was working as a general operative in a sheltered workshop in the Finglas area. She had a good relationship with her colleagues and supervisors.

Sylvia Sheils was sixty and had first been admitted to St Brendan's for a short period in 1980. Also a single woman, she was readmitted in 1983 with a diagnosis of chronic schizophrenia and severe borderline personality disorder and also epilepsy. In the mid-1980s she had been moved out of the hospital into sheltered accommodation in nearby Stanhope Terrace and in 1994 moved to Orchard View.

In 1987 Sylvia had been made redundant by the civil service. With a modest pension, she lived frugally, though she was considered by her peers to be 'well off' because she had both a pension and a bank account! Described by them as a bubbly and friendly person, she was well liked. She was also an avid reader. She was one of three children from a close-knit and supportive family, all of whom stayed in touch with one another.

Sylvia's bedroom adjoined that of Mary, and she worked in the same sheltered workshop. She was well known in the locality and regularly called in to the nearby Clarke's bakery to buy confectionery as a treat for the other residents. The workers in the bakery described her as being very pleasant as well as thoughtful.

Ann Mernagh, the third resident, had moved into the house only in late 1996. She was considerably younger than the other two women, being forty-six at the time. However, they all mixed well together and were close friends. Ann had first come to the attention of the psychiatric services as early as 1973, when she was twenty-two, following an unsuccessful attempt to take her own life. A severe borderline personality disorder was diagnosed, and she also suffered from epilepsy. She had a long history of unstable moods and a tendency to self-harm. She claimed to have been sexually abused as a child, some of her episodes of self-harm resulting in mutilation of her genital area. She had been transferred to St Brendan's in 1986, having been found to be generally unmanageable. By 1990, however, she had graduated to sheltered accommodation and in September 1996 moved into number 1 Orchard View. (The date of her moving into the house will be shown later to have played a significant role in this investigation.) She worked in a sheltered workshop in the hospital grounds.

Ann's bedroom was at the end of the short corridor opening off the top of the stairs in the return portion of the building. Next to her bedroom was the bathroom and toilet. A sharp left turn at the top of the stairs led to the narrow hallway running towards the front of the house, off the right-hand side of which Mary's and Sylvia's rooms both opened, with the vacant bedroom facing directly onto the corridor.

Evidence of the length of time all the occupants had spent in sheltered accommodation was obvious throughout the house, including the regimented way in which items were neatly arranged and the manner in which the breakfast table was set in advance for the following morning. The house was spotless, entirely free of clutter and all surfaces gleaming. Each resident had her own delph and cutlery and her agreed space in the fridge and cupboards.

The downstairs front room had a television set and four armchairs arranged around a low coffee table. The middle room contained the dining-room table, all set for breakfast, and an ironing-board. These were the only items of furniture in the two rooms. The spotless kitchen was at the rear of the house; the only things out of place were those that had been disturbed by the intruder.

The kitchen window looked out onto the enclosed yard. It was a sash window with four separate panes of glass, each approximately two feet by one foot. Both the top and bottom sash could be opened only to a depth of about six inches; after an earlier break-in in December 1996 hospital maintenance workers had fastened pieces of wood to the frame to prevent it being opened any further. No-one was ever charged with that burglary, and nothing of any value was taken. It could never be established whether that break-in had any connection with the murders or was a random crime.

The back yard is enclosed by a six-foot wall. The wicket gate in the wall had no lock, but a discarded cooker kept it permanently closed. The Gardaí would subsequently establish, however, that any pressure on the door could force the cooker back enough to allow access to the yard.

Ann Mernagh was to be the sole survivor of the events that occurred in the house on the night of 6/7 March 1997. She married in 1999, to another former patient, and in 2001 they moved together into a Dublin City Council flat in Drumalee Grove off the North Circular Road. But tragedy was to follow her. In early 2005 Ann left home early in the morning to take her dog for a walk. On her return she found her flat ablaze and her husband, James, who at this time was partially bedridden, dead from injuries he received. It appears that he managed to crawl as far as the front door but had been unable to reach up to open the lock. It was later established that the fire had broken out in his bed when he had dozed off while smoking. Ann, whose own physical health had also deteriorated over the years, died the following year.

Chapter 3 ᔐ

THE DISCOVERY OF THE CRIME

A t 8 p.m. on the evening of Thursday 6 March 1997 Ann
Mernagh left the house at 1 Orchard View to attend a bingo
session in the parochial hall in nearby Prussia Street. As she
was leaving she said goodbye to Sylvia Sheils and Mary Callinan, who
were in the front room watching television. They had both declined
her offer to bring them back chips from the chip shop, saying they
intended retiring early, as they were both due at work the following
morning.

On her way to the parochial hall Ann met a resident from one of
the other houses. She asked him if he would call to her house and tell
Mary or Sylvia to make sure that Ann had unplugged the iron she had
been using. He called briefly and spoke to Sylvia, who made sure all
was in order while he was still there.

Ann had won about £10 at the session and was in great form when
leaving. The parochial hall is almost directly opposite a house set in
flats where, it was discovered many months later, Mark Nash, who
would later be arrested for a double murder in Co. Roscommon, was
then living with his partner and their young child. Ann called in to the
chip shop and bought two bags of chips, one for herself and one for
the nurse on night duty in number 5. This was a regular habit of Ann's.

As she walked along Kirwan Street towards Grangegorman she
walked past the entrance of a laneway, a cul de sac at the rear of
Stanhope Street Convent School. In 1986 a young local woman, coming

home from a disco in the Rumours night-club attached to the Gresham Hotel, had shared a taxi with a stranger as far as the corner of Kirwan Street and Manor Street. She had alighted and begun to walk towards home. Unknown to her, the stranger had also got out of the taxi and followed her into Kirwan Street, where he had dragged her down the laneway, sexually assaulted her, and then strangled her. He had then fled the scene. The following day, during technical examination of the scene, a pair of reading glasses was found. I was one of a party of gardaí who would spend several weeks trawling through the records of various opticians' offices throughout the city and adjoining counties. Eventually the owner of the glasses was found, and he admitted to the murder of the unfortunate young woman.

I have to admit that I was somewhat sceptical about that line of inquiry at the time, and I was not alone in this. However, Chief Superintendent John Courtney, the officer in charge of the then murder squad, was insistent on the job being done properly, having some years earlier solved the murder of an off-duty garda in much the same way.

Ann called into number 5 Orchard View and spoke briefly to the nurse after giving her the bag of chips. She then went into her own house, where she found that her two friends were in bed. She went into Sylvia's room and told her about her good luck at the bingo. Sylvia congratulated her, and Ann then went to bed. She did not disturb Mary. The time was 11:30 p.m.

Ann had always encountered great difficulty in getting to sleep. However, following advice from the various doctors she attended, she always had a personal cassette-player with her in bed, which she listened to through earphones. She also slept with her head covered by a blanket, a legacy, it is believed, of her being sexually abused in her youth. In a strange twist, it would possibly be these habits that, on this particular night, would save her life.

At 6 a.m. Ann got up and, putting on her dressing-gown against the early-morning chill, went downstairs to make breakfast for herself and her friends, a task she carried out every morning. As she walked downstairs she saw that her handbag, which she had left on the coffee table in the front room before going to bed, was lying on the ground at the foot of the stairs, its contents strewn on the floor. She gingerly stepped over the bag and walked towards the kitchen. As she passed the door of the dining-room she noticed that the light was on in the room. She would never have gone to bed the previous night or, with her training, any other night and left a light on. Now she saw what appeared to be smears of blood on the light-switch. Becoming increasingly apprehensive, she walked into the kitchen.

The first thing she saw on turning on the kitchen light was the curtain blowing in and out. One of the kitchen drawers had been removed from the unit and left lying on the floor. Beside it she saw what appeared to be shards of glass. Believing that the house had been burgled again, she ran out of the kitchen and up the stairs, calling out Sylvia's name at the top of her voice. Not receiving any answer, she burst in the bedroom door, turning on the light as she did so. She would later tell the liaison gardaí who were appointed to look after her, Chris Kelly and Ann Markey, that the sight that greeted her in Sylvia's room would stay in her mind for ever.

Sylvia lay across her bed, with her feet planted firmly apart on the floor, facing the door. Her nightdress was pushed up as far as her chest, which was exposed. Ann could clearly see that there was blood on her neck and chest and also on the sheets. She approached her friend and shook her gently, all the time calling out her name in a low voice. As she placed her hand on Sylvia she felt cold. She later said, 'I knew then that she was dead.'

Panicking, and fearing that the person who had done this to her friend might still be in the house, watching her and waiting to attack her, Ann rushed downstairs without going in to check on Mary. She threw open the front door—noticing as she did so that the safety chain she had engaged before going to bed was off—and ran out into the middle of the road. She would later be asked how long she had spent outside on the road but would be unable to estimate it. She said that the sight of Sylvia had made her frightened and disoriented. A lorry driver delivering a load to Nolan's fish factory nearby would later tell the Gardaí that he had observed a woman in a dressing-gown pacing up and down outside number 1, seeming to be in an agitated state. He had not taken any action, believing that she was a patient in the hospital.

Slowly regaining some control, Ann began to realise that she had not checked on Mary. Fearing also that Sylvia's attacker might still be in the house, she ran to number 5, screaming for the nurse on duty to help her. When Nurse Mona Long (not her real name) answered the door she was faced with a hysterical Ann Mernagh, whom she brought inside and eventually managed to calm down sufficiently to make some sense of what she was trying to say.

By this time the noise and shouting had woken all the other residents in this and the adjoining houses. Fearing that Ann's behaviour and hysterical outbursts would upset all the others, Mona took her into a separate room. Ann told her that Sylvia was dead, that her throat had been cut and that her pillow and bedclothes were covered in blood.

Nurse Long rang the security office at the main gate of the hospital a short distance away and requested immediate assistance. She also, as protocol demanded, contacted the assistant chief nursing officer on duty in the hospital.

The two security men on duty at the main gate ran from the security hut to the house. Ann, when running out of the house, had left the front door open, and they both entered number 1. They stepped over the discarded handbag and went upstairs, shouting as they climbed that they were hospital security.

The first room they entered was Ann's own room. Finding nothing untoward there, they went into the next room, which was the bathroom. Becoming somewhat sceptical, they turned the short corridor and walked towards the front of the house. The first room they passed had a light on, and looking in they saw the body of a woman partially on the bed. They then walked on into the next bedroom and on looking in saw an unmade bed. The room appeared to be empty, but as they were turning to leave the room one of the men glanced down and saw a pair of legs on the ground on the opposite side of the bed, protruding between the bed itself and the front wall of the house. Without going any further into the room, and satisfied that this person was also dead, they left and went back downstairs. There they met the chief nursing officer, who was accompanied by the hospital doctor on call. The doctor briefly visited both bedrooms and looked without success for any signs of life.

All those present in the house at this time also noticed the broken glass in the kitchen window.

The doctor immediately went to number 5, where he examined Ann, who was becoming increasingly distressed as the enormity of what had happened began to dawn on her. She was treated for shock and then taken into the main hospital for observation and further treatment. The other residents of the five houses, who were becoming disturbed as news of the horrific fate of their friends filtered down to them, were also becoming agitated, and further medical assistance was sought for them also. Given her fragile mental state, Ann would from then onwards, following an arrangement between the Gardaí and the hospital authorities, be interviewed only with a medical person present.

Chapter 4

THE ARRIVAL OF THE GARDAÍ AT THE SCENE

Gardaí at the nearby Bridewell Garda Station were alerted by telephone by the hospital authorities. A patrol car manned by Susan McLaughlin and Michael McGrath was immediately despatched to the scene. Also in the car was a recruit garda who was being mentored by Garda McLaughlin. The gruesome sight that greeted him on what must have been one of his first days on duty would lead to his tendering his resignation within weeks. Happily, having spent some years working abroad, he returned to Ireland and rejoined the Garda Síochána, where he forged a successful career.

The gardaí logged their time of arrival at the scene as 6:20 a.m.

The scene and its immediate environs were immediately secured, and the names of all those who had entered the house that morning were established. When the gravity of the situation was relayed to the Bridewell Station, Sergeant Gerry McCarthy was sent over to take charge of the preservation of the scene. Using a roll of crime-scene tape he cordoned off the scene, including a large area of the public road outside the house.

I was contacted by phone at home and directed by the sergeant in charge at the Bridewell to go directly to the scene and ensure that all the necessary procedures were followed. I arrived at 7 a.m. and immediately requested that an independent doctor be contacted and asked to come to the scene to formally pronounce death. This is a requirement that gardaí must comply with before contacting the coroner's office to obtain permission to engage the services of the state pathologist.

At 7:15 a.m. Dr Tom Flood (not his real name) arrived at the scene. I had worked with him on other murder investigations and knew him to be a reliable witness and one well versed in technical examination and in giving evidence. We both donned white forensic suits—overalls, gloves, masks and overshoes—a supply of which I kept in the boot of my car. Introducing ourselves for recording purposes to the garda in charge of scene preservation, we entered number 1.

The sight that greeted me there will remain etched on my memory for the rest of my life. I am often asked if gardaí and detectives ever get used to viewing murder scenes and murder victims. Having visited and viewed these two victims *in situ* I can honestly say that I hope never to regard any murder scene as normal.

On entering the scene, Dr Flood and myself went directly to the bedrooms, our role there being confined to the official pronouncing of death. In his subsequent report the doctor described in detail the various observable injuries suffered by the two victims and the positions in which they had been found. He would also make further comments about a number of strange details concerning Mary Callinan. He would note that her nightdress was pulled up around her breasts, and that she wore a slipper on one foot only. Most upsetting, however, was the presence of a red object protruding from her vagina, the blade of an electric carving-knife lying across her stomach, and a similar blade lying on the ground in close proximity to the body.

At 7:22 a.m. Sylvia Sheils was formally pronounced dead, and at 7:24 a.m. the doctor pronounced Mary Callinan dead also. He found that full rigor mortis was present in Sylvia's body, while the process had not yet begun in Mary's.

Rigor mortis—the 'stiffness of death'—is one of the most recognisable signs of death. A chemical change after death causes the limbs to become stiff and difficult to manipulate. It begins between two and six hours after death, starting with the eyelids, neck and jaw. Over the next four to six hours it spreads to all the muscles, including internal muscles. Maximum stiffness occurs within twelve hours, and then it begins to dissipate, which can take anything up to three days.

The presence of rigor mortis is considered an approximate indicator of time of death. However, it is far from exact, given that so many factors can affect it, including body mass, muscle mass, age, sex, and the surrounding temperature.

In this instance what we had achieved so far in our inquiry would be considered good 'textbook' investigation. Within an hour and a half of the discovery of the bodies the scene had been cordoned off, a number of witnesses to the finding of the bodies had been identified, the formal pronouncing of death had been made, and a witness who appeared to have been in the murder house and survived had been found, was medically treated and in hospital.

As I left the scene that morning to alert other members of the Bridewell Detective Unit and to brief my superiors I couldn't help but feel a bit smug about how the investigation was progressing at this early stage. Little did I know what lay ahead with this investigation, or that it would take fifteen years to resolve. Had I known I might not have felt so pleased with myself.

I returned to the scene at 10 a.m., where I met Prof. John Harbison, the chief state pathologist. A full team from the Garda Technical Bureau, consisting of members from the Photographic, Fingerprint, Mapping and Ballistics Sections, were present, having been requested by Superintendent James Joyce, then the officer in charge of the Bridewell Station.

In all instances where a body has been found and foul play is suspected the scene must be preserved and 'frozen' to allow the pathologist to view the body *in situ*. This takes precedence over all other procedures. There are some very special occasions when a body can be removed before this—for example when medical intervention might be attempted, when leaving a body might be a source of danger to other people, or when leaving it in place might cause it to suffer further damage or actual loss. Other than that, the body remains in the situation and in the position it was found in.

For the second time that morning I donned a forensic suit. I accompanied Prof. Harbison and briefed him about the extent and nature of the examination performed by the doctor earlier. By coincidence, we were joined that morning by Dr Marie Cassidy, who is now chief state pathologist, having succeeded Prof. Harbison. She had arrived at Dublin Airport that morning to begin her first day as deputy chief state pathologist. On learning of her impending arrival the Garda authorities had despatched a car and a fast driver to the airport to bring her directly to the scene. Instead of being met and briefed by Prof. Harbison about her new role she would find herself having to attend a double murder scene.

During his examination of the bodies *in situ* that morning Prof. Harbison, speaking in his usual clipped and formal manner, referred to what he found at the scene as 'carnage'. Despite this, however, he pointed out that the area surrounding the scenes showed 'remarkable cleanliness'. His preliminary examination of Sylvia's body established that she had suffered an incised wound to her throat, measuring some four inches in length. He pointed out a number of superficial knife strokes on her abdomen, with further bloodstaining visible on the inside of her thighs adjacent to her vulva. Although the body lay across the bed, there was, he said, very little spraying of blood on either the bed itself or the bedroom walls adjacent to the bed. He noted that she was dressed in a black slip and white vest. Around her left thigh was the leg opening of a pair of pants, with the rest hanging almost to the floor.

During the examination of Mary's body he found a number of what appeared to be puncture wounds to the front of her chest. A long incision ran from her upper lip across her cheek. There were a number of wounds to her left breast, and on her abdomen he noted a number of linear marks that appeared to have been made by at least two separate blades. He also remarked on the foreign object embedded in her vagina.

Throughout our visit to the scene I noticed that the pathologist was unusually quiet. He would normally maintain a running commentary on his observations, both at the scene and with the body, drawing attention to a particular type of injury or to a blood pattern or spattering. I found his silence disquieting. He always addressed plain-clothes gardaí he met when visiting scenes, no matter what their rank, by the formal title of Mister. As we left the scene that day he turned to me and said, 'You know, Mr Bailey, what we have just witnessed in that premises is outside my experience, built up in almost twenty years of visits to crime scenes and the examination of injuries inflicted on one human being by another.'

At this pronouncement I felt the hairs stand up on the back of my neck. Here was a man who must have visited 90 per cent of all the murder scenes in this jurisdiction since the early 1970s saying, in his own inimitable style, that he had never seen anything like the murders of Sylvia Sheils and Mary Callinan. Describing a scene as 'carnage' was not something you expected from him. I felt that one could not give a more chilling summation of a crime scene.

Those words would remain with me as we set out to establish who could have perpetrated such a crime and what that person would look like, think like, and be like.

Chapter 5

THE POST-MORTEM EXAMINATIONS

The bodies of Sylvia Sheils and Mary Callinan would remain at the scene until seven o'clock that evening. They were then removed to the City Morgue in Store Street, next door to Store Street Garda Station. Garda Michael McGrath, who had been at the scene almost continuously since shortly after 6 a.m., accompanied both bodies.

When a body is being removed for post-mortem examination a member of the Gardaí must accompany it. The reason for this policy is that the garda will subsequently give evidence at any trial, firstly that there was no incident en route that might have caused any of the injuries found on the body and secondly that the body had remained in police custody until the completion of all the examinations.

As the hearse was driven from the scene that evening I was struck by the silence that descended on the huge crowd of onlookers that had been forming throughout the day. Certainly the reporters present were well used to attending at such venues, yet even they seemed moved by it all. They watched as the bodies of the two innocent victims, who had endured savagery almost beyond comprehension, were taken from their home, a home that should have been theirs to enjoy for many more years.

Even at that early stage the rumour machine was in full swing. Bloodcurdling tales of cannibalism and trophy-taking of body parts were circulating freely. Given that, before total lock-down by our team, the scene had been visited by at least five people, this was understandable. The enormity of the crimes committed against two gentle and defenceless elderly souls appeared to have left everyone shocked.

For my own part, the scenes I witnessed at first hand in that house—the carnage, as Prof. Harbison had called it—were ones that I would never forget. The indignities caused by the wounds inflicted on those two gentle women were an abomination and, to my mind, a desecration of the human body. I believe that all of us who gathered that day to form the nucleus of the investigation team felt the same way. We further realised that, as with Prof. Harbison, they were completely outside our experience. All our training and knowledge, gained over years of homicide investigation, could never have prepared us for this, despite our oft-stated belief that we had seen it all and were beyond shocking. My own first involvement in homicide investigations had been in 1973; but I would quickly realise that I still had a lot to learn.

The post-mortem examination of both bodies began on the morning of 8 March and would continue for two days. The examinations would be carried out by Prof. Harbison, and he would be assisted in his task by Garda experts from the Ballistics, Fingerprint and Photographic Sections. The same experts would also be directly involved in the examination of the scene. The intention of this crossing over of roles was to ensure that each garda involved in the examination of the scene would be thoroughly briefed in relation to the number and type of injuries inflicted, the number and type of weapons used, and the modus operandi of the perpetrator. Equally, they would be on hand to answer any questions relating to the scene posed by the pathologist.

Also present at the post-mortem examinations were two of our most experienced forensic scientists then attached to the Forensic Science Laboratory, Dr Louis McKenna and Dr Fiona Thornton. They attended both examinations and saw at first hand the extent of the mutilation caused to both victims. Their attendance was a most unusual departure from normal procedure, a reflection of the gravity with which the crimes were viewed. They would also spend a number of days at the scene, working in tandem with the Garda experts. Dr McKenna would be assigned exclusively to the actual investigation.

In the following paragraphs I describe in some detail the various injuries that were noted on the bodies of both victims during the post-mortem examinations. Some readers may find the details too graphic. I wish to make it clear, however, that they are not included to shock or to upset anyone; nor are they included for any gratuitous reason. Rather, I believe that it is important to show the extent of the depravity that was visited upon both victims.

Mary Callinan's was the first of the bodies to be examined. She was wearing a nightdress, and when the pathologist removed it he found that there were four openings in it that coincided with stab wounds to her chest area. What was immediately noticeable was that there were also a number of further stab wounds in the same area, suggesting that the perpetrator must have pulled up the nightdress before inflicting these further wounds. She also had a number of lacerations to her lips. He found a series of white horizontal scars on her abdomen, extending downwards into the pubic area.

Prof. Harbison counted a total of twelve stab wounds to the left chest area, three of which had penetrated the heart and lung. He found a fracture to her ribs on the left side of the lower chest area; this fracture corresponded to the imprint of a shoe or boot that was visible to the naked eye. A wound to the front of the throat had penetrated the larynx. There was also a four-inch incised wound to the throat, which had cut through the airway. Unbelievably, below this cut were a further thirty-six tentative incisions. The pathologist would find a further twenty-three similar incisions beneath the left breast.

During his internal examination Prof. Harbison finally succeeded in removing the foreign object that had been embedded in Mary's vagina. Efforts to physically remove it earlier had failed. After surgical removal it was found to be a kitchen carving-fork. The ferocity with which this had been plunged into her body had resulted in one of the steel prongs being bent backwards, which was what had prevented its earlier removal. The unique nature of this weapon meant that Prof. Harbison could say, without fear of contradiction, that before it was inserted in Mary Callinan's vagina it had been used to inflict the stab wound to her left breast that had penetrated the heart. He also found that it had been used to inflict wounds to her left shoulder, to her upper arm, and to the left side of her neck.

While dissecting her vaginal area when removing this implement the pathologist found a ragged incision. This incision had displaced and disconnected the clitoris. Despite the best efforts of all involved in the investigation, this item of information would shortly afterwards be leaked to the media, leading to wild speculation that the body part had either been taken as a trophy or even had been consumed. However, given the extensive damage that had been inflicted in that area, it could not be conclusively stated whether the body part had been removed or had been destroyed.

As in all cases of this nature, Prof. Harbison was asked to give a formal cause of death. If the case were ever to reach trial this would be required. He responded by saying that, in his opinion, death had been caused by a number of factors. These included haemothorax (the accumulation of blood in the chest cavity), caused by stab wounds to the lung; the cutting of the throat, including the cutting of the jugular vein; and no less than three stab wounds to the heart.

During his examination of the body of Sylvia Sheils he found that two knife slits in the vest she was wearing corresponded to stab wounds to her heart. She also had stab wounds to her forehead, her left eyebrow, and the right side of her nose. An incised wound to her throat was found to have cut completely through her airway and into the gullet behind it. As with Mary, a number of superficial incisions were found in the same area.

A stab wound to the right breast was found to have passed through the right lung and also to have incised the aorta. A further stab wound to the right side of the chest had penetrated the right lung. Also noted were two double punctures to her left arm.

In the pubic area the pathologist found signs of severe damage by some instrument to the lower area of her vagina. He would describe this damage as 'severe maiming'. These injuries, in his opinion, had been inflicted after death. He speculated that Sylvia died relatively quickly and that the cause of death had been bleeding to the chest from the stab wound to the right lung, together with the incised wound of the larynx and right vertebral artery.

He had taken the temperature of both bodies at the scene. They were remarkably similar, at 24°C. This suggested that the two killings had been carried out at about the same time. The assault on Sylvia had occurred first. Her body had been found lying across the bed, with her feet on the ground. Given the spattering of blood that was found in the same area, it is almost certain that she was still lying down when the fatal assault occurred. Similarly, Mary's body had been found lying on the floor between her bed and the wall. Again the spattering of blood proved that she too had been lying down when assaulted.

The double puncture wound found on Sylvia's arm had undoubtedly been caused by the carving-fork. Given that it had taken extensive surgery to remove it from Mary's vagina, it must have been used on Sylvia first. Tests were carried out on similar forks to establish the amount of force required to bend the prongs to the extent observed on the one found in the body. The ferocity of the blow required to cause the same amount of damage was found to be enormous. These forks are designed and manufactured to withstand both great heat and physical use; accidentally dropping one or striking it off a solid object would not have caused it to bend as it did.

Other items found at the scene that it was established had been used to inflict the various wounds on both women included two steak knives, the blade of one of which had been badly bent, and two serrated blades of the type used in an electric carving-knife. These are the type of blades that normally slot into one another and when fitted to the power handle perform a cross-cutting effect on whatever they are being used to carve.

All the weapons had originated in the house. They were later formally identified as having formed part of the equipment issued to the various households by the health board. They were normally kept in a drawer in the kitchen, the same drawer that had been removed from the kitchen unit and left lying on the floor.

The use of weapons acquired at a scene—referred to as weapons of opportunity—suggests that the perpetrator had been unarmed when entering the scene. People known to the police or familiar with police procedures will not, as a rule, carry a weapon concealed on their person when walking the streets: they would be well aware that a routine search might result in a lengthy prison sentence. In the same way you would regularly find, when searching people who appear to be acting in a suspicious manner, that they sometimes have a pair of stockings in their pocket. Stockings are much easier to explain away than gloves yet are equally effective in avoiding leaving fingermarks.

I know I am not alone when I suspect that in this instance there was an added aspect to both the choice and the origin of the various weapons used to inflict the horrific injuries on both women. Undoubtedly their assailant had spent some time going through the contents of the drawer that he had taken out and placed on the floor. The weapons he selected were not a random choice. Each was intended to inflict a maximum of damage: the serrated steak knives used to inflict the incised wounds, the serrated carving-blades used in the knife strokes and linear wounds to the chest and abdomen, and finally the most gruesome weapon of all, the carving-fork used to inflict the puncture wounds and then to heap further indignity on Mary's body. There seems little doubt that the time spent in his choosing of weapons had both heightened the perpetrator's anticipation and given an extra thrill to a very sick mind.

In a further break with the norm in a murder investigation, Prof. Harbison called to the incident room on a number of occasions to enquire about the progress of our investigation. During one of our conversations he speculated that these had been sexually motivated crimes, committed by an assailant with an extremely abnormal frame of mind. Both victims, he pointed out, had had their throats cut, both had suffered serious injuries to the genital area, and he had not found any defensive injuries on either of them. These are injuries that victims will suffer when trying to defend themselves. The classic defensive injury is found on the hands, where the victim has tried to grab a knife by the blade to prevent further injuries being inflicted; they are also regularly found on the forearms when an attempt has been made to ward off blows. In this instance it probably meant that death had occurred after the first few blows were struck, which was at least some consolation to know.

As he began putting his final report together, Prof. Harbison told me that it was his opinion that the murders had been the work of a single assailant, working alone. He based this opinion on the remarkable similarity of the injuries to the two victims, and said that he would have no difficulty in proving this if the matter came to trial.

The cutting of both victims' throats had also, he said, been quite deliberate, in that by doing so the perpetrator had prevented them from screaming or crying out and alerting the other occupants in the house. Once again this was proof, if it was needed, of the cold and calculating manner in which the murderer had approached the task. It certainly did not suggest that he was out of control.

According to the pathologist, the majority of the injuries to both bodies had been inflicted after death. This accounted for the absence of the copious amounts of blood that one would have expected, given the number of injuries inflicted. This suggested that, having killed his victims, our perverted killer had gone on to perform his bizarre rituals at his own pace.

Analysis of the blood flow on the bodies clearly showed that when the fatal blows were struck both victims had been lying down. Sylvia's position suggested that she had been awakened by something and was about to get out of bed when she was attacked. Mary would appear to have stepped out of bed and have been standing at the foot of the bed; it could have been some noise from Sylvia's room that had awakened her.

Words and descriptions that one seldom heard from a pathologist peppered Prof. Harbison's conversation. He would say that the genital mutilation in both cases was ritualistic in nature, with the damage in Mary's case being so severe that it could not be established whether a particular body part had been removed or had just been destroyed. The bizarre nature of the tentative cutting, of the horizontal scarring that ran down into the victim's pubic area and the sheer number of injuries inflicted were indicative of the culprit having spent some time with each body, 'in a frenzy fuelled by unnatural desires.'

I told him that a member of the public had contacted the incident room to tell us that on the night of the murders BBC television had broadcast a programme about the ritual genital mutilation of girls and young women in some African countries. The caller had also stated that there had been a programme on some other channel the same night that referred to a psychiatric hospital in Canada in which elderly women had been incarcerated for years. When I asked Prof. Harbison if a sick mind could have connected these programmes he said that we would probably never know, that the person themselves might not even know.

In an unguarded moment, he suggested that two injuries inflicted on Mary Callinan were indicative of the abnormal mentality of the attacker. These were the brute force and savagery required to drive the carving-fork into her vagina and the fractures to her rib cage. These fractures, he found, corresponded to the mark of a boot or shoe that he had noted on the left side of her chest. This suggested that the killer had stood over the dead body, possibly balancing himself on the windowsill, and driven his foot with such force onto her chest that it had left an imprint that was visible to the naked eye. Evidence would be established through the technical examination of the scene that the culprit may have been wearing Caterpillar boots, an expensive brand noted for its heavy-duty footwear.

If ever, the pathologist suggested, a particular injury was intended to convey the contempt a murderer held for their victim, either of these two injuries would qualify. Whether such contempt was the result of some personal motive against either of our victims specifically or was because of some deep-seated hatred of women in general, or a particular type of women, was something that the investigators would have to establish.

On another occasion I asked Prof. Harbison if he could estimate the approximate length of time that had been spent in mutilating the bodies, given the number and variety of their injuries. At this point, based on the information we had been supplied with by Ann Mernagh, we had an effective time frame of between midnight, when she had spoken briefly to Sylvia, and 6 a.m., when she had discovered the body. Dr Flood, while examining the bodies at 7:20 a.m., said that while rigor mortis had been present in Sylvia's body, the process had not begun in Mary's.

Prof. Harbison said he would be reluctant to give an opinion, because of how unreliable rigor mortis is in establishing time of death. Its absence in Mary's body would bear out his belief that Sylvia had been killed first. Given the frenzied nature of the first assault, the perpetrator would have had ample time, with little concern about being caught, to inflict the post-mortem wounds. He must then have had a certain cooling-off period, which had led him to decide not to kill Ann, even though we had established that he had gone into her room and had stood beside her bed.

Chapter 6 ⌒

THE USE OF CRIME-SCENE PROFILERS

Prof. Harbison contended that the genital mutilation, coupled with the nature and the extent of the other injuries to both bodies, suggested that this crime was sexually motivated, and equally he felt that it was outside his experience as a pathologist for more than twenty years. This caused some concern within the investigation team.

At an early stage, therefore, it was decided to seek the services of a specialised authority in the field of crime-scene profiling. It was hoped that such a person could assist in providing some background information that might help or at least provide guidelines in identifying the type of person being sought for the crimes. A crime-scene profiler, accredited by the Association of Chief Police Officers in Britain, was contacted and asked for assistance. The association recommended that we avail of the services of Dr Karl Roberts, a crime-scene profiler who was regularly employed by them. This would be the first time that such services had been used in an investigation in this jurisdiction.

All offender profiles that I have read begin by issuing a general warning. Police forces are informed that the profile is intended as just another investigative tool. The recipients are reminded that the findings are based on empirical research together with follow-up interviews with convicted offenders. They provide guidelines and parameters within which the perpetrator of a particular crime may fall. At its most simplistic, where entrance to a crime scene necessitates certain physical attributes, for example the ability to scale certain heights, one of the criteria would be that a disabled suspect could be safely eliminated. The completed profile will contain a number of criteria that, taken as a whole, can assist in narrowing the hunt for suspects.

———

To justify the expense involved in bringing such an expert in this field to Ireland it was decided that he would be asked to examine an unrelated and unresolved homicide within the Dublin North-Central Division. On 28 December 1996 the body of an English prostitute of Sri Lankan origin, Belinda Pereira, was found in a rented apartment in the city centre, having suffered severe head injuries. She lived in London, where she was studying to be a beautician and was supporting herself in her studies through prostitution. She was a regular visitor to Dublin, staying for two weeks at a time. During that time she would rarely leave the apartment, which would have been booked for her by her pimp. She would make as much money as possible in the short space of time that she stayed here.

Belinda had built up a large pool of regular customers through her visits to Dublin. On her arrival she would contact them by phone and make an appointment. She was careful to stay below the radar and not come to the attention of the Garda Vice Squad. She did not advertise her services in the books and magazines then available, preferring to get new customers through referrals from the established ones. She was very discreet, always ensuring that none of her customers were hanging around outside her apartment to the annoyance of her neighbours. By working alone in the apartment she also ensured that no charge of operating a brothel could be made against her, as the law at that time required that two or more women had to be operating in a premises before it could be considered a brothel.

On the night of 28 December 1996 two male associates of Belinda's called to the apartment she was using at Mellors Court, off Lower Liffey Street. When they received no response they forced the door and went in. They found her naked body lying on the bed, her upper torso and head covered with a duvet. She had received injuries to the head that were so severe that visual recognition was virtually impossible.

The fatal assault, it was later established, had not occurred there, which meant that she had been put onto the bed after being assaulted. The money she had accumulated during her visit was missing. She was in the habit of keeping the money in an unused kettle, a fact known only to her close associates. Nothing else had been touched or moved; this would suggest that her assailant was familiar with her routine.

She had used the phone in the flat to make her appointments with her customers. The investigators obtained details of all the traffic on the phone. All her customers were visited and asked to provide an alibi for her time of death, which led to some very red faces.

It is almost certain that she met her death at the hands of some person to whom she was known. The covering of the head and face of a murder victim is considered a classic sign of an association between victim and aggressor. However, no person has ever been made accountable for her death. Her case is now with the Garda Cold Case Unit.

Widespread concern was expressed by the public at the outset of the investigation over the murder of a lone woman in her home. However, this concern soon waned when word leaked out that she had been operating as a prostitute. The world-famous crime author John Connolly gives Belinda's death and the public reaction to it as the spur that drove him into writing his series of books about his fictional detective, Charlie Parker, and the murders he becomes embroiled in. On the night her body was found he was working in the nearby *Irish Times* office as a freelance journalist and had been despatched by the editor to cover the murder. He later described his books as 'an attempt to make sense of her murder, and, for that reason, they all fail.'

————

The profile created by Dr Roberts in relation to the murders of Sylvia Sheils and Mary Callinan would later take on an importance that it was never intended to and would ultimately be criticised in the report of the commission set up by the Government to study the investigation.

Dr Roberts would inform the commission that in his dealings with the Gardaí he found them to be totally inexperienced in the use of criminal profilers. As I have said, with all such profiles there is a warning at the outset. Dr Roberts' report states: 'This is a preliminary offender profile based on information provided to date. It may be subject to change depending on the availability of new information. This material is intended as an investigative tool for the senior investigating officer. It should not be used alone to direct the investigation, neither can it be considered as a piece of evidence.' This warning was clear and unambiguous.

The profiler was facilitated with a number of visits to the scene. All photographs, including post-mortem photographs, were made available to him. Important statements, which included the discovery of the body and the scientific examination of the scene, were also supplied. A number of case conferences were held, all of which I attended. The only matter that could not be discussed was the status of any suspects who had come to our notice.

A preliminary report was submitted by Dr Roberts on 14 April 1997. A summary of his findings is set out below; they are not listed in any particular order.

1. Both crimes were the work of one culprit.
2. Given the presence and extent of the mutilation of the genital area, this was a sexual attack. The possibility of the perpetrator being female was dismissed out of hand.
3. Given the extent and nature of the post-mortem mutilation, it was considered likely that the perpetrator suffered from violent fantasies about women.
4. The perpetrator would lack sexual experience.
5. The perpetrator would either be unaware of or afraid to engage in normal sexual intercourse.
6. He would have become even more sexually aroused as he inflicted the post-mortem injuries.
7. Given the number of exploratory and hesitation marks evident on the bodies, it was likely that this was the perpetrator's first serious offence.
8. The perpetrator would be in his early teens to mid-twenties.
9. The perpetrator would have poor social skills.
10. The selection of the type of victim, in this instance two vulnerable elderly women, suggested a culprit who was socially isolated and inadequate.
11. The victims could have been known to the culprit.
12. The culprit may reside or work near the scene.

13. The culprit either lives alone or is still with his parents.
14. He would have either a poor or non-existent work record and academically would have been an under-achiever, although at the same time he might be of average to high intelligence. Dr Roberts based this belief on the high fantasy level the killer displayed in his actions.
15. It was likely that he would have committed burglaries in the past and also that he could have committed acts of violence.
16. Since the offence he would have displayed minimal behavioural changes.
17. He would feel no remorse for his actions.
18. Lastly, and most importantly, the offender was 'extremely dangerous' and was likely to re-offend.

This last suggestion, given the high concentration of houses occupied by similar vulnerable former patients in the district, sent shivers down our spines. It meant in effect that we were now working against whatever internal clock was driving this monster.

A synopsis of the profile was created and was displayed in the incident room and made available to all the team. In the fullness of time we would establish that eleven of the eighteen characteristics mentioned above would apply to Dean Lyons, while nine of them could be applied to Mark Nash.

As time passed, given the failure to resolve the murders, some members of the investigation team, including myself, became increasingly concerned about the growing emphasis that some of our senior officers were placing on the profile itself, using it as a yardstick with which to measure and compartmentalise people who were identified as suspects.

During one of our briefing conferences with the profiler he suggested that we should establish definite physical boundaries to the scene at Orchard View. He stated that particular attention should be paid to any person of interest to the investigation who lived within or had close affiliations within the boundaries we selected. These boundaries would be physical limitations to casual access to the site. He suggested that one such obvious boundary was the River Liffey to the south of the crime scene. The North Circular Road, a busy thoroughfare, would form a boundary to the north, as would the Phibsborough Road to the east. The Phoenix Park would be the final geographical boundary to the west.

This hypothesis of an operational 'comfort zone' for first-time offenders was originally proposed by the world-famous profiler Dr David Canter. Using this system he had successfully profiled the railway killer John Duffy, who for years had abducted and killed his victims as they left the commuter train stations around London. By using the first recorded crime scene as the centre, he was able to show that, as the rapist and murderer became more and more daring in the areas where he picked his victims, there had been a progression outwards. Priority was given to suspects in close proximity to the first scene, and it didn't take the police long after this to stumble upon Duffy.

It would be established that almost 100 per cent of the personal attributes in the psychological profile created by Prof. Canter applied to John Duffy. He was found to live only a short distance from where he committed his first crime. With an accomplice, he had progressed from his earlier sexual assaults to the abduction and murder of his victims. In 2000 Duffy would give evidence in court against his accomplice, David Mulcachy. He would also admit to having personally committed a further seventeen rapes. It was his work on this case that had catapulted Prof. Canter to fame.

On a personal level, in that same year, while I was questioning a man who was considered a person of interest in the disappearance of a young woman, I found out during the course of our conversation that he was a nephew of John Duffy's.

Based on the proposition that the murders of Sylvia Sheils and Mary Callinan were the first crimes of this nature that our culprit had committed, it followed that they would have occurred in an area that he knew and also felt comfortable in. The profiler suggested that for his next murder he would in all probability cast his net slightly further afield. That he would re-offend was never in doubt as far as Dr Roberts was concerned. For the moment he would feed on his mental images of the murders of Mary and Sylvia. This would keep him going for a while, until his depraved mind sought further release in the bloody slaughter of other victims. Was he, we wondered, even now going around selecting a new killing field and even choosing his next innocent victim or victims?

In time we would find out that both Dean Lyons and Mark Nash lived within the geographical boundaries that we had set.

Chapter 7 ~

TECHNICAL EXAMINATION OF THE SCENE

Given the enormity of this crime, the scene and its environment were subjected to one of the most rigorous technical examinations that the Technical Bureau had ever undertaken. The head of that unit, Detective-Superintendent Liam Coen, offered to make all facilities at his disposal available to the examination. Two scientists from the Forensic Science Laboratory were also involved. The scene was preserved from the time of arrival of the first gardaí at 6:20 a.m. on 7 March 1997 until the completion of all the various examinations some eleven days later, on 18 March. The round-the-clock preservation of the scene would make a huge demand on local resources. However, all such requirements were supplied without question by Superintendent James Joyce, the officer in charge of the Bridewell Garda Station.

For a further three months from the withdrawal of the full-time garda from the scene, all beat gardaí and patrol units were required to visit the scene and ensure that there was no unauthorised interference. It was felt that the possibility existed that the perpetrator might return to the scene to relive his fantasies or to feed off the memory of the night. With the assistance of the Technical Support Unit and the co-operation of a local householder, surveillance cameras were mounted in the vicinity, which provided a complete overview of the scene. The tapes from the cameras were collected every few days and viewed. Any person seen displaying more than a passing interest was quickly traced and interviewed.

The Garda Photographic Section supplied one still photographer and a further expert in the videotaping of scenes to capture the various images connected with the scene. Two senior detectives were allocated from the Ballistics Section, with a further two senior members allocated from the Fingerprint Section.

A detective-garda attached to the Mapping Section prepared maps showing both the outside of the scene and precise drawings of the interior. These showed the exact position of the bodies, together with details of blood spattering and blood flow, and would form an essential part of any subsequent court case. Judges are reluctant to allow jurors access to or even to see photographs showing victims' bodies. It is believed that allowing the jury to see a body and the injuries it has received might colour a juror in their approach to the case. This creates a most unusual situation, whereby a jury are being asked to deliberate in a murder trial in which all evidence has to be produced and yet they are not allowed to see the item of evidence most central to the whole trial, namely the body. To surmount this problem the Gardaí rely heavily on the expertise of the garda from the Mapping Section, referred to throughout the job as the 'mapper'.

The early examination at a crime scene, which takes place while the body is *in situ*, is normally confined to photographing, with both still and video recording being employed. All aspects of the body are carefully preserved on film, together with the immediate area surrounding it. Only in extreme cases, such as contact with a live cable or a risk of flooding, will any further contact be made until after the attendance of the pathologist. If it proves necessary for the pathologist to move the body, for example to take the temperature or to check for rigor mortis, this too will be documented.

Before the removal of the body the forensic science team will cover all the extremities—head, hands and feet—with clear plastic evidence bags. This will ensure that no trace evidence, for example scrapings under nails, the culprit's hairs in the victim's hands, or body fluids, is lost in transporting the body to the morgue. At the post-mortem examination these bags will be removed and returned to the Gardaí for further examination. The body itself is carefully wrapped and secured in a heavy plastic sheet before being coffined for removal by hearse from the scene. Ambulances are seldom, if ever, used to transport bodies once death has been certified by a doctor.

The plastic sheet in which the body was wrapped is also returned for examination. The body will be escorted to the morgue, and a garda will remain with it until the completion of all the various tests and examinations. This, as can be imagined, is never the most sought-after role in an investigation.

Normally a member of the deceased's family will identify the body to the garda at the morgue. This garda must then, before the examination begins, formally identify the body to the pathologist. This will guarantee a chain of evidence that begins with the body of the victim or victims being taken from the scene and culminates in the post-mortem examination.

In Sylvia's and Mary's case the formal identification of both bodies was made directly to Prof. Harbison by a senior member of the hospital medical staff who had been acquainted with them both for a number of years. A number of days later Mary Callinan, who had no living relatives, would be further identified to Prof. Harbison by two former school friends who had been traced. This was done to ensure that no issue in relation to her identification could ever arise in the future.

The full team of Garda experts, augmented by the two forensic scientists, assisted Prof. Harbison throughout his examinations of both bodies. The attendance of the team who are involved in the examination of the scene is considered good practice, given that when they return to the scene they are in a position to tie in blood pooling and spattering with different injuries. Other signs, for example drag marks on floors, tears in clothing, or damage to furniture, can be tied in with what they have learnt during the post-mortem examination. Clothing, body samples and foreign objects removed by the pathologist will be handed by him directly to the Garda team for transmission to the laboratory, so ensuring a continuous chain of possession. Equally, the team can assist the pathologist with any query he may have relating to the scene itself.

One matter arose at the outset of the examination of the Grangegorman scene. The point of entry to the premises had undoubtedly been the broken kitchen window, which looked out onto the small enclosed yard. One of the panes of glass had been broken and removed from the frame. However, the majority of the broken glass was lying on the ground in the yard itself. Beside the broken glass was an unopened can of Campbell's soup. This led to some confusion, because it appeared that, given the presence of so much broken glass on the outside, the glass had been broken from the inside outwards, possibly with the can of soup. We identified the can as having been bought by Mary Callinan in a local shop some days earlier. The glazier who had repaired the window after the previous break-in in December 1996 had said that in his opinion the glass on that occasion had been broken from the inside outwards.

Detective-Sergeant Eugene Gilligan was the member of the Garda Ballistics Section in charge of the scientific examination of the scene. He was considered to be one of the foremost crime-scene examiners in the Gardaí. Having worked with him on a large number of serious crime investigations I can vouch for his expertise and his thoroughness.

Eugene removed the entire lower window frame. He then painstakingly gathered together every piece of glass from both inside and outside the house. Each piece collected was labelled to identify both its origin and whether it had been found facing downwards or upwards. Back in the laboratory, using a technique of light refraction, Eugene carefully rebuilt the entire pane of glass. He thus established that the glass had in fact been broken from the outside in, possibly by a blow to the lower left-hand corner. The culprit had then taken out the glass shards and placed them on the ground. The window frame is retained to this day at the Technical Bureau.

Eugene's work in reassembling the pane of glass is still referred to in training seminars and classrooms. Years later, when this case had eventually moved on, Eugene, now retired, would give many hours of his own time to ensuring that all the exhibits he had dealt with were available to us.

In his examination of the unoccupied bedroom, Eugene discovered a partial footwear impression on the otherwise spotlessly clean linoleum. He cut out and retained the piece of lino after first having it photographed *in situ*. He again had the piece photographed in studio conditions. He was thus able to enhance the image to provide an instantly recognisable sole impression. The Forensic Science Laboratory maintains a library of photographs of footwear impressions, gathered from all kinds of sources, including shoe manufacturers, wholesalers, retailers, and others involved in the footwear industry. They also regularly receive photographic examples of different sole types from other laboratories throughout the world. From his examination of the impression left at the scene Eugene established that it had been made by a boot with a pattern similar to that found on boots bearing the Caterpillar brand.

He then examined the footwear worn by every person who it was established had entered the crime scene. This was to discount the possibility that the impression could have been innocently left there. The blood that formed the impression had been identified as having come from Mary Callinan. It was safe to assume, therefore, that the mark had been made after the crime was committed. Those who had to supply their footwear for comparison included all the nursing and other medical staff who had access to the house, the security guards, all the gardaí who had entered the scene, and the pathologist. After examination it was established that none of this footwear matched the impression that had been left on the floor in Mary's blood. This then took on a huge significance.

Sole impressions left by footwear at the scene of a crime can be used in evidence to link a suspect to the crime. However, it can be used only in conjunction with other evidence, for instance visual or fingerprint evidence: no court would convict a person solely on the grounds that their shoes matched an impression left at the scene. In this it is similar to the evidence relating to mobile phones: while we can say that a person's phone was in use in the vicinity of a particular crime, it cannot be conclusively said, without other evidence, that it was in the owner's possession at that time.

Of equal importance to the possibility of the footwear impression being useful evidence is, naturally, the length of time that has passed between the crime and the shoe itself being found. Given the hardship that our shoes often endure, an obvious pattern present on a shoe today may be totally changed or gone altogether after a month or two of continuous wear.

The identification of the type of footwear that the perpetrator of this crime had been wearing would later take on further significance. Firstly, it can be stated without fear of contradiction that Caterpillar footwear would not normally be worn by homeless people or drug addicts, favouring as they do, for the most part, casual and less expensive types of footwear. Dean Lyons would certainly belong to that category.

After the arrest of Mark Nash in August 1997 for the murders of Catherine and Carl Doyle it would be established that he was the owner of a pair of Caterpillar boots. Nash would also make a number of verifiable admissions to the murder of Sylvia Sheils and Mary Callinan. One of the longest-established footwear retailers in Dublin is Heather's shoe shop at Arran Quay. They are also one of the main suppliers of Caterpillar boots. One of the shop assistants readily identified Mark Nash as having bought a pair of these boots some months before the murders of Sylvia Sheils and Mary Callinan. A pair of these boots was found by gardaí after the search of his flat at Clonliffe Road following his arrest for the murders of Catherine and Carl Doyle. Unfortunately it was too late to make a comparison with the impression found at Orchard View.

Detective-Sergeant Christy O'Brien was the latent-fingermark expert at the crime scene, one of the most experienced in his field. (To avoid confusion, it should be understood that a 'fingerprint' is the inked reproduction on paper taken from a person's hand, while a 'fingermark' is a print left at the scene, which may subsequently be lifted by the fingerprint expert.) Detective-Sergeant O'Brien developed marks on the kitchen window, at the point of entry. When microscopically examined, these were found to have been created by a gloved hand, possibly a hand wearing a woollen or woven type of glove.

Stains consistent with bloodstains were also present on the window frame. Given the level of DNA expertise in 1997, the amount of bloodstaining present was not considered usable for the kind of testing then available. Fingerprint powder had therefore been applied to them, in the hope of developing latent fingermarks. Once again a patterned surface was found. Years later attempts would be made to 'grow' the bloodstaining, that is, to reproduce it sufficiently to allow a DNA profile to be created from it. Unfortunately, it was found that as the blood itself was reproduced so too was the fingerprint powder.

Given the thoroughness of the technical examination of the scene, together with the duration of the tests, the various experts expressed amazement at how clean the scene was. Other than the trace evidence that I have described, there was nothing of significance at the scene.

Whether this can be attributed to a scientifically aware culprit or to just plain luck can only be speculated upon.

Bloodstaining was found also on a light-switch in the dining-room. This was the room in which Ann Mernagh had noticed the light switched on when she went downstairs that morning. When analysed, this stain was found to contain a mixture of the blood of Sylvia and Mary. This suggested that after he had murdered both women the perpetrator had gone downstairs to have a look around.

More sinister, however, is the fact that when Ann Mernagh's bedroom was scientifically examined, bloodstaining was found on the inside of her bedroom door and also on the edge of the mattress. This blood was identified as belonging to Mary Callinan. For the blood to have been found in these two places it can only mean that the culprit, after the murders, had gone into Ann's bedroom and, with the blood of his victims on his hands or dripping from whatever weapon he was carrying, had stood looking down on her as she slept. He had then turned and left the room. Given what he had done to the other two women as they lay sleeping, it is hard to imagine what had changed in his sick mind in the short walk between the bedrooms.

————

Before I leave the question of the scientific examination of the scene there is one further issue that I feel I must mention, which I believe clearly demonstrates the mentality of some of the senior officers on the investigation.

I have said that there was some confusion about whether the window had been broken from the outside or the inside, leaving us with the possibility that we had a staged crime scene on our hands. Because of the sterling work of Eugene Gilligan, this had been resolved beyond any doubt. This important nugget of information had been brought to our notice by the crime scene co-ordinator, Detective-Inspector Brendan McArdle of the Ballistics Section. Brendan had passed on the news to us at a conference attended by all the members involved in the investigation. The news was greeted with some relief by all present. When the conference ended and everyone got up to leave, a very senior officer who had been present asked Brendan to stay behind. I assumed that he intended to compliment him on the work done by his unit. To my amazement, he took issue with him, telling him that the information should not have been announced in front of all the others but should have been conveyed to him in private. I could not believe my ears. Brendan, a highly respected and long-serving member of the Ballistics Section, did not attend another conference.

This behaviour was surely an omen of things to come.

Chapter 8 ∼

PROGRESSING THE INVESTIGATION

In my capacity as a full-time incident room co-ordinator I had been contacted by the duty sergeant at the Bridewell immediately after the discovery of the bodies at Grangegorman and was directed to go to the scene to liaise with the gardaí already there. I arrived at 7 a.m. Being the first detective to attend, I ensured that sufficient personnel were on hand to cordon off and secure the scene. Then, having established all details that were immediately available, I drove to the Bridewell, where I arranged for a crime scene log book to be delivered to the scene. This log is completed by the garda who is preserving the scene. The times that the garda comes on and goes off duty are entered in it; in addition, they will enter details of all those who request entry to the scene, the times they entered and left, and the nature of their duties while there.

Up to very recently the gardaí who carried out preservation duties at a crime scene were required to attend the trial and give evidence of their duties at the scene. This was a huge drain on personnel resources, often requiring gardaí whose only evidence would be that they had been on duty there to spend days, and sometimes weeks, in a courtroom. Recent legislative changes have provided for the appointment of a senior garda, usually a sergeant, to take charge of scene preservation. Each garda carrying out duties there will complete a certificate, which includes all the relevant details. The garda in charge of the scene can then present the signed certificate as evidence at the trial.

I briefed my senior officers by phone and requested permission to call in all available gardaí. I then made contact with my colleagues in the District Detective Unit at the Bridewell and told them to report for duty. Given the seriousness of the case, this applied equally whether they were due to be on or off duty that day. Contact was then made with neighbouring stations to establish what personnel they had available to assist us.

Viewers of news or current affairs programmes will be familiar with the expression 'An incident room has been set up,' often accompanied by a picture of a grim-faced reporter standing outside a particular Garda station. What it refers to is the fact that a special team has been established at a particular station to co-ordinate the investigation of a crime or incident. The local team is normally augmented by detectives from the National Bureau of Criminal Investigation. Local resources, such as transport, office accommodation and clerical staff, will also be made available.

Given the large number of murders that occurred within the Bridewell area in the previous five years, an office in the station had been acquired, through the assistance of the district officer, Superintendent Joyce, as a permanent incident room, complete with its own phone lines and other facilities. (At one time there had been so many murders in and around the stretch of the North Circular Road from the Phoenix Park gate to St Peter's Church in Phibsborough that it became known in police circles as the 'Murder Mile'.) The Bridewell station at that time was unique in having such a facility.

Over the years I have worked as incident room co-ordinator in other stations around the country. On my arrival at the station a trawl would be made to establish which office could be made available for use as an incident room. The term 'available' was interpreted very broadly and often meant no more than that the unfortunate occupant of an office was on a day off and would return to find all their current work neatly dumped in a box and left with the garda in charge, who had probably just gone on holidays. The official occupant might remain without an office for the duration of the investigation. This sometimes led to the unfortunate IRC having to run a daily gauntlet of the evicted garda and their colleagues. What would often make a bad situation worse was the fitting of a new lock to the office door because of the sensitivity of a particular investigation.

The IRC has a clearly defined role in all major investigations. Firstly they will ensure that the scene has been properly preserved and arrangements made to have it examined. They must also request additional personnel and other resources. At the outset of every inquiry they open what is commonly called the jobs book. This usually consists of a hardback ledger, in which on every second page is fixed the original of every action sheet issued from the incident room. These ledgers normally hold in the region of 150 action sheets. For the Grangegorman murders I filled twelve separate ledgers.

Every step in any major investigation is clearly defined and arises from instructions contained in an action sheet. These sheets are completed in triplicate, the original being retained at the incident room, a copy given to the garda given the task of completing the inquiry or carrying out the investigative step as set out on the sheet, and a second copy given to the officer in charge of the investigation, known as the senior investigating officer or SIO. In this way the SIO will not alone know what phase an inquiry is at but will also know what each member of their team is doing at any given time. Only in extreme cases or in a rapidly developing situation will a detective take an action without authorisation from the incident room in the form of an action sheet.

On the completion of a particular action the designated garda will return the sheet to the incident room. A report describing what steps were taken and the outcome of the job will be attached, as will any statements or other documents arising from it. A brief résumé of the outcome is then written on the blank facing page in the jobs book.

If this system is adhered to strictly and conscientiously it is possible to follow the progression of any investigation to its natural conclusion, that is, the appearance in court of the person charged, just through reading the jobs book.

The first twenty to thirty actions in any major investigation are, for the most part, generic. They involve establishing the identity of the first person to discover the crime and contact the emergency services and the arrival of emergency personnel at the scene and the duties they performed there. They also deal with establishing the identity of all first-responders, crime-scene preservation, the identity of the victim, the last known movements of the victim, and preliminary house-to-house inquiries. Other jobs include the pronouncing of death, the removal of the body, requests for CCTV footage, and the appointment of media spokespersons. By the time of the first formal conference in relation to the investigation, normally within hours of the discovery of a body, the IRC will have these action sheets ready to distribute to various gardaí for completion.

As statements and information begin to arrive in the incident room they are read and scrutinised by the IRC. Actions arising from them are then distributed for completion. This is a process that self-perpetuates: the more queries you send out, the more fields of inquiry you complete. Within the first 24 to 48 hours of any inquiry an enormous volume of work can be generated in this way. It is important, therefore, that a careful check is maintained and that nothing is lost through the system being swamped with information in such a small space of time.

The inquiry team itself is subdivided, and various sections are given specific roles. These will include house-to-house inquiries in the vicinity of the scene or areas associated with it; suspect profiles, to include 'persons of interest' (a term I will explain later); family liaison (a field that, in the past, the Gardaí have fallen down on); and witness interviews.

For the most part, investigators will try to avoid being put on the house-to-house teams. This can be a tedious process, often requiring interminable calling back to houses where you received no response or where some of the residents were not immediately available, cross-referencing the details of movements supplied by people, and following up details on visitors.

I have been on investigations where a supervisor assigned a garda to these inquiries as punishment for some infringement or other—real or imagined. I have always argued strenuously against this practice, which will almost invariably ensure that a job that can often provide the most valuable leads will be, at best, half done.

In 1999 I was involved as IRC in the 'cold case' review of the abduction and murder in 1979 of a Co. Kildare woman, Phyllis Murphy. A suspect, John Crerar, was identified from a DNA test we had carried out on samples taken from his unfortunate victim. Her body had been found in the mountains at the Wicklow Gap some weeks after she went missing. Unbelievably, because this area was above the freezing line the culprit's trace evidence had been frozen and perfectly preserved.

While examining the documents from the original investigation I came upon the folder containing the house-to-house inquiry forms.

The form completed by the sergeant who called to Crerar's house had a note written across the top stating that, in his opinion, Crerar should be fully checked out. This had led to a blood sample being taken from him at the time, which was retained on file. When this garda, long since retired, was asked by the review team what had led him to pencil this prophetic remark on the completed form he said that it had been a 'gut feeling' he received after interviewing Crerar.

Regularly, while reading through these forms, some huge anomaly or discrepancy will almost jump out at you. Simple things, such as a witness saying they left the house at 6 p.m. to go to the local shop and had met a particular person en route, can take on a huge significance if this other person claims not to have been in the area. For the most part, these can be caused by human error and are based on genuinely held beliefs. In one murder case that I am aware of it took the culprit entering a plea of guilty to convince a witness who claimed to have met him elsewhere that he was wrong!

Every incident room will have a specific garda to filter and cross-check all the information in the completed questionnaires. During the investigation into the murder of Sylvia Sheils and Mary Callinan we were very lucky to have had the services of Sergeant Matt Mulhall in this role. Matt was one of the first gardaí I made contact with on the morning of 7 March 1997. I had worked on other murders with him and had seen how he operated. Every form the team completed in the Grangegorman area was collated, checked and then rechecked by him. The number of these forms would run into four figures, but not one nugget of information would be overlooked by him.

His pet hate was those questionnaires on which the recording garda had written that the person being interviewed said they had not seen any strangers in the area. The unfortunate garda would be greeted with the rejoinder: 'Listen, sunshine, go back and ask him who exactly he did see.' When someone had given a description of a person they met as being five foot six or seven the completing garda would be asked to explain how the informant had come by this precise height.

Murder inquiries, as a general rule, attract and create a huge volume of work. Almost every query generated in the incident room will create another. Empirical research would suggest that, given the wide parameters that accompany the setting up of an investigation, in almost 80 per cent of cases either the culprit or someone very close to them will have come, in some way or other, to the attention of the inquiry team. Recognising this fact and progressing the matter are, of course, entirely different things. It is imperative, therefore, that the incident room team remain in control of and *au fait* with all the information passing through the system.

During a recent review of an unsolved murder in the Dublin area I drew attention to the fact that in the first twenty-three days of the inquiry almost two thousand statements had been received at the incident room, which was operated by one garda who had limited involvement in murder investigation. To successfully analyse and assess that volume of information is impossible, no matter what the commitment of the person is.

The British police have a specialist computer network that is used in all incident rooms within the forty-two separate police forces in that jurisdiction. Known as the Home Office Large Major Enquiry System (HOLMES), it ensures that all information gathered is added to the data-base for analysis by experts. The system was introduced after three separate police forces had investigated the rape and murder of thirteen women by Peter Sutcliffe, dubbed the 'Yorkshire Ripper' by the media. In the subsequent review it was established that Sutcliffe had come to the attention of the police at an early stage on at least four occasions during the separate investigations, but the information about his behaviour had not been linked. How many of his victims might have been saved had this information been acted upon earlier is open to speculation.

There is, however, one important difference between the Garda Síochána and the various British police forces, and that is that the Garda is a national force with a countrywide mandate. As a consequence, gardaí attached to certain sections, for example the National Bureau of Criminal Investigation and the Technical Bureau, regularly work on investigations throughout the country. This system should ensure that any knowledge or information obtained in one investigation that is relevant to another should be immediately available through this cross-referencing. Certain investigators who were involved in the inquiry into the murders of Sylvia Sheils and Mary Callinan would in time become involved also in the investigation into the murders of Catherine and Carl Doyle. The problem, however, lies in how the information is disseminated and to whom.

The role of incident room co-ordinator is considered one of the most important cogs in the investigative system. This person initiates all actions and inquiries and is ultimately responsible for ensuring their successful conclusion. To this end, the IRC must be privy to all information coming into the possession of other units and to all facets and nuances of the inquiry.

An overview system has recently been established to assist the IRC. The 'ownership' of an investigation lies with the superintendent of the area in which it occurs. Given the huge demands on that office, it is normally the local detective-superintendent or, where one has been appointed, the local detective-inspector who will take overall charge as senior investigating officer. This officer will receive copies of all job sheets and a full copy of the investigation file as it grows. For their part they must maintain a decision log for each inquiry they instigate, setting out their reasons for taking, or not taking, a particular course of action. They must also be up to date with the day-to-day progress. I was part of the working group that drew up the decision log system. The roles performed by the IRC and the SIO are interlinked and complementary to one another.

The good 'bookman' (as the IRC is often called) is born, it is said, to the role. Nowadays IRC courses are given in the Garda Training College. Selection for the course is based on the aptitude shown by a particular garda in previous investigations. The course lasts several months and comprises a number of modules as well as field training. The generation of bookmen that I come from had no courses available to them: instead we learnt our trade through serving an apprenticeship with an established bookman. This was a difficult learning process, as our mentor would often make it abundantly clear to us that they had enough to do to run an investigation without having to wet-nurse an amateur detective. Any display of incompetence could lead to either a tirade of abuse or removal from the inquiry. The system ensured that you either met the requirements or were never again entrusted with the role.

The old-style bookman demanded, and received, the same deference that would be shown to much more senior gardaí. What is remarkable about the role is that the system has remained virtually unchanged over all the years. The bookmen with whom I served my apprenticeship learnt their trade from investigators who had in turn been trained by officers who had served in the Dublin Metropolitan Police and the Royal Irish Constabulary before the foundation of this state. I have attended incident room management courses given by some of the British police forces and by the Royal Canadian Mounted Police and can say that what is most remarkable about their training is how similar it is to our own.

My reason for digressing briefly on the role of the IRC is to show the importance that is attached to their role in any major investigation. Though my appointment as co-ordinator in the case of Sylvia Sheils and Mary Callinan would have been anticipated, there is no doubt that if any of my superiors had felt that I was not up to it, or that the role was too demanding, I would either have been removed or moved sideways. I have witnessed this being done to bookmen in the past, and have seen the effect the move ultimately had on their careers. The same thing could have been done at any stage during this investigation. The fact that, despite all the turns the inquiry would eventually take, no consideration was ever given to my removal suggests that they were satisfied throughout with how I performed this duty. In fact on two occasions during this investigation two gardaí studying to be co-ordinators were sent to me to be shown how to do the job.

————

By 10 a.m. on 7 March 1997 the team had been gathered and the first conference got under way. Conferences are an integral part of any major investigation. They are a way of seeing what progress is being made in the various inquiries; they are also a great way of keeping everyone in the picture, given that all actions are discussed in their presence. This team comprised all the detectives attached to the Bridewell Station, a total of six, augmented by detectives from neighbouring stations, from the NBCI and from the Technical Bureau. A number of uniformed gardaí were also present, seconded to the Detective Branch to assist in the investigation. In total, we had twenty-one gardaí gathered in that room.

A lot of those present would have worked together on other inquiries but would probably not have met since then. However, the usual greetings and banter associated with colleagues meeting after a time were totally absent that morning. Veteran investigators sat in stunned silence as details of the horrendous acts perpetrated on the two victims were outlined to them by Detective-Superintendent Cormac Gordon. Many of those detectives were people I would have thought had heard and seen it all.

As further details were imparted one could see the shock slowly giving way to a grim determination to ensure that they played their part in bringing the culprit to justice. After all my years attending murder conferences I believe that the customary direction to 'go out there and get him' did not, on this occasion, appear necessary.

Gardaí were paired off in teams of two and their different roles allocated. The pairings were based on who had shown in the past an ability to work well together, on experience and seniority, and on expertise in particular fields. One detective-sergeant was put in charge of dealing with suspects and persons of interest, a second in charge of witnesses, a third in charge of questionnaires. Another detective-sergeant was designated to liaise with Ann Mernagh. Sergeant Matt Mulhall and myself were appointed to co-ordinate all information as it came in to the incident room, with the instruction that no matter how insignificant a snippet of information might appear to be it was to be fully investigated. We were further told that any resources that we identified as being required would be made available to us, and that we should compile a list of personnel and other resources that we felt were needed and to have it ready by lunchtime the same day.

As we all went our separate way at the close of the conference, the time for the next one was set at 7 p.m. that same evening. It was further arranged that daily conferences would be held at 9 a.m., and that all involved in the investigation must attend them, unless engaged in important inquiries. All holidays and days off were suspended for the foreseeable future. Gardaí who had holidays booked were to let us know, and they would be replaced immediately. This to me was proof, if proof were needed, of the gravity with which our superiors were treating this crime.

————

A regular complaint made by gardaí involved in an investigation is the reluctance shown by some senior officers to share information about developments with all those involved. Oftentimes, in what is referred to in Garda circles as the 'top table only' syndrome, information is not filtered down to the gardaí involved in the mundane inquiries. This leads to the suggestion of an 'inner circle' in operation during certain investigations. It is a practice that I have bitterly opposed throughout my service. Although I can see the need to keep a tight rein on certain information, I believe it is a total contradiction to tell a garda that you can trust them with this or that piece of information only. It is difficult to get the best out of anyone if they feel they are not trusted.

Certain senior officers were notorious for having this attitude. It sends out the wrong message to an investigator if you are expecting them to put their family and social life on hold and at the same time that you don't really trust them. Given the unique nature of this particular investigation, I was hopeful that this policy would not apply. I was mistaken.

In spite of our collective expertise and experience, none of the team that gathered at the Bridewell that fateful day could ever, in their wildest dreams, have envisaged the journey we were about to set out upon. This investigation would come to dominate all our lives, leading to cancelled leave and family holidays, thus putting further strains on marriages and relationships. And how many of us, I have often wondered, would have made our excuses and sought removal from the investigation if we had known the turbulent road that lay ahead for us. We would face internal investigations, trial by media, an official commission of investigation, criticism from some of our more senior colleagues, one of our colleagues being convicted of an offence connected with the investigation and being summarily dismissed, the charging of the wrong man, and finally the charging of a second man and the efforts to have this second person convicted.

Yet at all times what was uppermost in our minds was the carnage that had been visited upon two defenceless victims and the need to bring someone to justice.

———

The various inquiries carried out at and around the scene, including house-to-house inquiries, traffic stops, field interviews and media appeals, quickly identified a total of seventy-five people who had either been in or passed through the immediate area on the Thursday night or Friday morning. Some thirty-seven would tell us that they had observed suspicious people or activities or heard unusual noises. People who had been identified as acting suspiciously had to be traced, implicated or eliminated ('TIE') from the investigation, which can be a slow, ponderous and time-consuming process. It is vitally important, however, to tie up such loose ends, which regularly occur in all investigations, as they can have huge consequences when presented to a jury at a subsequent trial if left open or unanswered.

Early information received suggested that three homeless men had been seen acting suspiciously in the vicinity during the night and into the early hours of the morning. It was proving impossible to find them until two nights later the garda on duty at the scene observed three people climbing into the back of an abandoned container lorry parked a short distance away. It turned out that these were the same three men, and in fact that they had slept in the lorry on the night of the murders.

A local garda, Paul Maher, was on beat duty in the area in the early part of the morning. On checking his notebook he would tell us that he had passed the scene at 11 p.m., at midnight and again at 1 a.m. Nothing of a suspicious nature was noticed by him around the house. A number of youths that he had had occasion to stop and search during the the night were found and fully investigated.

We would also learn that about a fortnight before the murders a man had been observed behaving in a suspicious manner opposite the scene. Our source suggested that the man appeared to be 'casing' the house. Inquiries turned up a number of other witnesses who also recalled seeing this person. Strangely enough, one of these witnesses would prove to have been the culprit in the first murder case I had been involved in, back in the early 1970s.

By using the various descriptions given of the person who had been acting suspiciously we were able to have a Compusketch made showing a possible likeness of him. This was given to the media in an attempt to have the man identified. I am one of those detectives who subscribe to the view that the value of such aids is questionable and in fact that they can be more of a hindrance than a help. By fixating on or being influenced by a particular description, facial feature or the like I believe that a person having genuine information can be influenced into not passing it on, believing that their evidence does not match what we appear to know already. This was never more so than in the review of a cold case I was involved in where it quickly became obvious to us that both investigators and public had become fixated upon a particular hairstyle as sported by a certain cult figure from a description given by one witness, to such an extent that certain other evidence began to be either ignored or summarily dismissed.

The publication of the Compusketch image of the Grangegorman suspect created a huge interest among the public and generated a large number of further inquiries. Sightings were reported as far apart as Galway, Cork, Waterford and Dublin. Each such sighting, of course, had to be fully investigated, the person identified had to be found, and then the TIE process had to be applied to them. We would eventually present the Compusketch image individually to each of the seventy-five people who had been at or near the scene on the night of the murders; all were adamant that they had not observed anyone that even remotely fitted it. All these inquiries had taken up considerable hours of investigation and had yielded absolutely nothing of interest to us.

Not surprisingly, given all the publicity that the discovery of the mutilated bodies had created, a huge number of people were nominated as 'persons of interest' to the inquiry. These were made by sources as diverse as members of the public, gardaí, prison officers, probation officers, medical staff from a number of institutions, informants, anonymous sources, and others, based on the person's genuinely held belief, perceptions, suspicions or simply 'feeling'. Undoubtedly a few were nominated for the sole purpose of causing the maximum inconvenience to another person. A total of 265 people would be nominated in this way. In each case the nominated person had to undergo the full gamut of the TIE process: they would be interviewed, their alibi investigated and, with their permission, their fingerprints and body samples taken. It is a testament to the abhorrence that was felt at these murders that not one of the 265 refused to co-operate. Given that a number of them had served long prison sentences for serious sexual offences or murder, and that a further number were held in various psychiatric institutions, we would have expected some resistance to our requests. Without exception, appointments were filled, blood and hair samples were freely given, and access to friends and partners was provided.

———

In July and August two momentous events occurred, beginning with the charging of a prisoner, followed within weeks by a different person making viable admissions. By then more than 1,800 jobs had been issued from the incident room, one of the largest number ever recorded for a murder investigation. The charging of Dean Lyons with the murders, rather than providing closure to the investigation, as one would have expected, would prove itself to be a watershed in Garda history and ensure that some fifteen years later we would still be living under the shadow of the Grangegorman murders.

Chapter 9

AN UNRELATED INCIDENT ON THE NIGHT OF THE MURDERS

During an investigative trawl of the magnitude of this inquiry a number of unrelated issues, some of which would never otherwise have been reported, surface and come to the attention of the investigators. We at the incident room were told of one such incident that, given the nature of the crime we were investigating, took on a huge significance and became a full investigation in itself; in fact at first it appeared that the outcome of that investigation might solve the murders for us.

The incident was the attempted abduction of a young woman a short distance from the scene of the double murder, some time between 10 and 11 p.m. on the night of 6 March. The intended victim operated as a prostitute in the nearby Benburb Street area. She later told us that, given the nature of her occupation and the fact that it often brought her into conflict with the police, she regularly received threats of one type or another but would not normally report them. In this instance, however, and given what had occurred such a short distance away, she felt it was important that it be reported.

Claire Smith (not her real name) had been working the Benburb Street beat at about 9:30 p.m. Her clientele consisted for the most part of drivers who approached her in their cars and, after agreeing a price for a particular service, drove with her to an area selected by her. One of the laneways she regularly used was a mere twenty to thirty yards from the scene of the murders at Orchard View.

On this particular night 'business' had been very slow. There had been a Garda operation against drunk drivers in the area the previous week, and there was no doubt that this had an effect on the men who would normally visit Benburb Street. Claire said she saw a Volkswagen Polo pull up a short distance from her. The driver sat in his car watching her for a few minutes. Something about his behaviour 'spooked' her; and her finely tuned instinct, honed by years of surviving on the streets, prevented her from approaching the car, as she would normally have done.

After a few minutes the driver got out of the car and approached her. As he drew nearer she noticed that he was only about twenty and was scruffily dressed and certainly did not seem the type to own a relatively new car. He greeted her with the age-old enquiry, familiar to all in the sex trade, by asking her if she was 'doing business' but never once looking her in the face. He remained in the shadow with the street lamp behind him, and she could not distinguish his features.

Claire told him she was not, that she was waiting for her boy-friend, who had gone into the laneway opposite to go to the toilet. On hearing this the young man returned to the car. He did not drive away, however, but sat there and continued to watch her. The intensity of his stare made her feel both frightened and vulnerable, and she decided to get off the street altogether for a while. She walked from Benburb Street into Stonybatter and on towards Manor Street. There were quite a few people walking about and she slowly began to feel safer. But the whole incident had an unsettling effect on her, and she decided to walk to her flat on the North Circular Road. She quickened her pace, anxious now to get home.

As she reached the junction of Manor Street and Prussia Street she stopped briefly, debating with herself whether or not to call in to the nearby chip shop to get something to eat—the same chip shop that a little over an hour later Ann Mernagh would visit to buy chips for herself and the nurse on duty at Orchard View. Standing on the footpath outside the shop, Claire glanced across the road and saw that the car, still with the young man behind the wheel, was parked partially on the footpath.

Becoming more and more frightened, she impulsively ran into Prussia Street, heading for home. Unfortunately, in doing this she would leave the safety of the well-lit and populated Manor Street area.

There was nobody to be seen in Prussia Street as she ran. Suddenly she heard the sound of squealing tyres and, looking briefly over her shoulder, saw that the car had mounted the footpath and was beginning to catch up with her.

The car then drove back onto the roadway and pulled in directly in front of her, blocking her escape route. The driver jumped from the car while it was still moving and, leaving the door open and the engine running, lunged at Claire and grabbed her coat. Shrugging free of the coat, she managed to evade him. She ran into a nearby cul-de-sac, Fingall Place, with the man still in pursuit. Realising that she had boxed herself in, and knowing that her only hope lay in attracting attention, she began banging on the front doors and windows of the houses as she ran past, all the time screaming at the top of her voice.

The people in some of the houses began opening their doors and coming out into the street. At this point the young man turned and ran back to his car and drove off at speed. One of the occupants took Claire into his house and calmed her down. After about twenty minutes he walked her home to her flat, a short distance away. There was no sign of the young man or the car. It was this householder who contacted us to tell us about the incident, and this would then lead us to Claire.

By another of those coincidences that bedevilled this inquiry, we would soon find out that the flat that Mark Nash was living in at the time, at 83 Prussia Street, was only a stone's throw from Fingall Place.

Given the proximity of this incident to our scene, coupled with what appeared on the face of it to be a failed attempt to abduct a woman, it was of course incumbent on us to investigate it in tandem with our other inquiries. At the outset we had identified the make of car and would soon discover that at about 6 p.m. the same day an incident involving a Volkswagen Polo had occurred on the Merrion Road. The driver had been approached by a young man on a bicycle, who told him he was an off-duty garda and was in pursuit of another car that had been involved in a crime. He requested that the driver allow him to take over driving the car and that he himself should sit in the front passenger seat beside him. Given the perceived urgency of the request, the driver had complied with it. They had driven away, leaving the bicycle that the young man had arrived on against a lamppost on the Merrion Road.

The erratic manner in which the man was driving the car soon led the owner to challenge him about his claim to be a garda. The young man made no response. The owner then asked him to produce identification, suspecting that he had lied to him. At this point the young man began to make some serious threats against him. He drove into the RDS showgrounds by way of the Simmonscourt Road gate and, again in a threatening manner, ordered the owner out of the car. He searched him and then jumped in and drove away.

We subsequently recovered the bicycle in the place in which it had been abandoned on the Merrion Road. We learnt that it had been stolen as long ago as 24 February from where the owner had locked and chained it at Crown Alley, off Dame Street, in the south inner city.

———

Shortly before midnight on 6 March a telephone caller to a Chinese restaurant requested a meal to be delivered to his home at Grangegorman Villas, an area close to our murder scene. Ann, a delivery woman working with the restaurant, was given the meal to deliver to the address supplied. She left the restaurant and drove to Grangegorman Villas, arriving there, according to the various parties involved, at 12:15 a.m. This time was considered extremely relevant by us, given that our culprit would either be inside the scene at that time or very close to it.

Ann had driven from the restaurant into Kirwan Street and from there out into Lower Grangegorman—the same route that Ann Mernagh had taken on her way home a short time previously. At the junction of Kirwan Street and Lower Grangegorman she observed a black Volkswagen Polo parked dangerously. The driver appeared to be slumped across the wheel; by the look of him she took him to be drunk. As she passed the same spot some ten minutes later, having delivered her order, she saw the car again, this time on the opposite side of the road and apparently freewheeling. As she drove past it the brake lights came on. She drove back to the restaurant and gave no further thought to the car until after she heard about the murders.

Finding this car and its occupant now became a priority. We sent out an all-station message, asking that a special search be begun with a view to finding the car. Gardaí were advised that if the car were observed they were not to approach it or its occupant without first contacting ourselves. A 'special search' is a citywide operation in which each mobile unit must search a designated area at an agreed time. On the completion of the search each team must report on the outcome to our radio control room. This is a mammoth undertaking, one that is used only in very special circumstances.

By the end of the search our car was found, parked in the public car park at St James's Hospital. This was one of the favoured spots for the criminal fraternity when leaving stolen cars that they intended to use again. There was a very good chance that a car could remain undiscovered for days on end in a busy car park. The crew that found the car had withdrawn and parked a safe distance away, from which they were able to keep it under observation.

When we were informed that the car was found, we immediately arranged for a specialist surveillance unit to stay with it. However, after the first twenty-fours, and following consultation with our forensic science experts, we decided to have the car removed for technical examination. This decision was made because of the importance of not losing any trace evidence that might be adhering to the car from our murder scene, given that the weather forecast had warned of very unsettled weather to come. We arranged for a low-loader to take the car to the secure vehicle examination facility then based at the former Garda Forensic Science Laboratory in St John's Road, Kilmainham.

At the Examination Unit the car was almost completely dismantled while a team of experts pored over every inch of it to establish whether any connection with the murder scene or with the victims could be found. To our huge disappointment, no such evidence was found.

Through sources in the criminal world we were told that the car had been stolen from its owner by Jerry Reilly (not his real name), a career criminal from the south inner city. A warrant to search his home for trace evidence that might link him to the murders was obtained in Dublin District Court by Detective-Inspector Michael Duggan. On 16 April 1997 he led a party of gardaí, accompanied by our forensic science team, in a search of the house. This search also proved fruitless.

Later the same day Reilly contacted us by phone and arranged to meet some of our team near his home. He readily admitted being involved in the various crimes connected with the bicycle, the car and the assault on Claire Smith. He also admitted having been in the car at Kirwan Street when it was observed by the delivery woman, Ann. He totally denied, however, any involvement in the murders of Sylvia Sheils and Mary Callinan. He told us he had left the Kirwan Street area after a few minutes and had driven directly to St James's Hospital car park, where he had left the car. Closed-circuit television footage would show him driving the car into the car park at 12:25 a.m. and then walking back out.

Given this evidence we had to eliminate Reilly, who for so long had seemed to be our culprit, from our inquiries.

Incidentally, Reilly had consented to our doctor taking oral swabs and samples of head and pubic hair from him. He had baulked, however, when asked if he would provide a blood sample, telling us that the plucked hair from his head would be enough for DNA comparison. I was impressed with his scientific knowledge until Matt Mulhall showed me that his record included the fact that he had received one of the first convictions in the country using DNA evidence following a serious sexual assault by him.

A humorous side of that incident came out when the investigating gardaí asked Reilly to give a blood sample and he had readily agreed. He later confided to associates that the blood sample would be no good to the gardaí, because, as everybody 'except them dumb coppers' was aware, 'blood is red and semen is white.'

Chapter 10 ∼

DEAN LYONS BECOMES A 'PERSON OF INTEREST'

A s the investigation progressed through the spring and into the summer of 1997, the number of people who, for one reason or another, became 'persons of interest' to the team continued to grow. Before the investigation was complete it would have grown to more than 250 people.

'Persons of interest' are those people identified by investigators who, though not themselves suspects, are nonetheless people we would be keen to eliminate from our inquiries. Actual suspects cannot be interviewed in the ordinary way without the legal caution being administered to them; were they to make some comment or admission while being interviewed without having been cautioned it would not be admissible in court. If such an admission were made, the garda involved would face rigorous questioning about his frame of mind when asking the question that brought on the response. If the question was asked to trick or obtain a confession from a person suspected of committing a crime, it could not be used.

A person of interest is just that; but were they to say anything to implicate themselves it might be admissible. This whole case would be based on just such a response.

Persons of interest can come to the attention of the Gardaí in a number of ways. These include confidential information from criminal sources, information from members of the public, and information from gardaí, prison officers, probation officers or others whose day-to-day work brings them into contact, and sometimes conflict, with criminal elements. It may be nothing more than a suggestion from an informant who feels there is something strange about the person they are nominating, or a garda expressing a personal suspicion based on dealings they may have had with a person they were arresting or otherwise dealing with. And we must always be careful that a person is not being nominated through vindictiveness or as pay-back for some injury or slight.

One sure way of encouraging information is through media appeals. It is, of course, what they are intended for. A number of appeals for assistance had been broadcast on various radio and television programmes in the early part of the investigation. The 'Crimeline' programme on RTE television in early July 1997 carried an appeal by Chief Superintendent Dick Kelly aimed directly at members of the public living in the vicinity of the scene. He asked for householders and others who had been victims of crime, especially those who for one reason or another might not have already reported the matter, to come forward and do so now. This appeal was based on the premise suggested by the crime-scene profiler that our culprit might live and be criminally active in the area. There was a chance that while local people might tolerate a neighbour who they were aware was engaging in minor crime—such as malicious damage, or stealing clothing from clothes lines or the like—they might be willing to anonymously pass on the person's details if they felt there might be some connection to the murders.

This appeal brought a huge response from the public. Among the calls received were two from two different householders in the area whose homes had been broken into. In one of these cases the Gardaí had arrested the culprit, while in the second instance the culprit had been known to the householder and had fled when challenged. This second incident had not previously been reported. I made out action sheets requesting that both youths be considered persons of interest and that they be investigated by the appropriate teams. It was quickly established, however, that one of them, John Whelan (not his real name), was then in custody in Mountjoy Prison.

On 11 July two gardaí called to Mountjoy. They met and spoke to Whelan in an area off the main visitors' area. At first he was very reluctant to engage with them, but when they told him they were involved in the Grangegorman murder inquiry he told them that he had been in custody on the night of the crime, serving a sentence that had been imposed on him the previous October. He added that he knew the area where the murders took place, as he used to frequent the nearby Benburb Street area, dealing drugs to the prostitutes there. He described himself as knowing nothing about the murders. A check with the prison authorities showed that he had indeed been in custody on the night of 6/7 March. To all intents and purposes this lead was a dead end.

It was found that the second person nominated to the investigating team by a member of the public was also serving a term of imprisonment. Éamonn White (not his real name) was incarcerated in Wheatfield Prison. On 18 July two detectives called to the prison and, through the prison governor, asked White if he would meet them, telling him that they wanted to talk to him in connection with the Grangegorman murders, as he had been nominated to them as a person of interest. He flatly refused to leave his cell or to talk to the gardaí. Given that it was his prerogative as a prisoner serving a sentence to refuse such a request, the detectives left the prison.

At the conference the following morning the gardaí involved updated those present on the outcome of their inquiries in both prisons. It was decided that they should find out when White was due for release and should meet him and interview him as he left the prison. The job was then put 'on hold', that is, categorised as pending and not completed.

Unknown to us, however, on the evening following our visit to the prison Whelan met some of his fellow-prisoners in the recreation area. By this time word had spread through the 'bush telegraph' in the prison that the coppers had called to interview him about the Grangegorman murders. Whelan told them that, while personally he had nothing to do with the crime, he did in fact possess information that he believed was relevant to it. He was not, however, going to 'grass anyone up to the coppers'; he had never done that before and would not do so now. In the discussion that followed, a consensus quickly emerged that in this exceptional instance Whelan should go back to the Gardaí and give them the information he had in his possession. This consensus was typical of the depth of feeling that existed in relation to these murders.

Whelan approached a prison officer whom he trusted and asked him if he would find out the names of the gardaí who had called to see him and if he would then ring their station and ask them to call back, that there was something he wished to talk to them about. The prison officer rang the incident room at the Bridewell and outlined to me his conversation with Whelan. He described Whelan as appearing to him to be anxious and worried and added that he had told him that he was in possession of important information about the murders that he was now prepared to pass on. Needless to say, this information caused great excitement among the team.

At the conference the following morning two of the more experienced detectives were told to visit Whelan and find out what his information was. They were also told that they would be expected to give an opinion about the veracity of the information as it was imparted to them. The prison authorities agreed that, given the nature of this crime, they would be facilitated on their arrival with an unsupervised private visit, away from the visitors' section.

When they met Whelan he appeared to them at first to be reluctant to engage with them. He told them that he had never in his life either admitted anything when being interviewed or given information about anyone else. He said he was finding it very difficult to do so now but that, given what had happened to the 'two old dears', he would not have been able to live with himself if the same things were to be done to someone else because he had held back information that might help. He also told them that he had discussed talking to the coppers with other prisoners before making up his mind.

He then said that his record, which the two detectives had with them, showing his various sentences and the times he had spent in prison, was not entirely true. The record showed that he had been serving a sentence at the time of the murders, a sentence he was still serving. What that record did not show, he said, was that on the day of the murders, 6 March 1997, he had been released from the prison, having served the greater part of the sentence he was in for. However, as he left the prison he had been met by gardaí who had been waiting for him to get out and had immediately arrested him for another matter, what is known in Garda parlance as a 'gate arrest'.

He had been taken directly to Kilmainham Garda Station, where he had been charged with aggravated burglary in a premises on the south side of the city some months previously. Aggravated burglary differs from the simple crime of burglary in that during the break-in the culprit offers or threatens violence towards the occupant, or the culprit is found to have been in possession of a weapon when carrying out the crime. This offence carries huge penalties. White had appeared that day at Kilmainham District Court and was remanded in custody. In effect, this meant that at no time on 6 March was he free to have committed the murders. On the other hand, the prison records did not show any break in his detention.

On 14 March 1997 White again appeared at Kilmainham District Court. The trial judge on this occasion granted him his own bail. Having signed the bail bond, he immediately left the court and went to the Benburb Street area and met his girl-friend, Marian Doyle (not her real name), who operated every day as a prostitute there to feed her heroin habit. Given that with Éamonn's arrival she now had two habits to feed, she decided to stay working the streets. He stayed close by in case any of her 'punters', as the women called them, offered her any violence or refused to pay her. At one point, he said, they had 'scored', that is, purchased some heroin, 'off the bloke who always sells the gear to the brassers [prostitutes]'. At first reluctant to name his dealer, he eventually said that it was a John Whelan. This was the prisoner we had interviewed in Mountjoy Prison on 11 July and who told us that he was in custody on the night of 6 March. Éamonn White and Marian Doyle had both 'shot up' in nearby waste ground, and Marian had then gone back to the street.

White said that later the same evening he had been standing at the doorway of the Model Hostel in Benburb Street. Marian had gone down a nearby laneway with one of her customers, and White was waiting for her to return. The Model Hostel caters for homeless men only and at that time was run by the Homeless Section of Dublin City Council. Given the strict guidelines laid down for occupancy—including signing in and out, rules for behaviour and a total ban on alcohol—coupled with the fact that a token nightly rent was paid, it was frequented for the most part by the older and more mature members of the homeless community. The younger generation, especially those with addiction problems, tended to avoid it altogether.

Éamonn White said that John Whelan, from whom he had bought the drugs earlier, was also outside the hostel. On this occasion Whelan was accompanied by three of his associates or customers who were also known to White. Two of these were Anthony Dunne (not his real name) and an Englishman called Liverpool Joe. (A suggestion that these two men might have been involved in the murders would surface as our inquiries were broadened.) The third person in Whelan's company was a heroin addict called 'Dino' Lyons, later identified as Dean Lyons. This was the first time that Dean's name had come to the attention of the investigation.

The group were discussing various incidents and, given that the scene at Grangegorman was very near to where they were gathered, together with the continuing police activity in the area, it was understandably the main topic of conversation. Anthony Dunne had commented that there had been 'no need to rape that granny.' The others told him that he was a 'dirty bastard' for referring to the victims in that way. White said that on hearing the comment Dino Lyons had begun laughing. Dunne had again commented that 'there had been no need to do it.' At this point White said that he began to feel very uncomfortable with the way the conversation appeared to be going.

At this stage Dino, according to White, appeared to become all 'hot and bothered'. He had stood in front of Dunne and told him to shut up, adding that 'one of these days' he would get his head punched for speaking like that. White then saw his girl-friend coming out of the laneway down which she had brought her client. She signalled to him, and he went over to her, believing her to be in trouble. He spoke to her and she told him that everything was all right and had given him money with which to try and 'score some more gear' for them both. He returned to the hostel door, but the group had dispersed. He was unable even to find Whelan to buy drugs from him.

Éamonn White said that this was the only information concerning the murders that he possessed, and he described himself as feeling better for having passed it on.

The interviewing gardaí thanked him and returned directly to the incident room. There the notes they had made of their conversation with Éamonn Whelan were discussed. On the face of it, we had two criminals falling out, in front of witnesses, about comments one of them had made about the murders.

The reaction of Dino Lyons to the comment about it not being necessary to rape one of the women did not appear to be a natural reaction and further suggested that this information could be significant. One group of detectives was set the task of obtaining information about his background and his present whereabouts. A full list of his friends and associates, including girl-friends, was also to be compiled. This task was to be undertaken as a matter of urgency.

We now also had a good reason for interviewing John Whelan again. When previously interviewed he had told us that he had been in custody on the night of the murders. This information had been borne out by the prison staff. However, given what we had learnt about White's sentence, we decided that we should double-check with the prison. To our surprise, we learnt that Whelan was due for release within the next two days. A separate team of gardaí was appointed to liaise with the prison and establish the exact time at which he was to be released. They were to meet him and tell him they wished to talk to him about a conversation in Benburb Street that he had participated in some days after the murders. They were to invite him to accompany them to the Bridewell. The reason for selecting a separate team was to ensure that Whelan's recollection would not be affected by people who had already heard one side of the alleged conversation.

On the morning of 22 July 1997, as Whelan stepped out of the main gate of the prison, he was met by our two gardaí. When told that they wished to speak to him in relation to knowledge he might have about the Grangegorman murders, he said he had already been interviewed and had given an alibi for the night of the murders. They told him they were aware of that but that what they wished to talk to him about was a certain conversation that had taken place outside the Model Hostel a few days after the murders. On hearing this he immediately said he would go with them to the station.

At the station he told the detectives he could clearly recall one evening being down in Benburb Street with his girl-friend, Patty Long (not her real name). They had been standing outside the hostel. Also present, he said, were Éamonn White, Marian Doyle, Anthony Dunne and Dean Lyons. They had all been talking about a robbery that had occurred that day in which they believed an associate of theirs had been involved. Dunne, according to Whelan, had said to them: 'You want to check out the yoke we did.' On hearing this, Dean Lyons had immediately intervened in the conversation and had shouted, 'It was just a burglary.'

This did not stop Dunne, who had continued talking. He said that he and Dean Lyons had broken into a house together. After they left the house they had discovered that one of them had dropped his social welfare card while they were inside the house. This is a card issued by the Department of Social Welfare and is required as identification when unemployment assistance or any other social welfare benefit is being claimed, and it carries some of the recipient's personal information. Leaving it at the scene of a crime would be like leaving your name and address behind. When they had gone back into the house there had been what Dunne described as a 'scuffle'. This house, he added, was up in the 'Gorman'.

Whelan said that at this point in the conversation Dean Lyons, who was normally the most timid and placid of young men, began to become very annoyed with Dunne. He grabbed Dunne around the neck, pushed him against the wall and screamed at him to shut up. Lyons appeared to him to have been very upset by the comments and also seemed afraid that Dunne would keep talking, revealing more of the story. The conversation had ended abruptly after this.

The following day Whelan had again met Dean Lyons and Anthony Dunne in the Benburb Street area. They were looking for a dealer to get their heroin. He said they had told him they were going to get out of the city; they mentioned 'going down the country.' He was aware that they had never actually left and believed they were deliberately avoiding him because he knew of their possible involvement in the murders.

When the revelations made by John Whelan were reported to us in the incident room it was decided that before going after Dean Lyons and Anthony Dunne we would firstly try to find the others who allegedly were present when this potentially very important conversation took place. In this way it was hoped that when the time came to put these matters to them we would have a number of people who would be in a position to support the stories of both Whelan and White. It is hardly necessary to say that at this point both Dean Lyons and Anthony Dunne qualified for inclusion in our list of 'persons of interest'.

Éamonn White had made reference to an Englishman called Liverpool Joe having been present during the conversation at the Model Hostel. His presence had not been adverted to by John Whelan.

Nevertheless it was decided that he should be interviewed and asked if he had any recollection of it. When it was put to him by the team he readily admitted that he was regularly in the company of some or all of those mentioned and often met them in the Benburb Street area. He was adamant that he had never been with them when any discussion had taken place about the murders and certainly had never been with them when they made any admissions to the actual crimes.

White's girl-friend, Marian Doyle, told us that it was true that she operated as a prostitute in the Benburb Street area to feed her growing heroin dependence. Her boy-friend was also an addict, and her earnings went to buy him his drugs also. All those mentioned by both White and Whelan were well known to her and she would regularly meet them in the area. The only conversation she had ever heard about the murders was one night when her boy-friend had an argument with another addict over splitting their heroin and this other person had suggested that her boy-friend was 'bad enough' to have committed them.

Equally, Whelan's girl-friend, Patty Long, told us that she had never taken part in or overheard any such conversation. On the day the conversation was alleged to have taken place she herself had been in custody in Mountjoy Prison over another matter.

To muddy the waters even further, Whelan had also told the gardaí during their interview with him that after their first visit to him in prison there had been a discussion between him and a number of his associates who were also serving sentences. Another prisoner who was well known to him had told him that he was wrong in saying that Dunne and Lyons had admitted the murders. This other prisoner, Noel Moore (not his real name), told him that he knew who had done them. He said that on the night of the murders he had broken into a different house in the Grangegorman area. After stealing some electrical equipment he had been going through some back lanes to avoid walking into the gardaí while carrying stolen property. In a laneway near the scene he had met the murderer. He knew this man to see and said that his name was Eddie Farrell (not his real name). They had greeted one another and then gone their separate ways. He said he had subsequently been arrested for the burglary by a named garda attached to the Bridewell Station and that all the property he had stolen was recovered.

Moore was, of course, questioned about this. Here he was admitting to having met the culprit near the scene of the crime! He told us that what he had said to White was merely a rumour that was rife around where he lived, and that Farrell was a well-known 'weirdo'. He absolutely denied being involved in any break-in in the area on the night of the murders. He had in fact been in custody at the time. Furthermore, the garda named said that he had not arrested Moore for a burglary or found him in possession of stolen property at that time.

Eddie Farrell, it was established, was in fact an in-patient in St Brendan's Hospital on the night of 6 March. The rumour about his involvement had originated after an argument between himself and another patient.

Anthony Dunne, who both Whelan and White had alleged had made the actual admissions during the conversation outside the Model Hostel, would later be arrested and interviewed in connection with the murders of Sylvia Sheils and Mary Callinan.

Liverpool Joe's name would also surface again. This time he would be nominated as the murderer by another person, a Pat Ryan, who had himself been nominated by Dean Lyons, who told his father Ryan been with him when he killed both women. He would be traced to Liverpool and interviewed. No evidence to suggest any involvement by either of these men was established. However, I will be referring to them again later.

On 22 September 1997 we revisited John Whelan. This was after the arrest of Anthony Dunne, which had been based on the information he had provided us. The purpose of this visit was to establish whether Whelan was still adamant about the conversation he alleged he had heard. This visit was also after the arrest and charging of Mark Nash with the murders of Catherine and Carl Doyle.

During this visit Whelan told the detectives that everything he had previously told us was completely untrue, including the admissions he claimed to have heard Dunne making. He further claimed that it had been his girl-friend, Patty, who had told him that Dean had admitted the murders. We immediately made contact with Patty, who denied that she had ever said anything like that to Whelan. She equally denied that Dean had made any admission to her. She offered to confront Whelan in our presence and to repeat this denial to him.

We went back to Whelan and told him that Patty said she had never said anything to him about the murders. We also told him that she was outside in the car and would come in and repeat the denial in front of him. Whelan backed down completely and told us that he had been lying when he claimed that Patty had said it to him. He had been told by Dean himself, he said, during one of their private conversations, that he had killed the two women in Grangegorman.

This was the third version of this whole event that Whelan had given us about how he became aware that Dean Lyons had been involved in the murders. His original version had been to some extent corroborated by Éamonn White; however, when the wider circle of associates that they claimed were present at the time were canvassed about the issue, they did not support the story.

Substance users and abusers, as all the members of this group were, are notorious not so much for telling lies to the police as for having a habit of telling us what they think we want to hear. A classic example of this was when we met Pat Ryan, who Dean Lyons would say was with him on the night. Instead of just making a blanket denial, Pat named an entirely different person as being Dean's accomplice. Dean, he told us, was so afraid of this second person that, rather than naming him, he had taken the soft option and blamed Pat instead.

Innuendo and gossip can very quickly, in the day-to-day life of the addict, take on the mantle of truth. Sometimes the line between reality and rumour can become blurred and unrecognisable. Their life will bring them into regular contact, and indeed conflict, with the judicial system. Sometimes their very freedom can be dependent on giving the arresting garda an earful. Certain addicts were notorious for telling us every crime each of their associates had committed but would never mention any of their own transgressions. They feel that to have a copper dependant on them for information is no bad thing when they are involved in illegal acts to feed their addiction. Every good policeman will number among his 'touts' or informants a few addicts like this. The important thing to remember when receiving information from these sources is that they come with a 'health warning' attached.

I believe that the two people who gave such damning evidence against Dean Lyons and Anthony Dunne did not do so out of any desire to wrong them. Undoubtedly there had been a conversation between them all in relation to the murders. Unfortunately, the interpretation of this conversation took on a life of its own, and it would prove to be the catalyst that led the investigation towards Dean Lyons and all the notoriety that ensued.

The information supplied to us by Whelan and White suggested that both Dean Lyons and Anthony Dunne should be fully investigated. Although the case against them was diminished substantially by the failure of the other witnesses who they claimed had been part of the conversation to corroborate their information—Patty Long, Marian Doyle and Liverpool Joe—we would have been remiss in our duty had we not followed the information to a conclusion.

Chapter 11

THE INITIAL INTERVIEW WITH DEAN LYONS

At the outset certain difficulties were encountered while we attempted to trace the whereabouts of Anthony Dunne. The investigation team learnt that Dean Lyons regularly slept at a hostel for homeless people run by the Salvation Army on the Broadstone side of the grounds of St Brendan's Hospital, known among the homeless fraternity as the 'Army Hostel'. Access to this part of the hospital grounds was through a tunnel that ran from the main hospital complex and under Grangegorman Road Upper. Access by road was through a gateway that opened off Morning Star Avenue.

The hostel was in a pre-fab building that had been erected in the late 1960s opposite the main ward complex. It was always referred to as the 'Army Hostel'. It is believed that this name derives not from the Salvation Army but from the fact that on the outbreak of violence in Northern Ireland in the late 1960s and early 70s these pre-fab buildings had been put up to provide temporary accommodation for families forced to flee their homes in the North, and when it was originally opened it was staffed by army personnel.

The various hospital wards had been closed for several years, and the huge granite buildings that had housed them had fallen into disrepair. All the windows and doors to the front of the derelict building that overlooked the pre-fab had been boarded up. The rear had been altered a few years earlier to resemble the GPO in O'Connell

Street for the making of the film *Michael Collins*. The false columns, tram lines and false cobblestones are there to this day.

Although boarded up, the main building in recent years had come to be used as a shelter by the city's rough sleepers and was known among themselves as the 'skipper'. These are the homeless people who would not stay in the ordinary hostels, either because of substance abuse, fear of other residents or a desire to remain independent of and outside the system. A number of them had been barred from other hostels because of recurring violent outbursts while staying in them.

The building was regularly checked by gardaí seeking people either wanted on warrant or wanted in connection with particular crimes. The offices and cordoned-off portions of the large Dickensian wards had been adapted as living areas. The original steel beds that had been left behind were upended to form physical barriers around the staked-out sleeping areas. Mattresses were strewn like carpeting on the ground. Fires would be lit on the concrete floors, and these were the only source of light in the dark, dank building. Personal belongings, meagre as they were, would be kept close at all times. 'Turf wars' were a regular feature, and personal safety and survival were totally dependent either on the occupant's reputation or on their connections.

The rear of the building looked out onto a large open area, which had been used to stage the various crowd scenes in the making of the film. This area also housed the abandoned nurses' home, and a separate portion was fenced off and used as storage space by the hospital maintenance department. The administrative offices were housed in the old eighteenth-century debtors' prison to the front of the site. At the top end of the site and at its furthest distance from the derelict hospital buildings is the back wall of number 1 Orchard View.

In the late 1980s the bodies of two rough sleepers, Danny Lyons and Pauline Leonard, were found lying side by side in a derelict site off nearby Benburb Street. Both had died from hypothermia after falling asleep in the open. The case caused a public outcry, with their joint funeral attracting huge attention. Given my relationship with homeless people, I read one of the epistles during their funeral mass.

Morning Star Avenue houses a further three hostels that provide accommodation for homeless and displaced persons. These are the Morning Star Hostel for men, the Regina Coeli Hostel for women and a separate hostel in the grounds of the Regina Coeli that provided shelter for families fleeing from abusive spouses. These were run by the Legion of Mary, whose founder, Frank Duff, had lived for many years in a large detached house adjacent to the hostels until his death in 1980.

On a given night this small area could be home to several hundred homeless, displaced or transient people, who brought with them a large number of addiction and other problems. It was an area best avoided unless you were unfortunate enough to require its services.

Shortly after 9 a.m. on Saturday 26 July 1997 two members of the murder investigation team, Detective-Garda Billy Mullis and Garda Joseph O'Connor, called to the entrance doorway of the Army Hostel. These were the two gardaí who had been designated to deal with Dean Lyons. Both were experienced gardaí who had previously been involved in a number of major investigations. They had been teamed together during this investigation as part of the group formed to trace, implicate or eliminate persons of interest.

As each of the residents left the hostel they carefully avoided all eye contact with the gardaí—a natural reaction, given their life circumstances. Dean Lyons came out alone and was immediately approached by the two gardaí, who introduced themselves to him. The other residents visibly relaxed as they realised that it was not them the coppers had been waiting for. In their lives, the adage that someone else's misfortune was their good fortune certainly applied.

When the gardaí introduced themselves to him, Dean replied, 'I think I know what this is about.' Mullis told him that they were investigating the murders of Mary Callinan and Sylvia Sheils and that they believed he possessed certain information in relation to the crimes. They asked him if he would consent to accompany them to the Bridewell Station, where, with his consent, they would take a set of his fingerprints and arrange for a doctor to take body samples from him for comparison with the crime scene. He would also be interviewed about his knowledge of the crime and asked to account for his movements on the night. It was emphasised to him that he was not being arrested. Dean readily agreed to go with the two gardaí.

Outside the station he was again reminded that he did not have to go in with the two gardaí and furthermore that if he did go into the station he was free to leave any time he wished. He was then brought to a room referred to as the doctor's room, a room outside the jail section that was regularly used by doctors when examining people in the station. Dr Jim Murphy (not his real name) was contacted, and he arrived at the station some twenty minutes later. Body samples were taken from Dean after he had given his consent to the doctor. Dr Murphy had previously taken similar samples from a number of the other persons of interest during this inquiry. Dean was then fingerprinted and photographed. After washing his hands, he returned to the doctor's room with Billy and Joe.

It should be explained here that the Bridewell Station consists of two quite separate sections, one part being the public area, which is overseen by the sergeant in charge. This is the part of the station where members of the public can call on business. The other part is the separate jail section, which is overseen by the prison sergeant. Access is through a locked steel gate from within the station; it also has a steel doorway giving access to the enclosed yard to the rear. Those awaiting their appearance in court or transfer to prison, as well as those detained for questioning, are held in one of its twenty cells, some of which, on a busy court morning, could hold as many as ten prisoners each.

The Bridewell was built in 1901 to serve as a detention centre for the nearby Police Courts, later to become Dublin District Court, which is still in use today. The building became a Garda station only in the mid-1960s, following the closure of the almost derelict station attached to the Special Criminal Court buildings in nearby Green Street. After being designated a Garda station the Bridewell was subdivided, the majority of its cells being converted to either offices or bedrooms. Having slept in some of those bedrooms during the early 1970s I can say that the alterations must have been minimal.

Joseph O'Connor gave Dean a cup of coffee, and the interviewing of him began. Between then and 1:30 p.m. an easy-going, relaxed atmosphere had developed between Dean and the gardaí. It would later be described by them as a conversation rather than a structured interview. Dean freely discussed with them his substance addiction problem, the difficulties this had caused in his home, his involvement in crime and his general life-style. He said that he could not at that point recall where he might have spent the night of 5/6 March. He suggested that he might have stayed in the Army Hostel. When told that his name did not appear on the attendance sheet, he shrugged his shoulders and said that at that point he could not dispute that. He vehemently denied, however, being involved in the murders. He also claimed not to have any information that could help the Gardaí. He conceded that he knew a man called Anthony Dunne and said that he hung around with him and regularly 'scored gear' with him.

Throughout this interview Dean remained relaxed and friendly. He continuously smoked cigarettes provided by the gardaí and laughed and joked with them. As their conversation drew to a close, Garda Joe O'Connor reminded Dean that the body samples taken from him would be submitted for analysis and that the fingerprints taken from him would be compared with any fingermarks developed and lifted at the murder scene. Dean, he told him, would have a lot of explaining to do if his fingerprints were identified at the scene.

At this point, on hearing what Joe had just said, Dean made a comment, the implications of which would reverberate through the Garda Síochána and Irish society for years to come. He said he had actually been inside the house at 1 Orchard View about a year and a half before the murders. A friend of his, Michael Flynn (not his real name), was a nephew of one of the women who lived in the house, and he had called with Michael to see her and to deliver a message to her from Michael's mother. He added that Michael's aunt was the woman who 'wasn't murdered' that night. This was taken to be a reference to Ann Mernagh. Dean then said that he could be making a mistake and that it might have been Michael Flynn's brother, Robbie (not his real name), that had called to the house with him on that particular day.

This was the first time the Gardaí had been aware of any connection, however tenuous, between Dean Lyons and any of the residents of the house at Orchard View; nor had the Flynns' relationship to Ann Mernagh been known to them.

Joe O'Connor told Dean that this information could not be true, as the Gardaí knew that Ann Mernagh had only moved into the house in September the previous year, some six months before the murder. To the amazement of both gardaí, this comment had an immediate effect on Dean. His whole demeanour changed in an instant. Gone was the casual banter and the rapport that had been established between them during the morning; he became visibly upset and nervous. He ceased all eye contact with the gardaí, bowed his head, and began to shake.

Billy Mullis leaned closer to Dean and asked him if he was all right and if there was something bothering him. He began to cry. Through his sobbing he said he had something to tell them. In a low, barely discernible voice he said, 'I killed the two old ladies.' He added that he was sorry.

In a matter of minutes a mundane interview, being carried out for the most part to ensure that all the necessary boxes were ticked, an interview that was being wound down, had undergone a sea change. With those few words Dean Lyons had progressed from 'person of interest' status to culprit. He continued to stare at the ground, sobbing gently; he became more and more distressed.

In accordance with the Judges' Rules, which govern admissions made during the course of a general conversation as opposed to during an interview with a person in custody, Detective-Garda Mullis, though taken aback by this development, applied the procedure instilled in him by years of experience and issued the legal caution to Dean. After being told that he was was not obliged to say anything unless he wished to do so and that anything he did say would be taken down in writing and could be given in evidence, Dean's sole reply was that his mother and family would never forgive him.

Chapter 12 ∽

THE ARREST AND DETENTION OF DEAN LYONS

Following his admission to a serious crime, Dean Lyons was told that he could no longer be treated as he had been up to then and that the Gardaí now intended to arrest him for the murders of Sylvia Sheils and Mary Callinan. Dean and the two gardaí left the 'doctor's room' and walked in silence out of the station into Chancery Street. Dean kept his head bowed, looking down at the ground, and continued to cry. Equally, neither Billy Mullis nor Joe O'Connor made eye contact with any colleagues they met while walking out of the station. The enormity of the moment was affecting them almost as much as it was Dean. They walked out through the front door of the station in a tight group and stepped onto the footpath outside. Billy then told Dean that he was now arresting him.

The reason for leaving the station was to ensure that the arrest occurred in a 'public place', as required by the legislation. Both Mullis and O'Connor were very mindful that one wrong act by them could jeopardise any evidence that had been established. They were also quite isolated, with no opportunity to discuss this development with their superiors or their colleagues. In arriving at the decision to arrest Dean Lyons they were aware that they were starting an irreversible chain of events but felt that, given the unsolicited admissions made by Dean, they were left with no other alternative.

Dean continued sobbing and kept his head lowered throughout. The time was 1:45 p.m.

Upstairs in the incident room Matt Mulhall and myself continued to work away, unaware of the drama that had developed only yards away. But word gradually filtered up that Billy had arrested Dean after he had admitted to the crime. We sat there in amazement, wondering if it could be true, if this case that we had lived with over the last few months and that at times had almost overwhelmed us with its sheer volume and scope was finally over. We then rushed down the stairs to witness the unfolding drama. Little did we know the twists and turns that this day was about to bring.

A lot of hypotheses and suggestions have been put forward about what may have caused Dean Lyons to respond as he did to the remark Joe O'Connor made about his fingerprints. Both Joe and Billy Mullis always expressed amazement afterwards when talking about it with their colleagues. Dean's relaxed, easy-going manner had changed in an instant. He had slumped forward onto the desk that separated him from the two gardaí, his head almost touching it, and wept bitterly. In a barely audible voice he admitted to having committed two of the most vicious murders ever committed in Ireland. The concerns he expressed for the effect his crimes would have on his family lent further credence to his admission.

Mullis and O'Connor had worked well together as a team since the beginning of this investigation. By the morning of 26 July they had interviewed and eliminated a large number of persons of interest. Before each interview they fully acquainted themselves with the contents of the briefing document and were in a position to put all the facts to each person; but nothing could have prepared them for the astounding admission in their interview of Dean Lyons.

After being arrested in Chancery Street, Dean was taken to an area adjacent to the public office in the Bridewell Station. He was introduced to the sergeant in charge, Tom O'Meara, to whom the details of Dean's admission and arrest were outlined by Billy. Under the Treatment of Persons in Custody Regulations (1987), Tom would be responsible for ensuring that Dean was properly treated while in his charge. He had a reputation throughout the city as an honourable and decent garda who treated all who came into contact with him in a fair and humane manner. In his long service he had dealt with hundreds of prisoners.

Tom told Dean that he would now be detained for up to six hours and that this period could, on the instructions of a superintendent, be extended for a further six hours. He was also informed of his right to have a solicitor contacted and asked to attend at the station, and further that he was entitled to have any person of his choice informed that he was being detained at the station. All this was explained in simple, everyday language to him to ensure that he was fully aware of his rights. In a barely audible voice Dean responded: 'I killed the two women in Grangegorman.' He declined the offer of a solicitor. Sergeant O'Meara told him that if at any time he changed his mind a solicitor would be contacted for him immediately.

In compliance with the Electronic Recording of Interviews Regulations (1997), Dean was then told that facilities existed in the Bridewell for the electronic recording of interviews with him while he was in custody. This could be either an audiovisual or audio-only recording. The system was then in its infancy, with the Bridewell Station being one of only three pilot stations in the country where these facilities were available.

One of the most important aspects of the pilot scheme was that any such recording could be made only with the express permission of the prisoner being interviewed. To prove to the courts that an offer to allow the interview be recorded had been made, if a prisoner declined to have an interview electronically recorded they must be electronically recorded making that refusal. They could also, at any point during a recorded interview, withdraw their consent to further participation, whereupon the recording must be stopped immediately.

By coincidence, this regulation was due to be changed after 1 September 1997. After that date the officer in charge of the Garda station would be the only person entitled to make this decision, and only in carefully regulated circumstances would interviews be allowed to proceed without being electronically recorded. The pilot scheme had found that there had been a high refusal rate among those being interviewed.

At the time of Dean's arrest, however, the only person who could decide to opt in or out of the system of recording the interviews was Dean himself. This was a situation that would take on a huge significance both as events unfolded on the afternoon of 26 July and for many years to come.

Dean made one request, and that was that he be allowed to contact his mother. Sergeant O'Meara assured him that immediately on his entering the jail section he would be facilitated with a phone call to his home. In the jail section Dean gave Joe O'Connor his home phone number. Joe rang the number, and it was answered by Dean's sister, who said that her mother was not then available. Dean was handed the phone and spoke briefly to his sister. He asked her to tell their mother that he had been arrested and was being detained in the Bridewell. He added that he had been arrested for murder. Seemingly unable to continue with the conversation, he then handed the phone back to Joe.

At Dean's request the sergeant in charge of the jail section, Sergeant Eddie Corry, arranged for the interview suite fitted with the audiovisual equipment to be made available for any subsequent interviewing. Eddie again established that Dean had been offered the services of a solicitor, and when Dean told him that he had been asked and that he did not want one, Eddie told him that if he felt at any time while he was being detained that he needed a solicitor he was to ask for one. The questioning, he was told, would then be suspended until the solicitor arrived.

At 3:27 p.m. Dean's mother phoned the station. Tom O'Meara put the call through to the jail section and Dean was brought to the phone. They had an emotionally charged conversation, during which Dean was clearly heard by the gardaí standing at the nearby desk to tell his mother, 'I did it. I'm sorry.' He began to shake and appeared to have difficulty in holding the phone. He then became so upset that he terminated the call and handed the phone back to the garda. He was then led back to his cell. Eddie Corry picked up the phone and told Dean's mother that if she called to the station she would be immediately facilitated with a visit to his son.

At 5:20 p.m. Dean's mother, Sheila Lyons, arrived at the station and met Sergeant O'Meara. On hearing who she was he brought her to the jail section and directed that she be permitted access to her son. The visit was supervised by Garda Adrian Murray, who attempted to remain as inconspicuous as possible, sitting at the opposite side of the visiting room. Dean was brought into the room and on seeing his mother began to cry. She took him in her arms and gently led him to a chair. Dean was convulsing, and his mother was hugging and kissing him and telling him that everything would be all right. Throughout this emotionally charged meeting, which lasted some fifteen minutes, Dean sobbed continuously, holding his mother's hand the whole time, mother and son sitting side by side. She continued to try to reassure her son, who was becoming ever more upset. Some weeks later I asked Adrian about this and he told me that, although the seating arrangements and physical contact ran contrary to all regulations, he could not bring himself to intrude on the enormous pain and anguish that the meeting was clearly causing both mother and son.

At one point Sheila turned and addressed Adrian directly. She asked him if the Gardaí would have any objection to her asking Dean to 'tell her to her face' that he had killed the two women. She said she had to know, that she wanted to hear Dean say it and that she wanted to see his face as he said it. Adrian was acutely aware that, given all the circumstances, it was unlikely that any comment by Dean that contained any admission of guilt would ever be admissible in a trial. He told Sheila that, like her, all the Gardaí wanted was to find out the truth.

She gently lifted Dean's chin until mother and son were looking directly into one another's eyes. Then, taking both her son's hands, and without breaking their eye contact, she addressed him directly and, in what must have been a moment of complete heartbreak for any mother, asked him to tell her the truth. In a barely audible voice Dean said: 'I'm sorry, Ma. I'm a scumbag. I killed the two women.' Although visibly paling as her son uttered these words, Sheila continued to hold Dean's hands for a further moment. They then embraced again, Sheila holding her son so tightly that it seemed he would snap in two. In a voice charged with grief she told her son that she, his father and the rest of his family would stand by him and would do all in their power to help him. Dean just continued to nod his head and to hold on tightly to his mother.

The meeting ended shortly afterwards, and Adrian Murray led a still-weeping Dean out of the room.

As Sheila was leaving the jail section she was met by both Sergeant Corry and Garda Murray. They told her that Dean had declined the offer of having a solicitor contacted on his behalf. Adrian suggested to her that she contact one herself on behalf of Dean.

At 10 p.m. on Saturday evening Dean's father, Jackie Lyons, arrived at the station. Again Sergeant O'Meara directed that he be facilitated with an immediate visit to son. Dean again broke down when he was taken into the interview room and saw his father standing there. This visit was supervised by Inspector Michael Burke, who remained as unobtrusive as was possible. Jackie addressed Dean directly and said that his mother, who was completely distraught, had told him that Dean had admitted to the murders to her. He asked Dean to tell him the truth, 'not to be telling any more of your lies.' Dean said: 'Dad, I did this crime.' Jackie told him that this simply wasn't true and that Dean was a 'dangerous liar'. However, Dean continued to insist to his father that he had committed the two murders. Jackie asked Dean why he hadn't told them about the murders when he visited the family home the previous Thursday. Dean replied that it would have been 'very hard' to have admitted to his parents and the rest of his family what he had done.

As the meeting, which had lasted some ten minutes, drew to a close, Jackie Lyons, who had become more and more upset at what had been said, again accused Dean of telling lies. He further suggested to him that those same lies would 'destroy the entire family.' In a comment that would prove to be eerily prophetic, Jackie advised Dean not to be saying he had done it if he had not committed the murders. Dean replied to his father's comment by saying, 'I did this crime.'

Before he left the room this brave man put his arms around his son, and Dean responded in a similar fashion. Both began to cry, their heads resting on one another's shoulder. Jackie gently patted his son on the head and, telling him he loved him, silently left the room.

————

Dean was detained in the Bridewell Garda Station from 1:46 p.m. on 26 July 1997 until 9:35 a.m. the following day, a total of nineteen hours and forty-five minutes. This included a period between 12:10 and 8 a.m. on the Saturday night and Sunday morning when, in accordance with regulations, he was allowed to sleep in a cell. No interviewing was permitted during that period.

Dean's initial six-hour period of detention, which was due to expire at 7:46 p.m. on the Saturday, had been extended by Superintendent James Joyce, the officer in charge of the Bridewell. The decision was taken in order to facilitate the proper investigation of the offence for which Dean had been arrested. Given that this second six-hour period was not due to expire until 1:36 a.m. on the Sunday, and that Dean could not be interviewed between midnight and 8 a.m., the time differential between midnight and 1:36 a.m. would be added on after 8 a.m. Dean would then be questioned until 9:36 a.m. on Sunday morning.

At 4:30 p.m. on Saturday afternoon Dean asked Sergeant Corry if he could contact a doctor on his behalf and ask him to visit him at the Bridewell. Given his drug dependence, he wanted to ask the doctor to give him something to help him with his withdrawal. This is a request that is regularly made by people with addiction problems detained in Garda custody. The visiting doctor invariably supplies the prisoner with a heroin substitute, such as Physeptone, a brand of methadone provided in liquid form, to help the detained person deal with any heroin withdrawal they are going through.

The doctor arrived at the station at 5:40 p.m. and, having examined Dean, decided there was no immediate need to give him any medicine. This was not the same doctor who had earlier that day taken the various body samples from Dean. He gave the garda in charge a supply of Physeptone with instructions on how and when it should be administered. It was given to Dean later that evening.

Formal interviewing was carried on between 2:15 and 3:25 p.m. on Saturday afternoon, a period of one hour and ten minutes. Dean was then given a rest period. Interviewing resumed at 5:45 and continued until 8:45 p.m., a total of three hours. The final session that day took place between 10:10 p.m. and midnight, one hour and fifty minutes. Between each period Dean was returned to the cell to rest, being brought out only to avail of the various visits from his parents and from the doctor.

On the Sunday morning interviewing resumed at 8:45 a.m. and concluded at 9:15. Before this interview Dean had gone in a patrol car with myself and other gardaí and pointed out the scene of the crime and various other places. This journey lasted from 8:10 to 8:34 a.m.

In effect, Dean had been formally interviewed only for a period of 6½ hours, although he had been incarcerated for nineteen hours and forty-five minutes. This means that he had been interviewed for a little less than a third of the total time he spent in custody. It should be noted that, given the various constraints imposed on the Gardaí in connection with the interviewing of people in custody, it would not be considered unusual for a prisoner to be interviewed for so short a period during the length of their incarceration.

The interview held during the early part of Saturday afternoon—that is, the first interview after his arrest—was recorded, with Dean's permission, on videotape. At the outset of this type of interview three new videotapes were opened in his presence by Sergeant Corry and inserted in the recording machine. At the termination of the interview all three tapes were removed in Dean's presence. One of these tapes, selected by him, had a permanent seal affixed that can be removed only on the direction of a trial judge. Dean signed the seal to certify that it had been affixed in his presence. He was told also that on his release he was entitled to apply for one of the other tapes.

Notes had not been maintained by the gardaí during this interview, but at its conclusion a full transcript of the videotaped interview was written out by Billy Mullis, who sat and watched the recording in its entirety. These written notes would run to fifty-eight pages. When this transcript was read over to Dean before his release on the Sunday morning he agreed it was a true account of the interview and signed it.

Before the interview scheduled for 5:45 p.m. began, Dean told Sergeant Corry that he did not want either this interview or any other interview recorded on audio or video. The reason for this change of mind has never been established. It certainly could not be suggested that Dean had been uncomfortable when the previous interview had been recorded. On the tape he appears relaxed and confident, often addressing the camera directly when making a response to questions. There was, of course, general speculation among ourselves about why he made this choice at that particular point. The consensus was that his decision may have been influenced by the visit from his mother a short time earlier.

At the conclusion of the last interview Eddie Corry had explained to Dean about the availability of a copy of the interview tape. It was felt that Dean might not have wanted his mother to see him making further admissions, admissions that in time would be shown to have been a complete fabrication, as his mother suspected even as he made them to her.

Dean was told that he would have to go on tape and be recorded making the request not to have the subsequent interview electronically recorded. The same procedure was followed, with three tapes being placed in the recording machine. This recording lasted some nine minutes and consisted of Dean, in response to a question from Eddie, telling the gardaí that he did not wish to have a solicitor contacted on his behalf and furthermore that he did not want his interview electronically recorded.

Between 5:45 p.m. and midnight Dean was interviewed at length, and both a memo of the interview and a formal statement of admission were taken from him. This was the interview that was suspended between 8:45 and 10:10 p.m.

On Sunday morning Dean was driven in an unmarked Garda car to point out various places he had mentioned in his admissions. He was then returned to the Bridewell, where a further short interview took place. A very contentious statement would be taken from him during that latter period. I was one of the gardaí who went on the trip with him and who took the final statement from him.

At 9:35 a.m., following directions received from the law officers, Dean Lyons was released from custody and then immediately arrested for the murder of Mary Callinan. The charge sheet was read over to him. He made no reply and was taken directly before a special sitting of the District Court and was remanded in custody.

Chapter 13 ~

DETAILS OF THE ADMISSIONS MADE BY DEAN LYONS

Throughout his period of detention Dean Lyons had made a number of admissions, both oral and written, about his involvement in the murders of Sylvia Sheils and Mary Callinan. To avoid any confusion in the reader's mind I will give each of these admissions a distinct reference.

'Dean A' is the lengthy transcript of the electronically recorded interview. The transcript runs to some sixty-two typed pages. This interview was conducted by Detective-Garda Billy Mullis and Garda Joe O'Connor.

'Dean B' is the memo of the interview early on Saturday evening following on Dean's refusal to allow the electronic recording of the interviews to continue. In its entirety it runs to some eight typed pages. The members of the interviewing team here were Detective-Sergeant Robbie McNulty and Detective-Garda Dominic Cox.

'Dean C' is the formal written statement taken late on Saturday night after Dean had received the visit from his father. This interview was also conducted by Detective-Sergeant Robbie McNulty and Detective-Garda Dominic Cox. This document, which contains the most specific of his admissions, runs to seven typed pages.

'Dean D' is a short handwritten statement taken from Dean after he returned from visiting the scene with us on the Sunday morning. On this occasion the members of the interview team were

Detective-Garda Alan Bailey (myself) and Detective-Garda Dave Lynch from the NBCI.

These various admissions would form the basis of a case presented in a phone call that Sunday morning by senior officers to the Director of Public Prosecutions, which would culminate in Dean being charged with the murder of Mary Callinan and appearing in court later the same day. I will give the details of each set of admissions so as to demonstrate the apparent strength of the case as it appeared at that time. To keep the entire issue in perspective, however, it is equally important to recall that this was the only evidence presented in that telephone call.

————

'Dean A' begins with Dean acknowledging that he was aware of the exact nature of the crimes for which he had been arrested. At the outset he said that when he was in the women's house he had stumbled and made a noise. The noise appeared to disturb one of the occupants. A woman had come out, and he had attacked her. A second woman had then appeared, and he had attacked her also. He could not recall what weapon he had used in attacking them.

In an attempt to put some structure on his admissions he was asked to describe how he got into the house. He said it was through a little window at the side of the house, which he had smashed. Billy repeated this description of 'at the side of the house,' and Dean responded that it was 'sort of round by the back.' The woman must have heard him stumble as he went up the stairs. After the assault on both women he had panicked and left the house. A short distance away he realised that his social welfare card was missing and, fearing that he had left it in the house, he went back into it again. He could not find the card. After leaving the house for the second time he met a female friend. He told this friend what he had done. They had both left the area together and had gone out to Inchicore.

Dean was asked if he had noticed anything as he climbed through the window, such as an object that might have been on the ground. This was an oblique reference to the large rubbish bin just inside the window, which he would have to circumvent to get in. He replied, 'Not that I can remember.' When he got in he had 'rooted around' in a cupboard, looking for items of value to steal. The only object he found was a Miraculous Medal—a commercially produced religious object that would be of no financial value. However, he had taken it. After he found the medal he had not been able to find anything else of value and had then left the house. When he was outside he discovered that his social welfare card was missing. After getting back into the house he went upstairs, where he attacked the women. After the attack he said his mind had gone blank.

Dean would make this same remark throughout his various interviews, always at a time when he ought to have been in a position to provide more detailed admissions.

In saying that he had assaulted the women on the second occasion on which he had entered the house he was somewhat contradicting his earlier statement, in which he appeared to be suggesting that it happened during his first time in the house. At this point in the interview he was not corrected: this would be normal practice, in the hope of building up a rapport at the outset of any such interview.

When he was asked if the two women could have been on the landing on the second occasion on which he entered the house and that it was when he was going upstairs that he had met them there, Dean repeated the word 'landing' and, after a moment, agreed that it had been at that stage. He added that he had told the two women to go back into the room. When he met them he had been carrying a knife with him that he had found in the kitchen. He 'stuck one of them' with this knife. When asked which doorway the woman had been standing in when this happened he said he didn't remember, that he hadn't been taking any particular notice.

Dean told Billy and Joe that after he stabbed the woman he ran from the house and had gone as far as Benburb Street. In an attempt to bring him back to talking about the assault they asked him to elaborate on what had taken place in the house and to tell them exactly where he had killed the woman. He replied, 'On the landing way.' What was most noticeable about this admission was that he appeared to be referring to having stabbed just one woman, and furthermore that the assault had taken place on the landing. All the evidence we possessed suggested that both women had been assaulted and killed where their bodies had been found, in their bedrooms. Joe asked Dean whether the assault had taken place on the landing or in the bedroom, and he replied that he had pulled the 'woman—women' into one of the rooms. When asked about the assault on the second woman he responded that he could not recall, as his mind was 'completely blank'.

Billy asked Dean to clarify what he was saying: was he in fact saying that the first woman was standing at the bedroom door and that, having stabbed her, he had then dragged her body back into the room? He agreed, and added that he had not put her on the bed but had left her lying on the floor. He had stabbed this woman several times: in his own words, he 'stuck the knife into her another time or three times.' When asked to elaborate on where on her body he inflicted the various stab wounds he was unable to recall.

When he was leaving the scene after the murders Dean said he met a man in his seventies, totally bald, who was walking an Alsatian dog. This man wished him goodnight, and he returned the greeting. After the murders he went to his skipper in the derelict hospital building, where he burnt his shoes and all the other clothes he had been wearing. From memory, these consisted of a black tracksuit top, black jeans and white runners. He had then put on other clothes that he had in the skipper and had stayed there for the rest of the night. During the commission of the crime, he said, he had also been wearing a pair of black leather gloves. Given that a weave pattern had been developed at the point of entry to the house, he was asked if any part of the glove was knitted, and he replied that they had been all leather.

When asked to talk about how he had gained entry to the house, Dean replied that he had broken the glass in the window with his elbow. He described it as being a 'small square window.' Given his small size, he had no difficulty in climbing through the broken window. With reference to the medal he had found in the house he said he had thrown it away shortly after arriving at Benburb Street. He had done so after being told that he would 'never have an ounce of luck' were he to hold on to it.

Going back to accounting for his movements after the crime, he said that after leaving the house he went directly to Benburb Street, where he met his friend Molly, who was a prostitute in the area. He estimated that it was then between 2 and 3 a.m., as Molly would always stop working around that time. The gardaí asked him if it would be correct to assume that it had been around midnight when he had gone into the house, and he agreed. On seeing his dishevelled state and all the blood on his clothing, Molly had immediately asked him what had happened to him. Dean said that he had 'broken down' and confessed to her what he had done. He described himself as having become emotionally upset, and Molly had attempted to console him. He told her he needed to go out to a place in Inchicore, as he really needed to get some drugs and he knew a dealer out there who would be operating at that hour of the night. She had advised him to get out of his blood-stained clothes before trying to get a taxi to bring him out there.

He had then gone up to the skipper and changed out of his clothes. He had hidden them under a blanket. When reminded that he had previously claimed to have burnt them, he said he had not done that until the following day. He had walked back down to Benburb Street and met Molly. They had hailed a passing taxi, a blue Sunny, and travelled together in it to an old graveyard in the Inchicore area where he knew the man he was looking for would be. They had obtained two heroin deals and had then 'shot up'. After about an hour he had gone out onto the road and flagged down a black Mercedes taxi, which took him back directly to the skipper in Grangegorman. Molly did not travel back with him.

Dean told the detectives that there had been whole parts of the day of the murders that he could not recall, because of the amount of heroin he had consumed over a short space of time. When asked, he readily agreed that he had told the Gardaí that after meeting the women on the stairs he had gone into the room with one of them and had stabbed her a few times. He was unable to recall any details whatsoever of an assault on a second woman. Later that day, on seeing the amount of blood that had saturated his clothes, he had realised that 'there must have been some damage done.'

Joe asked Dean if he was aware that there had been a third woman in the house throughout the time he had spent in it. Dean said he had found that out only a few weeks later, when his friend Michael Flynn, whose mother was related to the third woman, had told him. This, he said, was the same Michael Flynn that he had earlier told gardaí he had called to the house with about a year and a half ago.

In an effort to obtain as much information as possible from Dean, he was asked to describe the internal layout of the house. He replied that he could not remember it now. He added that he had the same difficulty recalling the layout of the house on the night of the murders, as he had been 'out of my head' from the heroin he had taken before going into the house. To the best of his recollection, he had gone out through the front door when leaving the house. Inside there had been a hallway with two or three rooms on the landing. The house was built in flats, with 'separate apartments.'

The kitchen where he had found the knife was beside the toilet. He had opened the drawers in the press but had not taken them out. In one of the drawers there had been a lot of cutlery. There had also been a number of books that, to him, looked like rent books. On the off chance that there might have been money in them, he had searched them, without success. He described the knife he had taken from the drawer and subsequently used in the assault as being a black-handled kitchen knife. This, he said, was the only weapon that he could recall having used. He had left it at the scene when he was leaving.

In a specific reference to the scene as it appeared the following morning, Dean was asked if he had found any handbag when in the house. He replied that he had not. He further insisted that at all times he had been alone when carrying out the crimes. He was then asked if he had admitted his part in the murders to anyone else. He said he had told Wayne Hunt (not his real name), whom he knew from the hostels he stayed in. On another occasion another associate of his had actually accused him of having committed the crime, and he had denied it completely.

Dean was then formally asked if he had ever said anything to Anthony Dunne about the murders. Dunne, he said, was well known to him, but he could not remember ever having told him about them. When asked if it was possible that he might have told Dunne, he said he could have 'when I was high.'

In total, Dean said, he had taken about £30 from the house. He had found this money under the bedroom carpet. This was the same bedroom into which he had dragged the woman he had stabbed. Later in the interview he said that he had taken only £25.

At this point in the interview Billy and Joe asked Dean to provide them with more specific details of the assault on both women. He responded by saying that about two days after the crime he had overheard a conversation between a few of his friends, during which rumours of the extent of the injuries to both victims were discussed.

He said he had become very upset on hearing them. He decided then that he was going to admit his involvement to a care worker at one of the hostels that he knew. At the last moment, however, he had changed his mind.

A direct question was then put to Dean. 'How many people did you kill?' In response he said: 'How many did I kill altogether in my whole life?' When told that the question was a direct reference to the house in Grangegorman only, he replied that he could only recall having killed one woman, that although he had told gardaí that he had met two women on the stairway, he had not known that he had killed them, that he had thought he had only wounded them. Furthermore, he said he was unable to describe the women.

Later that same morning, he said, he went up to the scene. By this time uniformed gardaí were in attendance, and the area was cordoned off. Dean joined the crowd of onlookers that had formed. He asked one of the gardaí what was going on, and the garda had given him a smart answer about some missing dog, or something like that. Dean said he had responded with a smart answer of his own and had then walked away.

Dean told Billy and Joe that he now felt much better for having admitted the murders to them. Since he had done them he had begun behaving in strange ways. Some of his friends had even commented on his behaviour. On two separate occasions since then he had attempted to take his own life with a heroin overdose. The murders had begun to play on his mind so much that he had contemplated giving himself up to the Gardaí. During a conversation he had with a friend, Pat Ryan (not his real name), he told him that he was going to turn himself in. When Ryan quizzed him about it he told him that there were warrants out for his arrest. Dean said he had gone as far as the front door of Pearse Street Station but had then turned away.

He described himself as now feeling 'ten times better' after admitting to the murders, that it was a load off his chest. Since the day of the murders he had been expecting to be arrested. In recent days some of his associates told him that the police were asking a lot of questions about him. He had considered leaving the country, believing it to be his only hope, but had not got any funds to do so. He said he deeply regretted the murders, adding that this was the first time he had ever killed anyone.

When asked about his general attitude towards women, and particularly his feelings towards older women, he described himself as 'having nothing against them.' He told Billy and Joe that he was in a relationship with a girl who was actually carrying his child and was due within the next month. She was living in the Walkinstown area, was only seventeen, and her name was Veronica (not her real name).

On being questioned further about the possibility that he had not been alone when he committed the murders, Dean was adamant that he had been. The house had been a completely random choice. He denied that he had previously broken into the same house, and added that on the occasion on which he had visited it with Michael Flynn to deliver a message for Michael's mother to Ann Mernagh he had not seen the other occupants.

Although describing himself as having been 'solely responsible' for the two murders, he could not provide any details about the death of the second woman. When breaking the glass in the window to get in he had given himself a minor cut to his elbow.

As the interview was about to conclude, an attempt was again made to get Dean to provide certain specific and verifiable facts. He was asked again to describe what he had observed as he climbed through the broken window at the point of entry. 'As far as I can remember,' he said, 'there were curtains on the window,' but he could not remember what kind they were. He was then asked if there had been any net curtains on the window, and he replied that there had been, and also that there had been no heavy curtains on the it. There might also, he added, have been two statuettes on the window ledge.

Again what the gardaí were attempting to get Dean to refer to was the presence of the large refuse bin just inside the window. Billy Mullis was aware that were he to refer specifically to the bin both the question and, more importantly, the answer would be ruled as inadmissible. To circumvent this possibility he asked Dean to describe what he had seen directly in front of the window, and whether he had fallen over anything as he got in through the window. He answered: 'I'm not sure. I can't remember.'

The final question posed to Dean in this interview related to the remark he had made to the two gardaí that morning as they approached him outside the hostel. He had told them then that he knew what they wanted to talk to him about. Joe asked him what exactly he had meant, and Dean replied that it was either about his having broken into a car a few days ago or about the 'murder case'.

This would be Billy Mullis and Joe O'Connor's final interview with Dean. They had been with him almost continuously throughout that morning and into the early afternoon. An easy, informal relationship had been built up between them during that time. The light-hearted atmosphere of the early morning, however, had to change to reflect the seriousness of the admissions that Dean was making. Nevertheless the friendship they had built up would continue. On several subsequent occasions, when appearing at the courts on remand, Dean would meet Joe, who was a full-time jailer in the Bridewell prison section, and greet him effusively.

The entire recorded interview was transcribed by Billy Mullis and read over to Dean on the Sunday morning before his release. He agreed that it was a true and accurate account of the interview, and signed the notes.

––––

The next interview with Dean took place after he had been given a break of almost two hours. We refer to the notes of this interview as 'Dean B'. This is the interview that followed upon his asking that it be no longer electronically recorded. The interviewing gardaí were Detective-Sergeant Robbie McNulty and Detective-Garda Dominic Cox.

At the outset Dean outlined his movements on Thursday 6 March. Early that morning, he said, he took some drugs with friends of his in the skipper. (A feature of a heroin addict's use of drugs is that they will seldom take them when alone. This is a precaution taken in case the user has a reaction to the drug and requires medical help.) After taking the drugs he went into the city centre. During the day he stole a mobile phone from a car parked in Henry Street. He got a second one from a parked car near the Grand Canal. He sold both phones and got £75 for them (a little less than €100). He immediately headed out to Inchicore to the graveyard where he had 'scored' drugs, which he shared with Molly.

Later in the day he attempted to gain admission to the Army Hostel but was refused because he was still 'high' on the heroin he had taken. He then walked down to Benburb Street and spent a while talking to the prostitutes there. He shared a deal of heroin with one of them. After that he went back to the skipper and slept for a few hours. When he woke up he decided to go looking for a house to break into to get money. He walked up through Grangegorman and smashed a window in a house and went in.

A direct question was put to Dean at this point by Robbie. Had all the glass fallen out when he broke it? He said it hadn't: he had to pull some of it out with his hand. At the time he was wearing leather gloves. When asked if he knew where the gloves were now he said he left them with a friend, Helen (not her real name), who was living in Haven House, a hostel in Morning Star Avenue for single homeless women. The gloves were in a blue bag, which held a number of other items of clothing.

Dean said that when he was climbing through the window he had to move an ornament out of his way; there had also been a press under the window. This comment was undoubtedly a response to the questions that Billy had earlier asked him about 'something' being inside the window. As he climbed through the window, he said, he had fallen to the floor. While searching a cupboard he found a Miraculous Medal, and he had then left the house, going back out through the broken window. He had to go back in, however, when he realised he had left his social welfare card behind. He told Robbie and Dominic that, on the second entry, he took a knife from the drawer and went upstairs looking for money. At the top of the stairs he met two women. They began screaming, and he stabbed them.

Robbie told Dean that he didn't believe that he was telling them the full truth and asked if his reluctance to do so was because he didn't remember, or rather that he didn't want to remember. In response Dean said that his head had been all 'fucked up' by all the drugs he had been taking.

Dean was now asked to describe the first woman, and also to tell the detectives which room she came out of. He said she had stepped out of the second room from the top of the staircase. He described her as being stout, smaller in height than himself, and with grey hair. She was wearing a light-coloured nightdress. She began to scream, and he stabbed her only to stop her screaming.

It was then suggested to Dean that the stabbing must have occurred in the bedroom rather than out on the landing, and he replied, 'Yes.'

He then told the two gardaí that when he entered the room the woman was fast asleep in bed. He began to search the room, and during the search he found the money under the carpet. The woman had woken up and, on seeing Dean, began to scream. He described himself as panicking and said he 'stabbed her a few times to stop her screaming.' The woman had still been lying on her bed when he was stabbing her.

He said he left that bedroom and went into the room beside it. As he pushed the door open he saw a woman getting out of the bed. He rushed at her and pushed her onto the floor. She began screaming. Describing himself as having 'lost the head,' he began stabbing this woman also. He continued to stab her even after she had stopped screaming. This second woman had been wearing a nightdress, bra and pants.

When asked if he had become sexually aroused while carrying out the assaults on both women he replied, 'No. I can't remember. I might have.' In response to further questions about this issue he said he had not masturbated while in the house with the victims but had done so some hours later when alone in his skipper. He agreed that both the killing and the sight of all the blood on his clothes had sexually aroused him. This line of questioning was based on the advice received from the crime-scene profiler, Dr Roberts, when classifying the assaults as sexual in nature.

At this juncture the gardaí asked Dean if he was prepared to make a formal statement to them, describing his full part in the murders, which would be taken down in writing. This would be in a totally different format from the question-and-answer sessions that had formed the basis of the other interviews up to this point. Statements, for the most part, are a narration of the events as given by a suspect or a witness, with the gardaí interrupting only to clear up any ambiguities, to fix certain times and dates, or other details. Dean agreed, and the taking of the statement began. When it was completed it would run to seven typed pages. The taking of the statement was suspended for a while to allow Dean to avail of a rest period and also to meet his father. The statement and the admissions it contains we are referring to as 'Dean c'.

———

This comprehensive statement begins with Dean saying: 'I want to tell you about the two murders in Grangegorman. God help me but I did those murders. I just needed money for drugs and I decided to rob the corner house in Grangegorman.' He had to get both killings out of his mind so he could get on with his life, and he described himself as being happy that it was finally 'out in the open.' He then gave the gardaí a lot of background information about himself, describing in detail his relations with his family and his peers. He was open about his descent into drug addiction and his growing reliance on crime to feed his dependence on drugs.

Again returning to the subject of the night of the murders, he spoke about returning to the house after leaving it, thinking he might have lost his social welfare card there and fearing that it would be found and could lead directly back to him. He gave further details about going upstairs and going into a bedroom that he searched and where he had found €25 under the carpet. There had been a woman asleep in the bed and she had awoken and on seeing him had begun to scream. He had punched and stabbed her repeatedly in an attempt to get her to stop screaming. She was still in the bed when he attacked her. He had then gone into the room next door, where he had met a second woman, whom he had pushed to the floor and stabbed a number of times.

The break in taking the statement occurred at this point. The interview resumed after Dean had a meeting with his father and availed of a period of rest.

On the resumption of the interview Dean said to the two gardaí: 'I want to tell you the truth about what happened in the house. It's all out now anyway. I've told my father I killed the two women.' He now began providing details that he had not previously given. He said he had taken a total of four knives from the drawer in the kitchen. These had included a couple of carving-knives, a black-handled steak knife and a big fork. He described the fork as 'the type you stick into meat when you want to cut it.' He had gone upstairs and into a bedroom, turning on the light as he went in. There was an elderly woman asleep in bed. He searched the room and found £25 under the carpet. At this point the woman in the bed woke up and, on seeing him, began screaming. Dean described himself as jumping on the woman; he 'smacked her in the face until she went out.' He then pushed her onto the floor and sat on her. He described himself as placing his hand over her mouth in case she screamed again and had then cut her throat with the carving-knife.

He said he then pulled up the woman's nightdress and tore off her underwear. 'I started to cut off one of her tits. I think it was the left tit. I don't know why I did this.' He then tried to cut her 'down around her waist.' Just before he left the bedroom he took the long fork and 'stuck it into her vagina. I had thumped it with my open palm, like hammering a nail in so I got it right up.' He then left the room, leaving her lying on the floor.

After walking out of that bedroom he went into the room beside it. There was also a woman in the bed in this room, and she woke as he stood over her and began to scream. He then attacked her. He prevented her from getting up out of the bed. He pulled off her bra and pants. All this time he kept his hand firmly over her mouth. While he was doing this the woman kept 'looking up at me.' As he was stabbing and cutting the woman he had become very excited and was also sexually aroused. 'I came in my pants I was so excited. I got lots of pleasure out of it when I was doing it. It was later on that I began to regret what I had done.'

When he left this second bedroom he went downstairs and went into the dining-room. He switched on the light and had a look around but found nothing of value. He then left the house, going out through the front door, which he opened by turning the latch on the lock. There had been a key on the inside of the lock, and once he got outside he threw this key away.

The taking of this statement concluded at midnight. In his concluding remark Dean said: 'I killed these women and I'm sorry. God rest their souls.'

———

Before I deal with the last set of admissions made by Dean there is one matter I would like to address. The first team to interview him, Billy Mullis and Joe O'Connor, almost selected itself, given their involvement with him since early morning. Robbie McNulty and Dominic Cox spent almost six hours with him, the maximum that could be expected of any team. As Saturday evening moved into

Saturday night it became apparent to us in the incident room that a further team of interviewers would be required to take over that role at 8 o'clock on Sunday morning.

Shortly before midnight on Saturday I approached Detective Chief Superintendent Seán Camon, head of the NBCI, and asked him if he had any preference for the detectives to interview Dean from 8 a.m. the following morning. He told me that Detective-Garda Dave Lynch from the NBCI would be one of the members. I had known Dave for many years. He was a highly experienced garda and had worked with our team almost from the beginning of the investigation. In my opinion he was a good choice. However, Camon's next comment really took me by surprise. He told me that I was to join Detective-Garda Lynch and be the second person on the team. I couldn't believe my ears.

At the purely physical level I had worked through that Saturday since 9 a.m. and, more importantly, it would be at least 2 a.m. before we would be in a position to close the incident room, what with all the teams we had out in the field attempting to corroborate the various admissions. Furthermore, in my role as an incident-room co-ordinator it was not normal practice for me to engage in the interviewing of prisoners. I had never been told to do so in any of the other investigations on which I had been the IRC. Normally, in fulfilling that particular role you would operate at one remove from the day-to-day details, thus ensuring that at all times you were able to maintain an unprejudiced overview of the investigation.

When I said as much to the chief superintendent I was told in no uncertain terms that this was a direct order from him, and that I was to carry out the duty as directed. Given that there always existed a far more relaxed atmosphere among the different ranks in plain clothes, and especially towards 'bookmen', I was surprised at the manner in which I was addressed. He further ordered that I was to be available first thing next morning to go for a trip with Dean and other gardaí to allow him to point out certain areas to us. On our return I was to assist Dave Lynch in formally interviewing Dean after caution and ensuring that any admissions he might make were properly recorded.

The reason for this departure from the accepted investigative norms has never been explained to me. Given that the Garda Síochána is a disciplined force, I certainly could not openly question or challenge an order from such a senior officer. Some of my colleagues later suggested to me that it could have been a direct consequence of my questioning the truthfulness and reliability of Dean's admissions. As that night had worn on, the contents of the admissions being made by him only tended to increase our scepticism and feed our concerns. Matt Mulhall and myself had openly voiced our concerns to our senior officers at every opportunity. Each failure on our part to corroborate any single shred of the admissions, we believed, should have added credence to our view.

It was certainly not a lack of personnel that had led to my being appointed to the interview team: by this time we had drafted in a lot of extra assistance to help out. I cannot say that my questioning these matters was what contributed to this position, and I certainly have never been told that this was the reason for it.

Before going into the next set of admissions made by Dean I will set out some of the attempts that were going on, both while Dean was being interviewed and throughout the night, to back up the various admissions he was making. In any trial in which the only evidence against the accused is his own admissions, the trial judge will give a warning to the jury about the danger of finding someone guilty solely on their own testimony. The outcome of our efforts to obtain corroboration would influence my approach when it came time for me to sit down and interview Dean; and that is why I feel it is important to show just what we had established by that stage.

Corroborating evidence is defined as evidence that tends to support a proposition that is already supported by some initial evidence and therefore confirms the evidence. In this instance we had Dean's admissions, and any further evidence would add to its reliability. It is where one item of evidence boosts another piece.

The various admissions made by Dean up to 8 p.m. that Saturday evening could best be described as being short on both specifics and verifiable facts. He had, however supplied certain details that could and were actioned by the incident room for the purpose of supporting or otherwise those same admissions.

On different occasions Dean had told us that after he left the scene of the crime he had gone directly to Benburb Street, where he met Molly, a prostitute who was well known to him and whom he trusted. She had noticed, he said, that his clothes were covered in blood, and he said he had admitted the murders to her. They had then gone to

Inchicore together to buy drugs. If we were to find Molly, and if she corroborated all he had told us, that would undoubtedly have silenced the naysayers—including myself—for ever and, given the importance that the law officers would place on her evidence, no doubt convict Dean outright. An all-out effort to find her while Dean was still in custody was therefore made.

An extensive index of all the women operating as prostitutes in the Benburb Street area was maintained at the collator's office in the Bridewell. It was regularly updated by Matt and his staff on information received from gardaí patrolling the area. Some two hundred women were listed in it. Of course this is not to say that at any one time all or most of that number would be in the area plying their trade. The street vice scene in that area was most unusual, in that a lot of women operated there only at certain times of the year. For instance, we could have mothers under financial pressure with children going back to school who might spend a few nights there; we would have an influx at certain other times of the year also, for example coming up to Christmas. The involvement of people like these in the vice trade is something that we may have difficulty grasping but was quite common in the area. Certainly there were half a dozen women to be found at any given time working the beat there. It is also significant that years of police pressure, enhanced social welfare benefits, abhorrence and condemnation by society, economic improvements and education, together with the daily fear of violence, could not deter women from working the streets in the area. What actually brought about the virtual demise of the trade there was when the Luas tram line was built along the street, blocking access by passing traffic, the life blood of the business.

We did find that we had a young woman called Molly Jones (not her real name) who regularly operated in the area. Her history sheet also showed that she was a drug addict who was known to purchase her drugs in the Inchicore area. This seemed to be a good lead. Gardaí were despatched to the area and, as luck would have it, found her working there. She readily agreed to come back to the Bridewell with the gardaí when she was told there might be an issue in relation to the Grangegorman murders that she could help us with.

We asked Molly if she knew Dean Lyons, and she replied that she did not know anyone of that name. She appeared to be honest and willing to help us but remained adamant that she did not know him. When shown a photograph of him she said he was vaguely familiar as one of the druggies who hung around the area with the younger girls, that is to say teenagers. Molly herself was thirty. He had certainly never admitted any murders to her, nor had she ever gone with him to Inchicore to buy drugs, although, like the majority of the substance users who frequented the area, including herself, she did go out there to buy drugs. She told us she had spent the week of 6 March in the Rotunda Hospital. This was verified by her appointment card, which she had in her possession, and a quick check with the hospital.

At our request Molly agreed to confront Dean and make these denials to him. Dean was asked if he would agree to meet her. He did so, and Molly was brought into the jail section. It was immediately obvious to the gardaí present that, from her reaction to him, she did not know Dean. What was even more obvious was that Dean had no idea who she was either.

An album containing photographs of the almost two hundred women who worked the area was shown to Dean. Though readily identifying a lot of the drug addicts in the album, he told us that the woman he knew as Molly was not in it. In time we would discover that a neighbour of Dean's, for whom he seemed to have had a mild infatuation in the past, was also called Molly. She could certainly not be the one he was talking about—being neither a drug addict nor a prostitute—and, it would further emerge, had never in her life carried on a conversation with Dean Lyons.

Dean had claimed to have visited the scene at Orchard View some months before the murders with one of two brothers, either Michael or Robbie Flynn. These were the youths who were related to Ann Mernagh, and he alleged that they called to see her with a message from the boys' mother. When questioned by our team, both separately denied ever having been at the scene and claimed that they became aware only after the murders that their aunt lived in the house, when their mother told them. They did say, however, that they had openly discussed their relationship with Ann Mernagh after learning about it among their peers, who included Dean Lyons.

Dean had also told us that he was in a sexual relationship with a seventeen-year-old girl called Veronica (not her real name), and that she was due to have his child. When interviewed she would tell gardaí that, though Dean was known to her, she had never had any relationship with him and was certainly not pregnant by him, or indeed anyone else. She knew Dean only because he hung around occasionally on the periphery of a group of addicts that she associated with. She added that he was tolerated by the group only because he was considered a 'soft touch' when he had drugs. He had never been seen by her in the company of any woman. In her opinion Dean always seemed a little odd.

The area of the derelict hospital ward in Grangegorman that Dean slept in—his skipper—was identified through directions given by him and information given by some of the other residents. A search team was quickly assembled and was sent in to look for fire debris from the clothing that Dean said he had burned. The team included qualified scene-of-crime examiners and were provided with emergency lighting. Despite an extensive and intensive search, no such fire debris was found. To confirm this, a further search was carried out in daylight, and again no such fire scene was found.

From inquiries made at the Regina Coeli Hostel in Morning Star Avenue it was established that Dean had left a bag of clothing with the girl-friend of one of his friends. Dean had claimed that this bag contained the gloves he had worn when breaking into the house. This girl, Helen, told us she had met her boy-friend with Dean the previous Wednesday, 23 July. They had both been going to buy drugs and had asked her to mind two bags of new clothes they had just been given in the Capuchin Day Centre. Dean had never bothered to collect the bag. When opened it was found to contain only two new T-shirts. Both the bag and its contents were scientifically examined, but no trace of bloodstaining to link its contents to the scene were found.

Any of these claims by Dean that I have set out above would, as I have said, be considered important corroboration of his story if they were found to be true or to have any substance. Not one of them had withstood even the minimum of investigation.

———

I met Dean personally for the first time at eight o'clock that Sunday morning. As I introduced myself and we shook hands I could not help but think, Is this timid, quiet person the monster that we have been hunting for the last six months? I know that if police work teaches you nothing else it is that you should never take anything for granted. However, it would be fair to say that Dean Lyons could not be regarded as the most physically intimidating person one could meet. Somehow or other, meeting him in the flesh I found it difficult to conjure up an image of him committing the vicious and sadistic assaults on Sylvia Sheils and Mary Callinan.

Given the formal nature and the evidential value of the journey it was proposed to take in the car with him, Robbie McNulty addressed Dean directly and asked him if he was prepared to leave the station with us and to point out those areas he had mentioned in his various statements. He was further told that he was not obliged to accompany us but that if he did, any information we established could be given in evidence. He agreed to come with us.

I would later look upon this meeting as being Dean's second-last opportunity to end this whole sorry episode. Having had the full night to think about what he was saying and doing, I half-expected him to say 'enough is enough' and to ask that a solicitor be brought in to him straight away. Instead of that he complied with our request.

I drove the Garda car out of the station yard; Dean sat in the back beside Robbie with his head partly covered in case we met any of his associates. Our journey was taken in almost total silence, broken only by terse directions from Dean to turn here or go there. During the journey he became increasingly introspective and withdrawn.

We drove first to the skipper in the old hospital grounds. I drove up Morning Star Avenue and in through the open gateway, and we pulled up at a point between the Army Hostel and the derelict hospital building. Dean asked me not to go any closer, fearing that some of his associates might come out and see him with us. I could not help but think that a little less than twenty-four hours earlier Billy and Joe must have parked near this same spot waiting to meet Dean as he left the hostel, and how much had changed for us in that short period. Little did I know just how prophetic this was to prove.

Dean pointed to a window in the building and said that his skipper was just inside. He then redirected me back into North Brunswick Street and up through Lower Grangegorman. Outside number 1 Orchard View he told me to stop the car. He pointed at the side wall and said he had climbed over this wall and then broken the window beside the drainpipes. I tried the wicket door in the wall and found that it was locked. I then climbed over the wall and opened the gate to let Dean come in.

The window that we knew had been the point of entry had been boarded over after Eugene Gilligan had removed the frame to assist him in reconstructing the glass pane. The building had been empty since the murders. It is empty to this day, as are the other four houses that comprise the terrace. No attempt was ever made to rehouse any other patients in it as a mark of respect to Sylvia and Mary, and it has fallen into disrepair. There are now plans to demolish the houses and redevelop the site. Over the years, when I had cause to revisit the house or the immediate area I often noticed local people make the sign of the cross as they walked by; some even crossed to the other side of the road to avoid having to walk directly in front of it.

On that Sunday morning, as we stood in a group in the back yard, Robbie asked Dean to point out the window he had broken to gain entry. He pointed to a completely different window. However, when asked if he was sure this was the correct window he said he could not be, because the other window near where he stood was boarded up.

We walked around to the front of the house and stood at the front door. Robbie asked Dean to point out where he had discarded the key he told us he had taken from inside the front door as he left the scene after the murders. Dean pointed to his left, in the general direction of Lower Grangegorman.

About a month after the murders local children, playing in a nearby garden, had found a front-door key under the hedge. Their parents, realising that it might be significant, had handed it over to us. It turned out to be Ann Mernagh's key, taken from her handbag on the night of the murders. Dean was pointing in the wrong direction as he stood outside the house; however, when he was asked if he was sure about this he immediately changed his mind and pointed in the opposite direction, towards where the key had in fact been found; but the garden where the key was found is more than seventy feet from the front door where Dean was standing.

Dean then directed me to drive to Benburb Street, where he pointed out an area on the roadway where, he said, he had discarded the Miraculous Medal. He then told us that he wanted to go back to the skipper in the hospital grounds. Here he pointed to the window beside the one he had pointed out to us earlier. He said he had burnt the clothes he had been wearing in that room. We then returned to the station. The room would later be searched by a forensic science team, who would not find anything of significance. It had also been examined during other searches that had taken place the previous night.

———

Dave Lynch and myself got together before we went in to interview Dean for what would be the final formal session with him. We were due to start at 8:45 a.m. I had spent some time with Matt Mulhall earlier that morning discussing how I should approach this whole interview. I should say that he was as surprised as I had been when I told him that I had been directed to interview Dean.

The consensus we arrived at was that I had to be true to my suspicion about the admissions. It would be very easy for me, we agreed, to just refuse point-blank to take part and then face the consequences within the job; as Matt put it so succinctly, 'They can't make you pregnant, and even if they could you don't have to love the child!' We decided I had no choice but to ensure that my questions reflected my beliefs.

I outlined my doubts and concerns to Dave Lynch. He in turn told me that he too felt uneasy about the veracity of some of the admissions Dean had made earlier. Hearing this being said by a detective with Dave's experience in the investigation of serious crimes, and with whom I had worked in the past, would make me feel very relieved.

We agreed that I should maintain the notes of any comments or admissions Dean might make to us. We further decided that we would, to coin a phrase, take the bull by the horns and tell Dean, in no uncertain terms, that we were not satisfied that he was telling the truth when he claimed to have committed the murders. In adopting this approach we were aware that, in the eyes of some of our senior officers, we would be crossing a line that could have serious repercussions for years to come and for our careers. However, we felt it was incumbent on us to take this stance. Imagine my disgust when, years later, I learnt that one of our senior officers, in response to questions asked of him about the approach to the interview taken by Dave and myself, had stated that it was no more than a 'ploy' or an 'interview technique.'

At the opening of the interview we offered Dean the option of having it electronically recorded. Deep down we both felt that he would take this opportunity, which would be his last chance, to deny before the cameras that he had any involvement in the murders. It would have been powerful evidence in his favour had he done so. However, he declined our offer and said he did not want it recorded. The notes of this part of our interview with him are what I am referring to as 'Dean D'.

I told Dean that, having watched the tape of his interview and having read the various statements he made to us, I was not satisfied that he was telling us the truth about the murders. He made no response, just sat across the table from us looking at a point above our heads. Dave then said to him that if, as he had claimed, he had committed both murders he should have been in a position to give us a lot more information but he did not seem to be able to. Dean asked us, in amazement, 'Do you not believe me when I say I done it?' I told him that, at most, he might have been in the house but that it did not appear to be him that had committed the murders. This, I added, might be why he could not supply the important information and why he was omitting so many details. He again made no reply.

Dave and myself, as we had arranged, now sat back and awaited a response from Dean. This, we felt, would now be make or break for Dean. We had clearly and unequivocally expressed our doubts to him about his guilt and by so doing just might have done irreparable damage to our case against him. There is no doubt that any defence solicitor worth their salt would have homed in on our line of questioning and cast a huge doubt over his guilt. The way was now open to him to begin denying his involvement.

Dean just continued to stare straight ahead, avoiding all eye contact with us. Dave then addressed him quietly and asked him to tell us the truth. 'Did you really kill the two women, Dean, or are you only saying you did?' I asked him to keep in mind the effects that his admissions had had on his mother and his father when he told them that he had committed the murders, adding that in spite of this they genuinely believed that he had not killed Sylvia and Mary.

On hearing this, Dean became quite annoyed. He pushed back the chair and threw the cigarette he had been smoking on the floor. Pointing his finger at me, he shouted at me to stop writing. I put down my pen and sat back. He was becoming more and more visibly aggressive, and for a moment I thought he was going to launch himself across the desk at us. He began to shout at us. We told him to calm down. He was becoming more and more physically aggressive. Dave asked him if he wanted to take a five-minute break; he replied: 'I'll make a statement to yous and you can fuck off then.' He continued standing and waving his fist aggressively in our direction. We again told him to stay calm. He sat back down and nodded at me to start writing. This statement, 'Dean E', is certainly one of the shortest and most unusual statements of admission I ever took in my police career.

———

Dean began this statement with the following comment: 'I want to tell you about what I did in the gaff [house] in the Gorman. I know you don't believe me but I'm telling the truth. I done the two old women.' He said there had been more blood on the woman who had been on the bed than the woman on the ground, with the greater part of the blood being around her vagina. He told us he had gone into the bedroom to 'prowl around', when the woman began to get out of the bed. He described her as putting her feet out onto the floor. He had pounced on her, putting his hand over her mouth and striking her on the side of the head with his elbow. He had stabbed her 'a good few times', and he might 'have slit her throat.' Then, removing her pants, he had 'cut her in the vagina a few times.'

He stopped talking for a moment and then he addressed us both directly. 'I know you don't believe me but I'm telling you I did. Because yous don't believe me I'm saying nothing more to you. I'm exercising my rights.' He then sat back into the chair and folded his arms across his chest.

I read the statement back to him and asked him to sign it, which he did. I then read over to him the notes I had been taking before the statement. When I asked him to sign these notes he told me to 'fuck off.' He lit a cigarette and refused either to look up at us or to acknowledge our questions. We then left the interview room.

Dave and myself had gone into that interview room with our minds fairly well made up that Dean Lyons had not committed the murders; within half an hour we were leaving the interview room with a further statement of admission signed by him. Nothing in what he had said to us would convince us that he had committed the murders; it would, however, suggest to us that he had convinced himself that he had done so.

We left the jail section and returned to find the incident room in uproar. Word had just been passed through to us that Dean was to be formally charged with the murder of Mary Callinan; a charge of murdering Sylvia Sheils would be preferred as soon as the file was sent to the law officers. He was due to appear in court that same morning.

I could not believe my ears. I honestly believed that, given that some of the team had expressed reservations about Dean's admissions, the question of charging him would have been left until after the law officers had studied the file. The approach Dave and myself had taken in our questioning of Dean would at least have drawn attention to that concern.

Chapter 14

CONCERNS ABOUT THE CONTENT OF THE ADMISSIONS

A fter the first interview with Dean had been completed, Billy Mullis and Joe O'Connor came back to the incident room with a copy of the videotape. I should say that the then incident room was a small room, actually a former single cell, even down to still having bars on the windows. It had been fitted out with floor-to-ceiling shelving, containing file copies of all major investigations in the Bridewell for several years. There were also two desks, which ran the full length of the wall. At the best of times there would have been room for only two or three people to fit comfortably.

That evening the room was full, with detectives jammed into it, all waiting to watch the videotape of the interview on the monitor in the room. We could barely conceal our excitement at the thought that the long, hard slog over that summer was finally coming to an end.

Our numbers were swelled even further with the return of some of our teams from their inquiries as the news continued to spread. In the end we had to announce that after we had viewed it in its entirety with the senior officers we would bring out the equipment and set it up in the main office so that everybody could view it. We told everyone to be available at 5:15 p.m. Matt Mulhall and myself, with some of the senior officers, sat or stood around the monitor, watching spellbound as the interview unfolded.

Dean's opening comment, that he remembered going into the house and, while going up the stairs, had stumbled and wakened one of the women who was about to come out and had attacked her, was greeted with audible sighs of relief all around. This was beginning to look good. On screen Dean was coming across as relaxed and eager to talk. He was, for the most part, talking directly to the camera and was not showing any signs of being under pressure.

As the interview progressed, however, my delight would soon start turning to concern. I looked at Matt and he silently mouthed the expression 'What the fuck!' My growing feeling of doubt was mirrored in his face. Only a few minutes into the interview these doubts were being fuelled even further.

In response to the question about there being an object in front of the window at the point of entry, Dean could not recall there being anything there. I had been at the scene and observed the large litter bin directly in front of the window, and it was hard to visualise a person pulling themselves through the broken glass and not being, at the very least, slowed down by this bin. Not alone could Dean not recall its presence but he did not even seem to have encountered it. Given that by this time he was telling us that he had climbed in the window, climbed back out through it and climbed back through it again, it seemed highly unlikely that he had not seen it there.

Towards the end of the interview this issue would be revisited, when Dean would say that there were two statuettes on the windowsill as he climbed through it. This also was totally wrong.

Dean told us that as he was walking up the stairs he met two women, and he ordered them to go back into the bedroom. He then claimed to have killed them on the landing and to have dragged their bodies back into one of the bedrooms. He could not recall having actually killed a second woman in the house and when questioned had described his mind as going 'blank'. In response to further questioning he told Billy and Joe that the first victim had been standing at the bedroom door, where he stabbed her. He said he then dragged her back into the room, where he had left her lying on the floor.

This information was totally at variance with the evidence that had already been established through the scientific examination of the murder scene—a scene that is indelibly printed on my brain. As I listened I began to wonder if Dean was even talking about the same crime. Blood spattering, coupled with the direction of blood flow, found in the immediate vicinity of where both bodies had been lying showed, beyond doubt, that both victims had been assaulted in their own bedrooms, Sylvia as she lay on her bed and Mary as she stood up from her bed in the confined space between her bed and the outer wall of the house.

At this point, while still watching the video, I began to make notes of the various anomalies in Dean's statement. I saw that Matt was doing the same thing.

When asked if he had been wearing anything on his hands while in the house, Dean replied that he had been wearing leather gloves. The evidence developed by our fingerprint expert, Christy O'Brien, clearly showed that whatever the culprit had been wearing on his hands had a weave or knitted pattern, unlike the flat surface of a leather glove. Billy had tried to elicit some information about the make-up of the glove from Dean, asking if any part of the glove surface had a knitted pattern. Dean told him that, to the best of his recollection, the glove surfaces had been all leather.

Dean's attempts at describing the interior of the house were completely wrong. He had described it as a house that was divided into flats or separate apartments. This could not be further from the truth: it had retained all its original features and layout and resembled nothing more than an ordinary four-bedroom house.

He stated that he had not completely removed the drawer from the press in the kitchen, in answer to being asked directly about it. This is the same drawer in which he said he had found the murder weapon. To me this was one of the more telling questions. Given the significance that our murderer had attached to deliberately selecting particular weapons to inflict particular types of injury, he had in fact removed the drawer and placed it on the kitchen floor. This was hardly an action that he was going to forget.

Another significant omission from Dean's statement came when he was asked to talk about the weapon he had used during the murders. He said he had used only a steak knife that he had found in the kitchen drawer. We know that the weapons the murderer used included not one but two steak knives, two blades belonging to an electric carving-knife and the long fork. Again, given their significance in our culprit's twisted mind, they were a huge omission.

Ann Mernagh's handbag, which she had left in the sitting-room, was found on the Friday morning upended in the hallway, near the foot of the stairs, with its contents strewn all over the floor. Given where it had been removed from and where it had been abandoned, I found it extremely difficult to comprehend how a man could admit to two murders but not to searching through a handbag. When asked specifically if he had seen any handbag at the scene, Dean answered that he could not recall seeing one.

Ann Mernagh said she had left her front-door key in her handbag when she was going to bed. This is the key the children found in the garden some seventy yards from the scene. It is the same key that Dean claimed to have taken out of the inside of the front door. The lock, in fact, was of the Yale type, with no facility for inserting it on the inside.

As the interview progressed there was one reply from Dean that, above all the other answers he had given, really brought my misgivings to a head. As he answered the question I actually heard Matt saying, 'Am I right? Did he actually say what I think he just said?' To me it started alarm bells ringing so loudly that I imagined everyone gathered in the room could hear them. Given the vagueness of some of his responses, Dean was asked directly by Joe O'Connor, 'How many people did you kill?' Dean looked Joe in the eye and answered that question with the following response: 'How many people did I kill altogether in my whole life?' Joe replied that he was referring to how many people he had killed while in number 1 Orchard View. Dean answered that he could only remember killing one woman, and even then said that he could not recall what she looked like.

Throughout this interview Dean had maintained that the clothes he was wearing had been covered in blood. Even Molly Jones, whom he had met in Benburb Street immediately after the murders, had commented on their condition, he said, and had advised him to change them. It had been established during both post-mortem examinations that the fatal wounds, to the throat and chest, had been among the very first of the injuries inflicted and that the majority of the wounds had been inflicted after death. Given this fact, both the forensic scientists and the chief state pathologist had always insisted that it was extremely unlikely that the culprit would have a significant amount of blood either on himself or on his clothing.

As the tape of the interview finished, both Matt and myself openly expressed our doubts and reservations about Dean having played any role in the two murders. On occasions during the interview I honestly felt that Dean Lyons had not got the remotest clue about what he was talking about.

Chief Superintendent Kelly had stated that, in his opinion, Dean appeared to be genuinely upset and remorseful and that his inability to recall all the details and the confusion he sometimes displayed was to a great extent a result of his drug dependence. He further directed that, in the interests of Dean's health and well-being, we were to ensure that a doctor was summoned and asked to attend him. Dean himself would also request that a doctor be contacted on his behalf.

The next team of detectives that interviewed Dean comprised Detective-Sergeant Robbie McNulty and Detective-Garda Dominic Cox, both attached to the Bridewell DDU. Both had been with the investigation from the outset and were also highly experienced detectives. Before they met Dean, Chief Superintendent Kelly and Detective-Superintendent Gordon briefed them on the contents of the taped admissions. In addition, Matt and myself would express our reservations to Robbie, advising him to be very careful. He immediately agreed to approach the interview and Dean's admissions with an open mind. Given that a little more than six hours would be available in total for interviewing before the midnight moratorium, it was decided to hold their interview in two sessions, thereby allowing Dean to avail of a lengthy break in between.

In the first part of the interview, notes of the questions put to him and his responses were maintained. In the second session a formal statement was taken. These are the admissions at 'Dean B' and 'Dean c', respectively, that I have summarised already. The break in the interview came at 8:45 p.m.

At that stage a very worried-looking Dominic came directly from the interview room into the incident room. Robbie was with him. Dominic said that he was very concerned about Dean's admissions, describing Dean as a 'Walter Mitty' type—a fantasist, someone who attempts to pass themselves off as something they are not and will never be. Dominic was letting us know that he was genuinely concerned that Dean was not telling us the truth when he claimed to have committed the murders. He told us that at one point he had put it to Dean directly that he was not telling us the truth. He asked him if his reluctance to be more specific was because he couldn't remember or didn't want to remember, or just didn't know. Dean had made no response to him. Given the bizarre nature of the crimes, Dean had also been asked if he had become sexually aroused while committing the murders. His response had been that he couldn't remember whether he did; he might have.

One further question, according to Dominic, was put to Dean, the response to which he had found the most worrying of all and that was leading him to think that Dean had no involvement at all in the Grangegorman murders. He put it to him that the assault on the woman had not, as previously stated by him, taken place on the landing. He told Dean that we were satisfied beyond all doubt that the assaults had taken place inside in the bedrooms. To his amazement, Dean immediately agreed with him and changed his story to accommodate this.

Robbie, the other half of the interview team, was then asked by us for his opinion of Dean and his admissions. He answered that in his opinion it was a matter of judgement, and one perhaps that we were not qualified to make. He said he was aware of Dominic's concern and also of the fact that these concerns had been growing as the interview progressed. While he agreed that the anomalies were worrying, it was nevertheless a fact that Dean was making the admissions freely and voluntarily and without any threat or inducement being made to him.

We decided that we would bring our concerns to Detective Chief Superintendent Camon. As head of the NBCI he was the highest-ranking detective in the country; he was also one of the most experienced. Since the discovery of the two bodies we had been assisted in the investigation by detectives from the NBCI, and the chief superintendent, in his usual hands-on approach, had taken an active interest in the case, regularly attending briefings and conferences. We were aware that he was due to attend an impromptu conference arranged for the Bridewell for 9 p.m. that night.

I should explain here that the whole question of whether this conference even occurred would become a source of division in the various inquiries and investigations that would be set up when the charges against Dean Lyons were eventually withdrawn. It would emerge that there was almost a straight split, with the senior officers denying that any such conference had taken place while the middle and lower ranks insisted that it had. During the sitting of the subsequent commission of investigation I listed those senior officers whom I said were present and had chaired the conference. The commission would eventually agree with us that the conference had indeed taken place.

As we headed into the conference we met Chief Superintendent Camon in the short corridor outside the room. He asked Robbie and Dominic how the interview was progressing. Robbie told him that the taking of a formal statement of admission had only begun a short time earlier and had been suspended to allow Dean a rest period. Dominic then voiced his concerns about the veracity of the admissions to the chief superintendent. He said he felt that Dean was not telling the truth when he was claiming to have murdered Sylvia and Mary and that in his opinion he was making up the admissions as he went along. It further appeared to him that Dean was using the questions asked of him to fill in the blanks in his answers. He added that when Dean was challenged about his lack of knowledge he would immediately hide behind his drug addiction problems.

Matt and myself also voiced the concerns arising from our viewing of the interview tape. I was aware that the chief superintendent had also watched a portion of this tape following his arrival at the station, sitting in the incident room.

I was shocked at his response to our honestly expressed concerns. Drawing himself up to his not inconsiderable height, he addressed Dominic in a loud voice: 'What the fuck more do you want!' Extending his left hand, he began to enumerate his points as he pointed at each finger:

(1) You have two elderly women murdered in their beds.
(2) You have a prisoner downstairs who, of his own free will, has admitted to the murders.
(3) He has freely and voluntarily admitted to the crimes on camera.
(4) He has admitted to his mother that he killed the two women, and has apologised to her for it.
(5) He is a heroin addict and cannot be expected to remember every single fact of something that happened almost six months ago.

He finished his tirade by telling Robbie and Dominic that when Dean's rest period ended they were to resume the interview and to include in the statement as much detail as Dean could supply them with.

We then went into the conference room, and the chief superintendent addressed the dozen or so present, briefing them on the various developments that the day had brought. I was instructed to 'action' all matters appearing in the admissions we had up to this time for the purpose of obtaining as much corroboration as possible while Dean was still detained.

The fact that three of the gardaí centrally involved in the investigation had voiced doubts about Dean's admissions was not even referred to. The opinions of experienced detectives with more than seventy-five years' policing between them was not mentioned.

Before Robbie and Dominic returned to the interview room, Dominic told Matt and myself that the more he thought about what we had, the less convinced he was that Dean had played any part in the murders. Robbie said that as far as he was concerned we should continue to write down what Dean was telling them; it could then be presented to the law officers, warts and all, and let that office decide whether or not Dean was telling us the truth and whether or not he had a case to answer. They then returned to the jail section to continue their interviewing of Dean.

Matt and myself continued working in the incident room while Robbie and Dominic were carrying out their interview. As each team returned with the result of the actions we had allocated to them we became more and more convinced that nothing Dean had told us was going to be corroborated. As midnight approached, we were in a position to say that Dean had not confided in any woman called Molly, he had not burnt his clothing in the skipper, he had not given the gloves he had allegedly worn to someone to mind for him, and, more importantly, his knowledge of the interior of the crime scene and of the details of the assaults on both victims was negligible.

Any member of the team who visited the incident room during that night was left in no doubt about our opinion of the case. This included any of the senior officers who called in to us to ask about the progress of the interview and the various inquiries. It was against that background that I was directed to become part of the early-morning interview team.

St Brendan's Hospital, Grangegorman, main entrance. (© *Collins*)

Map showing the layout of the 75-acre Grangegorman complex. (© *Collins*)

The Grangegorman murder scene. (© *Collins*)

The state pathologist discusses details of the scene with Garda technical experts. (© *Collins*)

The state pathologist, Prof. John Harbison. (© *CourtPix*)

Gardaí remove the body of Sylvia Sheils from the scene at Grangegorman. (© *Collins*)

Gardaí remove the body of Mary Callinan from the scene. (© *Collins*)

Search of waste ground at St Brendan's Hospital. (© *Collins*)

Stella Nolan, sister of Sylvia Sheils, who led the campaign to have her sister's inquest heard. (© *CourtPix*)

Sylvia Sheils in happier times. (© *Irish Times*)

Ann Mernagh, sole survivor of the Grangegorman murders. (© *Collins*)

Dean Lyons attending on remand at the District Court, charged with murder. (© *Collins*)

Dean Lyons leaving the District Court after the murder charge is withdrawn. (© *Collins*)

Dean's parents, Sheila and John Lyons. (© *CourtPix*)

Catherine and Carl Doyle. (© *Collins*)

The home of Catherine and Carl Doyle. (© *Irish Times*)

Members of the Doyle family at the funerals of Catherine and Carl. (© *Irish Times*)

Mark Nash appearing in the District Court charged with the murder of Catherine and Carl Doyle. (© *CourtPix*)

Sarah Jane Doyle at the trial of Mark Nash. (© *Collins*)

Members of the Doyle family leaving the court after Nash's conviction. (© *Collins*)

Mark Nash during the trial for the murder of Catherine and Carl Doyle. (© *Collins*)

Counsel for the state, Barry Coffey SC, at the inquest into the deaths of Sylvia Sheils and Mary Callinan. (© *Collins*)

James McGuill, Nash's solicitor.
(© *Collins*)

George Bermingham sc, sole member of the Commission of Investigation. (© *Collins*)

ATTEMPTS TO ESTABLISH FURTHER EVIDENCE AGAINST DEAN LYONS

Whatever about our thoughts and reservations, Dean Lyons was charged with the murder of Mary Callinan and appeared at a special sitting of Dublin District Court at noon on 27 July. The direction to lay charges against him had been given by Niall Lombard of the Office of the Director of Public Prosecutions, whose consent to do so had been canvassed in a telephone call from Detective-Superintendent Gordon. Detective Chief Superintendent Camon was present when this call was made.

Murder and aggravated sexual assault are two of those charges that can be laid only after permission has been granted by a senior representative of the Office of the DPP. There will always be one member of that staff on call and available for consultation. There are no exceptions to the rule. Contact with the DPP's representative is normally made by the senior investigating officer on the case or other officer in charge. He will provide all the details of the investigation, together with the evidence established against the person they are seeking to charge. In an ideal situation, this evidence will be presented in the form of a written report.

The DPP must be satisfied that we have made a sufficient case before granting permission to lay charges. It regularly happens that the SIO will be told not to lay the charge, or to lay a lesser charge, for example one of assault, until the full investigation file has been submitted.

In this particular case Mr Lombard, being satisfied on the basis of the evidence presented to him, granted permission to charge

Dean Lyons with one of the murders. This direction, to lay only one murder charge for the moment, was not unusual.

In the normal course of events, charging a prisoner with murder attracts a lot of media attention. Given the interest that this particular case had attracted, it is not surprising that, as word began to filter out about a prisoner being due to attend court in connection with the Grangegorman murders, all hell broke loose. By 11:45 a.m., as the court garda opened the doors to District Court No. 4, he was almost knocked over in the rush to get in. The crowd of onlookers spilled over into the Bridewell yard and out into Chancery Street. Reporters unable to gain access conducted 'vox pop' interviews among the crowd. One of my colleagues commented that it was like one of those crowds you saw on television gathered outside an American prison waiting for word that the execution had just been completed.

At noon Judge Desmond Windle entered the courtroom and took his seat on the dais as the court garda called out 'Silence in the court!' Judge Windle was was one of the most experienced judges who sat in the Dublin Metropolitan Area. Now he looked out over his packed courtroom for a moment and then signalled the court clerk to call the case. The clerk picked up the charge sheet and then in a clear voice read out: 'The Director of Public Prosecutions versus Dean Lyons.' All was silent, and then footsteps could be heard ascending the staircase from the holding cell beneath the courts. Detective-Sergeant Robbie McNulty stepped into the room and then turned and motioned behind him. The packed courtroom fell eerily silent as everyone craned to get a look at the prisoner as he entered the dock.

Later, when talking to some colleagues who had come in from other stations just to 'be there', as it were, I realised that, given the hype that had surrounded this case from the beginning, the crowd were expecting to see a 'Hannibal Lecter' type being escorted into the dock by burly prison officers in riot gear. Instead this diminutive figure slunk into the court and stood behind the microphone in the dock. He looked around at the gathered crowd with a look of awe on his face while continuously playing with plastic rosary beads that he wore around his neck.

Robbie McNulty entered the witness box and gave evidence of having arrested Dean earlier that morning at the Bridewell Station and of reading over the charge sheet to him. Dean had made no reply after being cautioned and being given a copy of the charge sheet.

Judge Windle told Dean that he was remanding him in custody until the following Tuesday, 29 July. In accordance with the legislation, he was refusing to grant him bail: a prisoner charged with murder can be granted bail only on application to the High Court. The judge asked Dean if he wished to apply for legal representation, and Dean responded in a barely audible voice that he wished to have Garrett Sheehan appointed to defend him. Robbie told the judge that Dean had no income, so Judge Windle appointed Mr Sheehan under the free legal aid scheme.

Matt and myself stood together at the back of the packed courtroom. We stared in dismay at the drama being played out in front of us. I can safely say that at that point we could have put our hands on our hearts and said that of all the crimes Dean Lyons might have committed in his short criminal career, the murders of Sylvia Sheils and Mary Callinan were not among them.

The hearing, which lasted only a matter of minutes, then ended, and Dean was led back downstairs and into the tunnel that would take him back to the Bridewell. There was an exodus from the courtroom, with the media scrum vying to be first to relay the news to their respective offices.

When later talking among ourselves about Dean's behaviour in the court and his reaction to the circus that it had become, Matt and I were undecided whether he had been overwhelmed by the number of onlookers or just possibly might have been enjoying his moment in the sun. While on the one hand he looked like nothing more than a rabbit caught in the headlights, he now had ample opportunity, which he had not availed of, to shout 'stop' and to announce in front of the public and the media that this was all a terrible mistake, that he had not killed anyone.

The investigation team returned to the Bridewell Station at the conclusion of the hearing. There Detective-Superintendent Gordon told us that anyone who had no urgent inquiries should take the afternoon off to recharge their batteries, and that we were all to meet back at the Bridewell at 10 a.m. the following Monday for a conference. An afternoon off was a luxury we had not enjoyed since March, and the announcement was greeted with a few cheers.

There is a time-honoured tradition in most police forces that at the successful conclusion of a major investigation the team congregate in a local pub for a few hours. It was normally considered to be a successful conclusion when the culprit was brought before the courts. This was an opportunity to trade anecdotes and tall stories, vent various grievances built up throughout the investigation and, of course, enjoy a few drinks now that the pressure was lifted off our shoulders. This tradition was also viewed as part of the winding-down process as gradually over the next few weeks the team would be scaled down, with only a few members retained to finish inquiries. Very often a lot of us would not be together again until the next major investigation. As can be imagined, these were often very lively affairs.

What was significant about the Grangegorman murder team was how few of us stayed on to attend the event arranged for our local pub. The great majority of us went our separate ways; one colleague who did attend would later refer to it as the worst wake he was ever at.

Later that Sunday night my wife and myself went to our local pub for a quiet drink, something that we had not been able to do to any great extent over the previous few months. How much your family life is compromised when you are caught up in a major investigation is never properly quantified, either by our masters or by those outside the job. For the duration of the investigation life outside the inquiry is virtually suspended; early mornings, long days and late nights are the norm. The IRC is expected to be almost continuously available to answer any queries or problems as they arise. Breaking news must be recorded and actioned almost immediately. Matt and myself could operate as a team, with at least one of us always available. Both of us also lived in close proximity to the station.

As we sat in our local that Sunday night I was approached by two off-duty gardaí whom I knew well. One served in a city-centre station, while the second served in a rural station. I had in the past worked on inquiries with them. They expressed surprise at seeing me there and asked if we had not gone for a drink after our great breakthrough. I told them that I honestly didn't believe there was much cause for celebration, and they were able to tell me that a rumour was already circulating within the job, even at that early stage, that not everybody was convinced we had the right man. I told them that they could count me among those same people.

———

The team reconvened at ten o'clock on Monday morning at the Bridewell. Once a person has been charged with a crime, the investigators have forty-two days during which a file must be prepared and submitted to the law officers, containing all the evidence that has been established against the accused. If this report has not been submitted, counsel for the accused is entitled to ask that the charges be struck out and withdrawn from the court. This puts the incident room under pressure both to prepare the file and also to ensure that all the outstanding actions are complete. The first conference after a prisoner has appeared in court will, for the most part, centre on ensuring that all matters connected with the prisoner's arrest, detention, questioning and court appearance are fully addressed. The gardaí involved in any of those matters will be directed to have their statements completed and handed in as soon as possible.

Our conference that day was addressed by Chief Superintendent Kelly. He complimented all of us on our work in bringing Dean Lyons to justice. He also conveyed to us the congratulations of the Commissioner, who had asked him to pass on his best wishes to the team. The task of attempting to corroborate the admissions made by Dean Lyons would continue. In addition, all outstanding actions dating from before the arrest were to be completed as a matter of urgency. The incident room staff, he said, would be working flat out over the next few weeks, and any assistance we requested was to be given to us without question.

At the conclusion of the conference all the team members left to complete their various actions. As with all such conferences, Detective Chief Superintendent Camon and Chief Superintendent Kelly remained behind to discuss our various strategies. Both Matt and myself addressed our senior officers and again voiced our firmly held belief about Dean's admissions. We said that it was our belief that Dean had not committed the murders and that any limited knowledge of the crimes that he appeared to possess he had picked up from the various questions that we were putting to him. Matt suggested that Dominic's description of Dean as a 'Walter Mitty' type was appropriate.

Chief Superintendent Camon told us that he was satisfied from the evidence we had that Dean had committed the murders and that we should be striving to prove the case and not be undermining it by expressing our doubts to other gardaí. I suggested that any report we would submit to the law officers should also, in addition to presenting the various admissions made by Dean, reflect the genuinely held concerns of both ourselves and certain other members of the team who, we were aware, held similar concerns to our own but had not articulated them. Chief Superintendent Kelly said that we should be concentrating all our efforts on firming up the case that we had against Dean and not undermining it. Addressing me directly, he informed me that as the bookman it was my responsibility to ensure that a full report, including appropriate recommendations to ensure that a charge in relation to the murder of Sylvia Sheils would also be laid against Dean, should be prepared without delay.

The following Friday morning a further conference was held at the Bridewell for the purpose of establishing the up-to-date position in relation to the various inquiries that had not been completed. At the conclusion of the conference everyone was, as usual, canvassed for their opinions and views on any matter discussed during it. One of our colleagues, Detective-Garda Tony Whelan, asked if the doubts about Dean's involvement that were being expressed by a number of team members had been or would be brought to the attention of the law officers. The senior officer who was chairing the meeting stated unequivocally that no grounds existed for any such doubts. The conference then ended.

As the other members left the room the senior officer told Matt and myself that he wished to meet the two of us in Matt's office in five minutes. From his demeanour I believed he was annoyed with us. We waited in the office and after a few minutes the officer entered the room and closed the door firmly behind him. He stated that the comment that had just been made at the conference concerning Dean's admissions was a direct consequence of the negative attitude that we were openly displaying to the rest of the inquiry team. He told us, in no uncertain terms, that were we to continue with those remarks, irreparable damage would be done to a case that our colleagues had striven so zealously to solve. Our negative comments, he said, had even been mentioned to him when he was attending a conference about a different crime in another station.

Working to a strategy that we had decided on over the previous few days, Matt told the officer that we would continue to ensure that all inquiries were completed and that a full file would be ready within the statutory time limit for the law officers. We would insist, however, that the report included the various ambiguities in Dean's statements, together with a full list of those admissions that should have been but could not be corroborated.

As the days turned into weeks, all our attempts at building the case against Dean came to naught. Each line of his admissions would be meticulously checked and cross-checked. As we approached the mid-point of our statutory period, twenty-one days, we were no further on than when we had started out. I also began to list those claims and admissions made by Dean that were totally at variance with the known and established facts. I list a number of them here, not in any particular order of importance.

1. At the outset, Dean claimed to have used only one weapon, a steak knife, to inflict all the various injuries. Post-mortem evidence showed that a number of weapons had been used; these included the electric carving-knife blades, the two steak knives and the roasting-fork.

2. He had been unable to describe in any detail the injuries that had been inflicted on either of the victims, notwithstanding the fact that some of them had been quite specific.

3. In his video admissions he said that as he ascended the stairs he had stumbled and was then approached by one of the victims. Later in the same interview he changed this and said he met the two women on the landing.

4. He claimed to have killed the two victims on the landing and then to have dragged the bodies of the 'woman—women' into one of the bedrooms. The established evidence clearly showed that both victims had been assaulted at or near where their bodies were found, one on the bed and the other on the floor between her bed and the window.

5. He claimed to have burned his clothes in the skipper. Extensive searches of the building had been carried out by trained personnel. No fire residue or debris was found in any of the areas pointed out by Dean.

6. He claimed to have visited the house at Orchard View some months before the crime with either Michael or Robbie Flynn. They were, he said, delivering a message to Ann Mernagh. Both Flynns denied

that any such visit had ever taken place. They said they were not even aware that Ann lived there until after the murders.

7.   He had insisted throughout that he had confided in Molly Jones, the prostitute whom he had met immediately after the murders, telling her he had killed the two women. We had been unable to find any woman of that name who could confirm this. The one Molly Jones we had found denied that it had been her, and when she met Dean in our presence he agreed that she was not the right woman.

8.   He had not made any reference to the large refuse bin inside the window at the point of entry and when pressed on the matter had referred to the presence on the windowsill of two ornaments that did not exist.

9.   He claimed not to have removed the drawer from the kitchen press, yet it had been left in a prominent position on the kitchen floor.

10. He said he had not found any handbag at the scene, yet Ann Mernagh's handbag and its contents had been strewn across the floor in the hallway.

11. During the crimes he claimed to have worn leather gloves, yet the developed marks clearly showed that gloves with a knitted pattern had been worn.

12. He claimed that when searching the kitchen drawer he had found some rent books. There was no item of this nature in the drawer.

13. His description of the sequence of the murders was completely wrong. He described having murdered one woman and, before leaving her body, inserting the long fork in her vagina. He had then gone in and murdered the second woman. Given that the puncture wounds, it had been established, were caused by the fork on both victims, this could not be correct, as he would not have been able to remove the fork to inflict the wounds on the other victim.

14. He claimed that before inflicting the injury on Mary he had partially removed her underwear. When her body was discovered, Mary was not wearing any underwear, and none had been found on her body or near her.

15. He said that when he was leaving the house he had done so through the front door, the key of which had been on the inside

of the lock. There was no facility on this lock for fitting the key on the inside. This key had in fact been taken from Ann Mernagh's handbag.

16. While at the scene with us on the Sunday morning he had first pointed out the wrong place where he stated he had discarded the key.

17. Having changed the whereabouts of the key, he then said he had stood at the door and thrown it in a different direction. If that was correct he would have to be able to throw the key some seventy-five feet, a not inconsiderable distance.

From my experience in preparing files for the law officers and subsequently presenting evidence before the highest courts in the land, I would say that any *one* of the discrepancies I have identified could prove fatal when pointed out to a jury. There would be little or no chance of statements of admission that contained so many anomalies ever being put to a jury.

The frightening thing was that these self-same anomalies were well known to have been contained in the statements at least eighteen hours before Dean would stand in the dock charged with murder. Our work with the statements and with the preparation of a file for the law officers could not do anything to alter or improve them.

It would all prove to be moot, however, as a couple of days later another gruesome double murder in a remote area in the west of Ireland would affect our investigation and ultimately bring the case against Dean Lyons crashing down.

———

There are two further aspects of the investigation that I should deal with here. The first relates to the background information, referred to within the Garda Síochána as the 'antecedent history', established about Dean Lyons. This information is considered an integral part of any file and is required by the law officers before they issue their directions to charge. The second aspect deals with some further admissions to the murders made by Dean after being charged. These admissions were made to persons other than the Gardaí.

Chapter 16

THE ANTECEDENT HISTORY
OF DEAN LYONS

Dean Lyons was born on 20 April 1973 and at the time of his arrest for the murders of Sylvia Sheils and Mary Callinan was twenty-four years of age. He was the middle one of seven children, with three sisters and three brothers, born to Sheila and John (Jackie) Lyons. They were a close, united family. Throughout Dean's incarceration his family stood by him. Given the notoriety of the crime and the rumours that abounded, this could not have been easy for them. They always believed in Dean's innocence and that one day he would be able to walk away a free man.

At an early stage Sheila had become aware that Dean was having difficulties achieving even minimal educational levels. She began a long, hard battle with the school authorities to have Dean properly assessed. Her persistence finally paid off when he was taken in for assessment by the Children's Assessment Unit of St John of God's Hospital. He was quickly identified there as having special needs, in particular with basic literacy and numeracy. These problems required the services of a remedial teacher.

Dean then attended Scoil Aonghusa in Tallaght, where he would prove to be a willing and popular pupil. He was described by one of the teachers there as being 'more of a follower than a leader.' He did not, she said, possess a dominant personality. Considered quiet and well behaved, he had never engaged in disruptive behaviour.

From 1987 to 1990 Dean attended Tallaght Community School until he completed his Group Certificate. The vice-principal described Dean to us as one of the most pleasant children she had ever dealt with. This was high praise, considering that it was said at a time when the news was out about his being charged with the Grangegorman murders. Throughout his time in her school she said that Dean had never required disciplinary correction. This teacher went further in expressing her faith in Dean, telling us that she could not, for one moment, envisage Dean Lyons committing any murder.

Other teachers told us that Dean was certainly academically weak, with an IQ in the region of 70. He mixed well with his peers, was always pleasant towards staff and pupils alike and was never rough or violent. They all believed that Dean's biggest failure was his complete lack of cunning, that he would never be 'street-wise'. He was, at best, a passive individual to whom things happened, as opposed to his making them happen. Again these comments were made while Dean was before the courts.

Dean left school not long after his sixteenth birthday. Very little information about his work record exists. However, having left the safety net of the school system he began to hang around with people far 'wider' than himself and began to experiment with various drugs. This would eventually lead to a full drug dependence. He continued to live at home during that period and to have the support of his family and peers.

His drug habit eventually led to his having to leave the family home. Unusually enough in such a situation, his leaving would appear to have been by mutual consent. He continued to stay in touch with each member of his family and revisited the family home several times a week, where he would always find fresh clothes and a hot meal waiting for him.

As his drug dependence continued to grow, Dean began to drift into the homeless scene that was centred around the inner-city area, with its proliferation of hostels, methadone clinics and drop-in centres. He quickly became a regular in the hostels, where he mixed with and befriended people with similar dependence problems. Even among this group Dean was seen as a 'soft touch' when it came to being asked to share either his drugs or his money. When arrested for the murders he was receiving a social welfare payment of £62.40 (about €80) weekly.

But his drug addiction accounted for all this money, and to survive he turned to a life of petty crime, breaking into parked cars and stealing anything of value.

At that time criminals had identified a relatively new item that had been introduced into motoring, the mobile telephone. The models of the time were too big to be carried conveniently around for long periods, so nine times out of ten they were left in the cars. The 'dead give-away' was the special aerial that had to be mounted on the roof of the cars. There was a ready underground market for these phones.

FURTHER ADMISSIONS MADE BY DEAN LYONS

I have already dealt with the admissions made by Dean Lyons to his mother at 5:20 p.m. on 26 July and later that day, at 10 p.m., to his father. There were also the admissions he was supposed to have made to both John Whelan and Éamonn White when he met them and their friends outside the Model Hostel in Benburb Street, which alleged admission had led ultimately to his being arrested and charged.

On the Sunday morning, 27 July, Dean was released from detention and then rearrested for the purpose of being charged with the murder. He was held in the Bridewell jail section pending the arrival of Judge Windle to hear the case at a special sitting of Dublin District Court. It is important to note that we were no longer entitled to interview Dean, as he was not now being detained for questioning but rather waiting to appear in court.

Dean was allowed a visit from his brother John, who had been asked by his parents to call to see him. During a very emotional conversation Dean was clearly heard by the garda supervising the meeting apologising for the pain and distress he had caused his family. He added that he was 'relieved to have got the whole thing off my chest.' The conversation then returned to the situation at home. Even with all the trauma that he must have been going through personally, Dean's primary concern was for his parents and siblings.

After his initial court appearance on the Sunday morning Dean had been remanded in custody to Mountjoy Prison. Given the nature and notoriety of the charges against him, on his arrival at Mountjoy he was transferred, on the orders of the prison governor, to Arbour Hill Prison. Dean would be unlikely to survive unscathed in a general prison: it would only be a matter of time before some young blood, out to make a name for himself, would decide to mete out his own brand of justice to Dean for these horrific crimes. The prison population in Arbour Hill, a total of some 130 prisoners, is made up for the most part of murderers and rapists and would assimilate someone charged with a crime such as this far more quickly and safely.

On his second day in Arbour Hill prison—sometimes referred to by inmates as the Arbour Hilton, because of its more relaxed regime—Dean became acquainted with a prison officer, Jim Dolan (not his real name). Considered by both his fellow-officers and the prison inmates a fair and equitable man, Dolan was regularly confided in by the inmates. He had a long discussion with Dean, explaining the do's and dont's of life in the prison. He asked Dean what crime he had been charged with, and Dean replied, 'The Grangegorman murders.' Dolan had asked him, with incredulity, if he was serious, and when Dean replied that he was had asked if he had actually committed them. Dean replied, 'Yeah, I did.' When asked why he had committed the murders he replied that he had been 'stoned out of his head' and had gone in looking for mobile phones.

On 11 August, as Jim was escorting him back to his cell after a visit from his solicitor, Dean commented that his solicitor had told him that the only evidence the police had that linked him to the crimes was his own admission, and that this on its own was really not worth a whole lot. Dean appeared to him to be in good form and to have been bolstered by this news.

However, within two days Dean would tell him that he had been wearing gloves when he was in the house. He also said he had burnt the clothes he had been wearing when he murdered the two women, that immediately after the murders he met a prostitute called Molly, and that it was following her advice that he burnt the clothing. In relation to the gloves he had been wearing at the time he said he had given them to a female friend of his who had been staying in a nearby hostel. He added that the Gardaí had visited the hostel but had not found the gloves.

While Dean was on remand in Arbour Hill Prison an associate of his, Andy Devoy (not his real name), was also there. He was serving a lengthy sentence for a number of serious sexual assaults. Devoy would tell us that he had several conversations with Dean about the Grangegorman murders. He believed that Dean trusted him enough to confide in him. On one occasion he asked Dean how the police had finally caught him for the murders. Dean told him that he believed that another friend of his had overheard him admit them to his girl-friend and had told the police about it.

Devoy, a career criminal who would talk to gardaí only if he believed there might be something in it for him, would certainly have had a lot of difficulty in convincing a jury that he had reported these conversations to the gardaí out of a sense of civic duty. Given the reprehensible nature of his crimes, very few would believe that this was his motive. However, what he was telling us mirrored the admissions Dean had made.

Dean, he said, had shared one further matter with him. Dean confided in him that he had been with another person when committing the murders. He claimed it had been this other person who cut up the bodies. He himself had 'only stabbed them', and it had been his accomplice who had carried out the various mutilations.

On another occasion Devoy said that he and Dean had been sitting in Dean's cell, talking and smoking. He noticed that Dean had a newspaper partially concealed under his blankets and took it out to read it. The paper contained an article about a man called Mark Nash. There was a photograph of Nash, and in the accompanying article it stated that Nash had admitted to murdering the two women in Grangegorman. When Devoy asked Dean about this Dean told him that he knew Nash very well and that it had been Nash who was 'your man what did this with me.' When he made this comment Dean was entering his second month in custody for the murder of Mary Callinan.

——

Members of Dean's family remained steadfast in the support of their son and brother, and they regularly visited him while he was on remand in the prison. The rules governing visits to prisoners on remand are not as strict as they are for those serving a sentence. Dean's father was a frequent visitor. I have often thought what a harrowing experience it must be for a parent to sit in the communal visitors' room at Arbour Hill Prison, separated by a table five feet wide from their child and knowing that the prisoners seated on each side of him at the same table are serving sentences for rape, murder and other unimaginable crimes.

Jackie told us that he never for a moment believed Dean capable of committing the murders. He always felt that, at worst, Dean might have gone into the house to steal property with another person and that this second person had committed the murders. During one of his visits, on 14 August, Dean told him he had been with a man called Pat Ryan (not his real name) on the night of the murders. He also said that after the murders Ryan suggested that the two of them should 'get offside,' that is, leave the city for a while until everything had quietened down.

Ryan had been known to us as an associate of Dean's and had been interviewed on 31 July when we were putting together a background on Dean. Acting on the information given us by Jackie Lyons, we interviewed Ryan again on 15 August. He provided us with an alibi for the night of the murders, claiming that he stayed in the Salvation Army Hostel in York Street that night, having signed in and out of the hostel and not left it during the night. He said he would normally meet Dean at about nine o'clock every morning at the hostel at the back of Adam and Eve's Church, where they both would go for breakfast. This is a drop-in centre that caters almost exclusively for people with drug addiction problems. He recalled that Dean had not shown up at the centre on the morning the bodies had been found.

The suggestion by Dean to his father that Pat Ryan had been his accomplice was proved within hours to be just another one of the falsehoods that Dean was building up in his imagination.

Ryan then began to tell us about another friend of Dean's who, he said, was always hanging around with him and who had a reputation for having a vicious temper. He was also reputed to always carry a knife concealed on his person. Pat Ryan said that he had always suspected this person of committing the murders. He told us that the man was a native of England, that he (Ryan) didn't know his proper name but that he was known among the drug fraternity as Liverpool Joe. He said that Liverpool Joe had returned to England immediately after the murders but that Dean, who had been with Joe when he killed both women, refused to go with him. Ryan also told us that it was an open secret among the homeless community that both murder victims had had their heads and legs cut off and that those body parts had never been recovered!

Liverpool Joe was well known to us and had previously been interviewed. While we were talking to Pat Ryan this man in fact was in custody in Mountjoy Prison and not, as Ryan said, in England. After interviewing him we had discovered that he was wanted on warrant in relation to some other matter, and we had lodged him in the prison. He was due for release on 4 September, and an operation had been organised to arrest him for the murders as he left the prison.

When Liverpool Joe was interviewed following his arrest he had told us he met Dean on the Friday morning of the murders in the centre at Adam and Eve's Church. Dean, he said, had arrived in at 9 a.m., which was the time they normally met. He was wearing two jackets, and Joe noticed that there was blood on the sleeve of one of them. He had asked Dean where the blood had come from, and Dean had told him he had broken into a house at the 'back of the Gorman' with an associate called Stephen. Dean, he said, claimed to have had a 'blackout' after getting into the house and that when he came to he was covered in blood. He didn't know what had happened in the house after he had his blackout.

According to Joe, as Dean and himself were talking in the centre Stephen had come in and on seeing Dean in deep conversation had become upset, no doubt suspecting that Dean was talking about what they had done. On seeing Stephen, Dean immediately shut up. Joe believed that Dean was in physical fear of Stephen, and that it was this fear that had led to him nominating Joe as his accomplice during the murders, as opposed to Stephen. Joe said that from the moment he had first heard about the murders he had immediately suspected that they had been carried out by Dean and Stephen.

From inquiries made at the drop-in centre while Joe was still in custody we established that he had omitted to tell us that on that Friday morning another mutual friend, a drug addict called Noelie (not his real name), had also been with him when he was talking to Dean. Noelie told us that Dean definitely had some blood on the sleeve of one of the jackets he was wearing. He had been with Dean, he said, on the Wednesday before the murders. The two of them had been 'shooting up' when Dean let the syringe fall out of his vein, causing him to have a 'blow-out,' that is, venous bleeding. This would be a regular occurrence among 'mainlining' addicts. As proof of this having happened, Noelie gave us the jacket he himself was wearing during our interview, which bore bloodstains from their attempts to staunch Dean's blood flow. Analysis would later show that this blood was indeed Dean's.

Joe had told us that when he met Dean in the centre that morning the first thing he noticed was that Dean's face was badly scratched, as if he had been in a fight. He described the scratch marks as being very fresh and noticeable. Noelie now told us that this was totally untrue. He himself had met Dean in Morning Star Avenue at about 8:30 a.m that Friday. They would meet there most mornings at about the same time: Noelie would be coming out of the Army Hostel and Dean would be leaving his skipper at the same time. He had not noticed anything unusual in Dean's behaviour, and Dean, who would always talk about his 'strokes' or crimes, had certainly not mentioned to him being involved in any burglary or murders. He said that Dean could normally 'not hold his piss' and would have had to tell him about it if he had been involved in a crime as big as this. Equally, Noelie said he had been with Dean throughout the time he spent in the Adam and Eve's Centre, and the conversation and admissions made by Dean as recounted to us by Liverpool Joe had never taken place.

We believed that this information as supplied to us by Noelie was significant in many respects. Given that the murders had taken place between midnight and, at the outside, 6 a.m., we now had a witness who had met Dean only some 2½ hours afterwards and in whom Dean appeared to confide. Where they had met was also quite close to the scene of the crime; this fact alone would surely have elicited some comment if it were true. Unlike Liverpool Joe—whose name had been given to us as the accomplice and who in turn had provided us with another name as the accomplice—Noelie did not appear to have any reason to lie to us or to attempt to implicate either Dean or any other person in the murders.

However, what to our minds was far more compelling evidence that the story Liverpool Joe was telling us was a complete fabrication was a certain incident that had occurred at about noon that same Friday morning. From information given us by Noelie, we established that both himself and Dean had actually been arrested at that time. This vitally important piece of information had been omitted totally by Dean when giving us details of his movements immediately after the murders. Imagine our amazement when we were now told that Dean was in Garda custody only some six hours after the bodies at Orchard View were discovered.

The facts we established following both this revelation and other information supplied us by Noelie would, in my opinion, finally and conclusively disprove the story that Dean had told his father and that Jackie in turn had relayed to us and would equally remove any last vestige of reliability that could attach to anything Dean said, no matter who his audience was.

Some time around 10:30 a.m.—a time when we had been told by Liverpool Joe that Dean had been in the company of his accomplice Stephen—Dean had in fact been in the Grafton Street area with two other friends, John and Anto (not their real names). They had all gone into the HMV shop and stolen a number of discs. The other two would confirm this to us and also tell us that they were worried that Dean, who was in a bad way for a fix, would get them all caught. In the event they got away with the property and had gone along Grafton Street, selling the discs to passers-by. They then pooled the money and took a taxi out to the Dolphin's Barn area, where they 'scored' some heroin. They met two further friends, Benjie and Eamo (not their real names), and had then walked together down to Rialto to a vacant furnished house that was fast becoming a favourite haunt of homeless drug addicts in which to 'shoot up' in relative comfort and safety.

An off-duty garda walking past this house with his children had observed the youths going into the house and, knowing it to be vacant, had contacted his colleagues. When they arrived they found Dean and three other youths after they had taken one 'fix'. They were all arrested for being found in possession of drug-taking apparatus and were conveyed to Kilmainham Station, where they were charged with a number of public order offences. They were held in custody there until brought to court in the early afternoon the same day. We now had a situation where the person who would admit to having committed two of the most reprehensible murders this country has ever known was safely ensconced in Garda custody for a number of hours shortly after allegedly committing them. After their court appearance the same day Dean and his friends were admitted to bail.

All the gardaí involved in the arrest, charging and detention of Dean and his appearance in court that fateful day were quickly identified and formally interviewed. Each one of them would state that Dean had no scratch marks on his face or any other signs of having been involved in a serious assault. They had all been aware, of course, of the discovery of the two bodies earlier that day and the various stories in circulation about their horrific injuries. They would equally have had their suspicions aroused had they met any person displaying injuries that they could have obtained in a fight or assault. The presence of any bloodstains on the jackets that Dean was wearing was so insignificant as to warrant either not having been noticed by some of the gardaí or, alternatively, being no more than would be found on any drug addict who was regularly injecting himself. As trained observers, conscious that a major crime had been committed a short distance from their own area, none of those gardaí were going to overlook that evidence if such evidence was present.

For the sceptics among us, of course, this was further proof, if it were needed, of the total unreliability of anything Dean Lyons was telling us. And the number of sceptics was increasing daily.

On this occasion Dean had supplied the information not in a question put to him by the gardaí but in response to a question from his own father. It should also be remembered that at the time he supplied the information he was no longer in our custody, and it certainly cannot be suggested that we influenced his story in any way.

When we had interviewed the man Dean alleged had been with him at the time, he totally denied any such involvement and furthermore could supply us with a cast-iron alibi. He had spent the night of the murders in the Simon Community hostel at Usher's Quay and had not left until shortly before 9 a.m. Given the nature of the man, however, not content with denying any role for himself in the murders he had immediately nominated another person as Dean's accomplice. This is exactly the problem I was referring to when talking about the type, standard and reliability of information that would usually be forthcoming from informants with addiction problems. The information he gave us about the cuts to Dean's face and about his jacket being 'pebbledashed' with blood also sounded very good until we discovered that a number of gardaí had met and dealt with him during that day and had not seen anything of this nature.

We also established that Liverpool Joe had indeed fled the country after the discovery of both bodies. However, he was being sought for interview in relation to a firearms offence in the city centre at the time, and it was this that had prompted his flight.

On 12 August a known drug addict, Jock Carey (not his real name), approached a uniformed garda on duty outside the GPO. He said he had certain information in relation to the Grangegorman murders that he wanted to pass on. The garda brought him into the nearby Garda office in Upper O'Connell Street. There he said that on St Patrick's Day he had met Dean Lyons near the skipper in Grangegorman. This, he said, was the first time he had ever spoken to Dean. Both of them were 'strung out' on heroin and began talking about their respective habits and how they financed them. They had shared stories about the different 'strokes' they had pulled off.

Dean told him that he had broken into a house in the Grangegorman area and that while inside he met two elderly ladies. They had gone 'berserk', and one of them had been brandishing a knife, threatening him with it. Dean described himself as having tried to calm the two women down but the one with the knife had slashed out at him, cutting him on the arm. The other woman had scratched him a few times on the face. The woman with the knife had also cut him on the face. Carey said that he himself had been aware of some of the details of the crime through various press reports and had asked Dean if he had touched the woman. Dean, he said, told him that this third woman had begun to scream at the top of her voice. He also said to him, in response to his question about what exactly he had done to the victims: 'Fuck them, they shouldn't have had the knife.'

This story was even more far-fetched than any of the others that had been given us. We now had the suggestion that the women had in fact been in possession of the knife and that they had cut Dean, forcing him to retaliate in self-defence. We also now had Ann Mernagh allegedly screaming at the top of her voice. What all this does suggest, however, assuming of course that Carey could be believed, is that even at this point, only ten days after the murders, Dean was making admissions to the crimes.

Chapter 18 ❧

THE PSYCHOLOGICAL
ASSESSMENT OF DEAN LYONS

D ean's solicitor was the well-known and respected criminal defence solicitor Garrett Sheehan. Garrett, later to be appointed a High Court judge, had built up a reputation over the years as one of the best defence solicitors in the country, always ensuring that no stone would be left unturned in his defence of his client. He was equally respected by his clients, prosecuting gardaí and the courts.

On 21 August 1997, at Garrett's request, the director of the Central Mental Hospital, Dr Charles Smith, visited Dean Lyons at Arbour Hill Prison. The Dundrum hospital houses among its patients those who have been deemed by the judicial system to be criminally insane.

During his conversation with Dr Smith, Dean once again admitted to the two murders. In his report to Garrett Sheehan he would say that although these admissions were made to him he did not find them to be convincing. This opinion, as expressed by one of the leading psychiatrists in the country, mirrored exactly the opinion some of my colleagues and myself had expressed on the Saturday evening before Dean was charged.

On 9 September 1997, again at the request of Garrett Sheehan, Dean received a visit from Dr Gísli Gudjónsson, professor of forensic psychology at the Institute of Psychiatry at King's College, London, and an internationally renowned expert on the psychology of interrogations and admissions. His special field is the study of false and unreliable confessions. Prof. Gudjónsson's expert testimony would form the basis of the appeals that led to the overturning of the convictions in both the 'Birmingham Six' and 'Guildford Four' cases. He is the creator of the term 'memory distrust syndrome', now used in legal and medical circles to describe people who distrust their own recollection of events to such an extent that in recalling those events they come to rely almost exclusively on details supplied to them by others. He also created the 'Gudjónsson suggestibility scale', a weighting matrix used in the consideration of uncorroborated admissions made to the police, designed to measure the vulnerability of the person being interviewed. He has also drawn up the 'Gudjónsson compliance scale', which equally is used to measure the degree of compliance of a person. This 'eagerness to please' can be based on a number of conditions, including the avoidance of conflict or confrontation.

We were not at that point entitled to see the report that he would eventually submit following his meeting with Dean: it could be disclosed to us only if Dean gave his permission. This is a problem faced daily by investigators. Even when a prisoner alleges ill-treatment and the Gardaí summon a doctor to examine them for any evidence, the results of the examination cannot be disclosed to us by the doctor, notwithstanding the fact that it is we who arranged (and paid for) the treatment and that the findings may be of evidential value.

Years later I would have the opportunity to read a synopsis of Prof. Gudjónsson's report. In it he stated that he had applied a test, based on the research he had carried out, for measuring the extent to which he would consider Dean to have a suggestible personality. The same test can be used to show the extent to which a particular type of person can be misled, either through being asked leading questions or from interrogative pressures. From his examination he said he would place Dean in the top 5 per cent of the population with regard to suggestibility. He also estimated Dean's IQ to be in the region of 71.

Dean, he said, had told him that at the time of his arrest he had been living in the hostel. He was a heroin addict and had last 'shot up' at about six o'clock on the evening before. He claimed to have been arrested at 8:50 that morning, just as he was leaving. He had intended looking for something he could steal and sell to get money with which to buy heroin. When the police had asked him to give them an account of his movements on the day of the murder he was not able to remember anything. They told him they had statements that suggested that he had committed the murders.

Dean described himself as having made a false confession at a time when he was both going through drug withdrawal and anxious to get out of custody to try to score drugs. He told Prof. Gudjónsson that he admitted to the murders without giving any thought to what the consequences might be. He was so sick from withdrawal that his body ached all over, he had the shakes and was in a cold sweat. He had asked to see a doctor, and when one arrived, at about 11 a.m., he had prescribed methadone. The police, however, had not given it to him until he admitted on video committing the murders. He said that before the interview on video the police had shown him photographs of one of the victims and had also fed information to him.

Prof. Gudjónsson commented in his report that Dean had in fact been examined by the doctor at 5:40 that Saturday afternoon, and that the medication he had prescribed for Dean was given to him at 8:45. This meant that Dean, a recognised heroin addict, had been without a fix for almost twenty-four hours before being medically examined, and it would be some three hours more before he received any medication.

The DPP's office had requested that the defence allow them to have Dean assessed by Dr Adrian Grounds, a consultant psychologist. Dr Grounds is a senior lecturer in forensic psychiatry at the University of Cambridge. His speciality is the needs of mentally disordered prisoners, and his work on the psychological consequences of wrongful imprisonment is world-renowned. The DPP's office had hoped that Dr Grounds might be able to assist them by producing a report and assessment based on the admissions made by Dean. This request was turned down.

The law officers permitted Dr Grounds to view both the video recording of the interview and the various written admissions taken from Dean. In his report he would raise significant doubts about the reliability of the various confessions. He would further suggest that, given Dean's educational and intellectual levels, he was 'more than likely' to yield to leading questions.

Eventually Dr Grounds was permitted by the defence to meet and interview Dean. He also met his parents and siblings. On the completion of these interviews he submitted a further report, in which he raised further doubts about Dean's admissions, describing them as 'totally unreliable.' He identified a number of circumstances that could have contributed to Dean's vulnerability, including his low intelligence and his tendency to be easily led. He was 'eager to please' and had a history of making up believable stories. In fact in his opinion, Dr Grounds said, Dean was borderline mentally handicapped. He further found him to be 'unusually suggestible.'

Dr Grounds also commented on the significant length of time Dean had been without drugs. Dean had told him that he had believed that the police, when they met him at the hostel, had wanted to question him about a 'syringe robbery' (in which the victim is threatened with being injected with contaminated blood). Dean told him he had learnt that he was to be questioned about the Grangegorman murders only as he was being driven to the Bridewell. He claimed he had asked to be allowed telephone his mother and was allowed to do so only after he had admitted to the murders. He further stated that he was told he would be released if he admitted the murders.

His need for drugs had become so acute that he had told them he had killed the two women. He had then been taken out of the station and arrested. He also said that he had been told by the various detectives who interviewed him 'exactly what happened.' He was then able to use this information when he was admitting the murders.

Some years later Dean's admissions would be subjected to further psychological analysis. This examination was conducted by Prof. David Canter, whom I have previously mentioned, at that time director of the International Centre for Investigative Psychology at the University of Liverpool. This examination was requested by a commission of investigation, known as the Birmingham Commission, established by Government order in 2005. We will be dealing with the commission and its findings later.

On completing his examination and analysis Prof. Canter was asked to consider whether the admissions were consistent with the language skills that had been attributed to Dean. At the commission's request, Dean's family had made a large number of personal documents available to him for the purpose of comparison.

Prof. Canter established that Dean had a habit of 'mirroring'. This means that he would repeat words and expressions used by the person interviewing him; he would do this even if he didn't understand what the word or expression meant. This behaviour, Prof. Canter suggested, was obvious in the interview that was recorded on video. He said that Dean can be clearly observed using language far beyond his intellectual capacity. In addition, he found that the written statements contained grammar and vocabulary that were also far beyond his ability.

After their consideration of Prof. Canter's findings, the commission would state that they were in total agreement with them. They suggested that the structure and language to be found in his statements were 'far too sophisticated to be the spontaneous unprompted language of Dean Lyons.' However, they would add the caveat that every interview contains 'some element' of the 'interviewee embracing the language of the interviewer.'

The findings of all the psychologists and psychiatrists did no more than confirm the opinions both Matt Mulhall and myself had expressed about the reliability of Dean's admissions only hours after his arrest, using little more than our instincts and experience in dealing with interviews and admissions. These expert findings by all the learned and eminent professionals—made long after the event— were exactly as we had always maintained. Dominic Cox's remark that Dean was 'learning' from us throughout the interview was proved to be correct. If only our opinions had been listened to and acted upon when they were expressed, this whole sorry episode, together with the pain and suffering caused to both Dean and his family, could all have been avoided.

Chapter 19

THE MURDERS OF CATHERINE AND CARL DOYLE

In spite of what we might sometimes think, murders in Ireland are a relatively rare occurrence, averaging about one a week for most years. Even rarer are double murders: the total number of double murders committed in this jurisdiction, not related to the armed conflict in Northern Ireland, could be counted almost in single figures. An even rarer occurrence would be where two such double murders are linked. The Grangegorman murders, committed only a short distance from Dublin city centre, and the murders of Catherine and Carl Doyle in the rural area around Ballintober, Co. Roscommon, would be one such occurrence. Throughout my own career in the Garda Síochána I was involved in a total of three double-murder investigations.

In early 1996 Catherine and Carl Doyle, a Dublin couple, realised a lifetime ambition and secured a smallholding for themselves and their four small children, ranging in age from seven years to thirteen months, in the townland of Caran, near Ballintober. They were a close, loving couple who, as well as being husband and wife, were also, most unusually, first cousins. Relatives would always comment on how close they had been, even as children. Catherine was the eldest of seven children, while Carl had two brothers. The couple had hoped that the move to a rural area, facilitated under a rural resettlement venture, would provide them with a quality of life that might not have been available to them had they remained in Dublin.

The cottage they had been allocated was in need of some repair, a chore that they took on enthusiastically. They quickly settled in to the small, close-knit community, their children making friends with the local children. Carl secured work in the meat factory in nearby Ballyhaunis. They enjoyed an idyllic life and never for a moment regretted making the move from the city. Both stayed in close contact with their families in Dublin and were regularly visited by them.

The weekend of 15–17 August was earmarked for one such visit. Catherine's younger sister, Sarah Jane, was to come and spend the few days with them. She would be bringing her five-month-old child and her new partner, who would bring his own eleven-month-old child. That partner was Mark Nash. By the end of that weekend Nash would stand in the dock charged with the murder of Catherine and Carl Doyle. He would also have made a number of verifiable admissions to the Grangegorman murders.

Earlier that year Sarah Jane had ended her relationship with her son's father. By April she would meet and begin a new relationship with Nash, who had broken up with the mother of his child at about the same time. They had met in a night-club in Harcourt Street in Dublin. It was only a few weeks after Sarah Jane had given birth, and the couple had struck up a rapport and had spent the evening chatting about their children. They arranged to meet the following day. They both brought their children with them and had spent a pleasant afternoon together. Within a month they had moved in together.

They had first lived in a flat at 83 Prussia Street. Sarah Jane did not feel comfortable living there, as Nash's estranged partner was living in the same flat. By April 1997 she could no longer take this arrangement and they had moved out, first to a flat further down the road and then to 133 Clonliffe Road, where they were living on the occasion of their visit to Catherine and Carl.

However, theirs was a troubled and volatile relationship. They regularly argued, their rows lasting for hours at a time. The other residents of the house in Clonliffe Road would later tell us of constant bickering and arguing, which could be heard all over the house. One of them would describe hearing Sarah Jane screaming at Nash, after one particularly noisy argument, to 'get the fuck off me, let me go.' This neighbour had grown so concerned that he had knocked on the door, which appeared to end the argument. After another such row Nash had thrown a drawer full of his own excrement out the window of the flat into the back yard of the house—a singularly bizarre act, to say the least. By the weekend of 15 August the other tenants in the house had had their fill of his erratic behaviour and had lodged a number of complaints with the owner of the house.

Nash's relationship with his former partner had also been punctuated with violent outbursts. On one occasion, towards the end of their relationship, he had referred to her during an argument as a 'whore'. She had struck out at him, and in retaliation he had grabbed her by the throat and attempted to strangle her. He also threatened to hit her with a steam iron. He had gone so far as to say to some of their mutual friends that he would kill her, threatening to burn the house down while she was inside it.

His attitude towards Sarah Jane's family was equally aggressive. On occasion he had been verbally abusive towards them when he met them in their home. He had also had words with both Catherine and Carl, whom he had met on one of his visits to the house. However, Sarah Jane believed that of all her family, the ones that Mark respected most and who he might even listen to were Catherine and Carl. She had gone so far as to confide in a friend that she was hopeful that, over the weekend of their visit to the country together, Catherine, whom she revered, would 'sort Mark out.' Little did she know that by the end of the weekend she would be in Beaumont Hospital, being treated for life-threatening injuries, while Catherine and Carl would be found dead in their dream home, leaving four orphaned children.

———

Mark Nash left his place of work at about 4:30 p.m. on 15 August by taxi and went directly to the flat in Clonliffe Road, where Sarah Jane was waiting with the two children. At that time Nash was working for a telemarketing firm in the North Strand area. The taxi then took them all to Heuston Station, where they boarded the train for Castlerea. Other passengers would later recall Nash's erratic behaviour throughout the long rail journey. They said he appeared to be 'agitated' and that he regularly addressed the children in a loud, aggressive manner.

Carl Doyle was waiting at the station in Castlerea when the train pulled in at 8:35 p.m. By this time the children had fallen asleep, and

Nash and Sarah Jane carried them into the car. They drove to the Doyles' house, stopping en route in Kenny's pub, where they bought drink and cigarettes. Throughout the journey Nash remained quiet and morose.

When they arrived at the house the two sisters greeted each other joyfully, and the two men carried the sleeping children into the living-room and laid them down on the sofa, covering them with blankets. Catherine's four children were already asleep upstairs in the bedroom, and the two women decided to leave the other children on the sofa until they all went to bed.

The four stayed chatting and drinking in the living-room, with some music playing in the background. Nash began to relax as the night wore on and joined in the conversation, giving no hint of the dark thoughts that must have been running through his head. Some time around 1 a.m. he began to complain of feeling unwell and went into the bathroom, from where he could be clearly heard getting sick. By this time Carl had fallen asleep sitting up on the sofa, his packet of cigarettes and his lighter resting in his lap. The two women decided to sort out the sleeping arrangements for the two youngest children and, leaving them asleep on the sofa, had gone upstairs.

As they were making up the bed they heard a noise from the living-room, quickly followed by the sound of someone walking quietly up the stairs. The sound did not alarm them, as they presumed it was either Mark or Carl coming up to check on their progress. The bedroom door burst inwards and they both turned around. Mark stood there with what Sarah Jane later said was a 'scary, mad look in his eyes.' He carried what appeared to be a hammer in his hands. It would later be established that this was the tool used for lifting the top off the kitchen range when adding fuel.

Without any warning, Nash lashed out, striking Sarah Jane on the back of the head with the tool, saying to her as he struck her, in a calm and clear voice: 'You have to die, Sarah.' Catherine bravely intervened, throwing herself between Nash and her sister. He then turned his attention to Catherine and began to beat her repeatedly around the head with the tool.

Her six-year-old son was awakened by the screams of his mother but could only lie in bed watching in horror as Nash bludgeoned his mother at the foot of his bed. Sarah Jane tried to save her sister, but

Nash beat her away with the iron tool, landing a number of further blows on her head. He then continued to beat Catherine around the face and head, and she slumped towards the floor. He then hunkered down over her and beat her again a number of times.

Seizing her opportunity, Sarah Jane stumbled down the stairs to awaken Carl, whom she had last seen asleep on the sofa. She ran towards him, screaming at him to come and help Catherine. She stood over him, shouting his name and shaking him; then she saw that he had been stabbed through the heart and was dead. She gave an involuntary scream, realising at the same time that the noise upstairs had ceased. She heard the measured steps of someone descending the stairs and realised that Nash, having finished with her sister, was now coming to get her. He began calling out her name in a calm, 'sing-song' manner.

Sarah Jane realised that if she stayed in the room she would not live to see the morning. She also feared that, with her out of the equation, Nash could possibly start on the six defenceless children who were still in the house. She ran outside but, not wanting to go too far away from the children, hid in the long grass in the back garden, just outside the pool of light spilling out of the open doorway. She did not want to stray any further from the house, intending to attempt to intervene should he start assaulting any of the children.

To her horror, she saw Nash step out the door. He stood so close to where she lay hidden that she feared he must hear her laboured breathing as she pressed herself against the earth. Standing there, clearly silhouetted against the light, he began to calmly call out her name, asking her to come back into the house, saying that 'everything will be all right.' Listening to his calm, relaxed manner she was almost lulled into believing him. However, when he received no response he began to scream her name aloud, and began to run around the garden. After a few moments he ran back into the house, and she could hear him moving around downstairs.

Sarah Jane decided to try to look in and see what he was doing, but at that moment Nash ran back out of the house and jumped over the ditch surrounding the garden and ran off through the nearby fields, calling out her name as he ran.

Sarah Jane stood up and as she did so saw a light going on in a house a short distance away. Although not sure where Nash now was, and expecting him at any moment to jump out of the shadows that surrounded her, she half-crawled towards the light. As she did so she realised for the first time that she was bleeding profusely from the wounds to her head. Trying not to cry out in pain, she dragged herself, at times on her hands and knees, along the stony ground towards the light. She paused every so often to listen but could not hear any sound. Eventually, fearing that the longer she delayed the greater the chance of Nash returning to the house and to the defenceless children, she threw all caution to the winds and half-ran and half-walked the final few yards.

———

Seán and Theresa Hestor were asleep when they heard someone knocking and banging on their front door. They could also hear a female voice crying out for help. Seán ran and opened the door and found a young woman standing on the step, bleeding from wounds to her head and face and covered in earth and grass. She began screaming at him to get help for the children. He brought her into the house and closed the door. In a hysterical voice she begged him to allow her to use his phone to ring for the Gardaí. He dialled the number of Castlebar Garda Station and handed her the phone. Sarah Jane attempted to tell the garda who answered that she had been assaulted but became increasingly upset about the children. John took the phone from her and gave his address and the few details he could get from the woman, who he could now clearly see to have a number of serious injuries. The garda told him that help was on the way.

Theresa attempted to comfort the young woman as best she could and wrapped a blanket around her. The young woman told them her name was Sarah Jane Doyle. She expressed increasing concern for the safety of the children, who, she told them, she had left alone in the house.

Within twenty minutes a Garda car arrived at the house. Garda Thomas King and Garda Muireadach Colleary spoke briefly to Sarah Jane and then, having ensured that medical assistance had been summoned, drove to the Doyles' house, where they met an off-duty colleague, Sergeant John O'Gara, who had arrived there in his own car after being alerted by a call from the station.

As they pushed open the front door they were greeted by the plaintive sound of children crying and calling out for their parents. Although, through their conversation with Sarah Jane, they were aware that some terrible crime had been committed, they were taken aback by the sight that greeted them as they rushed into the house.

In a room to the left of the front door they found the body of Carl Doyle, still sitting upright on the sofa. Close to his body they saw the two infants, still sleeping peacefully.

The door to the right of the main door opened into the kitchen. There they found Catherine's body, lying on its back in the middle of the kitchen floor. Her head faced towards the stairs, which were to the rear of the kitchen, and her lower body faced towards the entrance doorway. Although still dressed, her legs were opened wide apart.

Carefully stepping over her body, the gardaí climbed the stairs, calling out to the screaming children that they were coming to help them. They found the terror-stricken six-year-old sitting up in the bed, cradling one of the younger children, who lay asleep in his arms. Not wanting to let the children see the bodies of their parents, they remained in the bedroom trying to reassure them. A local doctor, Dr Kearney, arrived at the scene minutes later and first examined both bodies for any signs of life. She then directed that all six children should be immediately brought to Roscommon County Hospital and be detained there for observation. Both Catherine and Carl Doyle and their children were well known to Dr Kearney, as she was their family doctor. The distraught mother of one of the children, Sarah Jane Doyle, had already been removed to the same hospital but would not permit the medical staff to begin treating her potentially life-threatening injuries until she was assured that the children had all arrived safely at the hospital.

The scene at the Doyle home was preserved by the gardaí, with the bodies of Catherine and Carl left in place until the arrival of the chief state pathologist, Prof. John Harbison.

On the completion of his preliminary assessment Prof. Harbison directed that the bodies be removed to the mortuary at Roscommon County Hospital. By this time Sarah Jane had been transferred to Beaumont Hospital in Dublin, where her extensive head injuries were treated. The six children, including the four who had been orphaned by Nash's actions, had also been discharged and were being cared for by members of the extended families.

The post-mortem examination of Carl Doyle's body revealed that he had received four stab wounds to the chest, one of the wounds having received two thrusts. Given the depth of the wounds, it was estimated that the knife used to inflict them had a blade at least 5½ inches long. It was established that he had died as a result of shock and loss of blood, with an accumulation of blood in the chest. One of the stab wounds had penetrated his aorta, while a second had penetrated his heart.

It was further found that at the time of his death Carl was moderately inebriated. This was certainly not to suggest that he was drunk to such an extent as to be unable to defend himself. As a consequence, Prof. Harbison concluded that the fatal blow had been struck while Carl was asleep. This proposition can be borne out by an examination of the photographs taken at the scene by Garda photographers. Carl can be clearly seen sitting back into the sofa, his cigarette lighter on his lap. This was the position in which Sarah Jane had last seen him when she and Catherine left the room to go upstairs to get the beds ready for the children.

Catherine's body was found in the kitchen, lying on the floor. When Sarah Jane ran out of the house, Catherine had still been upstairs, being subjected to a sustained assault by Nash. There is no real explanation, therefore, for how her body came to be on the kitchen floor. In my opinion her position, with her legs and arms outstretched, is suggestive of the body having been staged or posed rather than falling. One would then be forced to consider that Nash may have intended to inflict further injuries on the body, given the time and opportunity. Did his failure to find Sarah Jane interfere with some bizarre ritual he intended to carry out?

Catherine was found to have died from bleeding into her chest as a result of multiple stab wounds, which had penetrated her lungs and heart. A total of sixteen stab wounds were found, nine of which had been to the chest. In addition, bruising around her larynx was suggestive of an attempt either to strangle her or to prevent her from calling out. Prof. Harbison found two linear marks around her neck, which could have been caused, in his opinion, by a band-like instrument being pulled tightly against it from behind. In her case the cause of death was shock and haemothorax due to stab wounds to the lungs and to the heart.

It would later be established that during all three assaults Nash had used a variety of weapons, all of which were weapons of opportunity. They included a black-handled knife, the blade of which had snapped off, with parts of it found lying on Carl's body; the tool used for opening the top of the range; a dinner fork; a length of wood; and a second black-handled knife. The knives all came from the Doyles' kitchen.

When Sarah Jane was examined in Roscommon County Hospital she was found to have bruising to her shoulders, chest, arms and legs. She had also suffered a depressed fracture to her skull. Given the nature and extent of this latter injury she was immediately transferred to the care of a neurosurgical team at Beaumont Hospital. When examined there she was found to have suffered a second fracture to her skull. She was considered extremely lucky not to have died or to have suffered permanent brain damage.

Chapter 20 ∿

| THE HUNT FOR MARK NASH

The search for Mark Nash began immediately after Sarah Jane Doyle provided the Gardaí with his name and description. She told them he did not possess any form of transport, and a cordon was placed around the immediate area. A Garda helicopter was brought down to assist in the search, as were a number of dog units.

It was felt that Nash would be captured quickly, given that he did not know his way around the area and that with his distinctive Afro-Caribbean features he would be easily spotted. This was not so, however, and as the day progressed the limits of the dragnet were widened. Nash's name and description were broadcast on a number of local and national radio stations. The appeals for assistance from members of the public continued throughout the day, and would eventually lead to his capture.

The first reported sighting came some time between 11:40 and 11:45 a.m. A caller said there was a suspicious-looking man walking on the railway line at Ballymoe, heading in the direction of Castlerea.

Some fifteen minutes later a man whose house overlooked the railway line just outside Castlerea answered a knock at his back door. When he answered the door a foreign-looking youth who was standing in his rear porch told him that he had just got a puncture and asked him if there was anywhere that he might get it repaired. He then apologised for disturbing the man and, without waiting for an answer, walked away. Some fifteen minutes later the householder saw the same young man walking on the railway line.

This incident would later be the subject of widespread discussion among gardaí. The consensus was that had the person who answered the door been a woman or an older man Nash would have forced his way into the house and lain low there until the search for him died down.

Some time around 12:45 p.m. a woman walking her dog on the main road just outside Castlerea saw a youth walking on the railway line a short distance from the station. Nash at this point appeared to realise that his presence on the railway line was attracting unwanted attention. He left the line just outside the town, near the home of Mick Harte. Mick was away and returned at about 2 p.m. to find that his house had been broken into. The doors on a number of outhouses had also been forced open. His racing bicycle, together with his jacket and cap, were missing. Nash left behind the jacket he had been wearing, together with a pair of stockings. He had now changed his appearance and obtained a means of transport.

After leaving the house he cycled into the town. He must now have begun to feel confident of avoiding detection. As chance would have it, however, as he cycled along the main street he passed a friend of Mick Harte's, who recognised the bicycle. This recognition did not go unnoticed by Nash, who now began to cover his tracks more carefully.

Within the hour the Gardaí were receiving phone calls about a man attempting to hitch a lift on the Castlerea–Williamstown road. This man was on foot. Previous to this, the route he had been taking followed the main road to Ballyhaunis and on towards Knock. The sighting on the Williamstown Road suggested that he had changed direction and was taking to the secondary roads, heading towards Galway. Were he to reach the city he would find it much easier to blend in with the large student and tourist population that swells the city all year round.

His attempts at hitching a lift proved unsuccessful, as people were reluctant to pick up any strangers after the publicity that the crimes and subsequent flight had attracted. There followed a number of sightings of him, again cycling towards Williamstown and on towards Galway. His behaviour became even more erratic as the afternoon progressed towards evening.

Regina Flynn was working that day in Glynn's shop and filling station in Williamstown. Some time after 2 p.m. a young man cycled onto the forecourt, dropped his bicycle on the ground and ran into the shop. This stranger's attitude and demeanour frightened Regina. He asked for cigarettes. Throwing the money onto the counter, he grabbed the cigarettes and ran back out of the shop. She saw him jump up on the bicycle and pedal furiously away in the direction of Dunmore, the next village on the road to Galway.

Minutes later Karen Feeney was working in her father's pub and shop on the other side of Williamstown when a stranger who spoke with a strong English accent came in. He bought some writing paper and a ballpoint pen and then left. Nash would subsequently use the writing material to write a number of letters of apology to Sarah Jane. These would become very relevant to the inquiry into the Grangegorman murders.

Valerie Kearney was working in Egan's shop and filling station in Dunmore when a man walked in and asked her if they sold sandwiches. The look on the man's face frightened her, and she noticed the handle of a hammer protruding from his jacket pocket. When she told him that they did not sell sandwiches he bought some sweets and chocolates and walked out of the shop. Valerie followed him out and saw him cycle off in the direction of Tuam.

A few minutes later a stranger was observed by a number of people sitting by the bank of the Sinking River just outside Dunmore. The man seemed to be writing a letter while eating a bar of chocolate. A bicycle was lying on the grass margin beside him.

At about four o'clock that Saturday afternoon Felix O'Rourke, whose house was on the main road about half way between Dunmore and Tuam, answered a knock to his front door. When he answered it he was confronted by a young man who was carrying an empty plastic bottle. He asked Felix if he would fill the bottle with water for him. He did so, and the man then cycled away.

Nash called to another house on the Tuam–Galway road at about 6 p.m. and again asked for a bottle of water. On this occasion he had not knocked at the front door but was found by the occupant standing in the open back door. The sound of voices from a back room filled the kitchen, and Nash handed the startled woman a plastic bottle and asked if she would fill it for him. In a pronounced English accent he told her that he was 'tired from cycling.'

By 6:45 p.m. Nash had reached the village of Claregalway, only a few miles outside Galway. He walked into Moran's shop and asked the proprietor, Bernie Moran, if she had any 'meat sandwiches' for sale. When she told him that she hadn't he muttered something under his breath and left the shop. She saw him cycle off in the direction of Galway.

Shortly after 7 p.m. Garda Aoife Moran received a phone call at Tuam Garda Station. The caller told her that he was driving from Claregalway towards the city and had just passed a man on a bicycle who he believed to be Mark Nash. The caller was using a mobile phone—a rare enough facility in 1997—and so had Nash in his line of vision, unlike the majority of the other calls that had been received at the various Garda stations during that afternoon, which were dependent on the caller being close to or having access to a phone. Garda Moran immediately despatched a patrol car, manned by Garda Curtin and Garda Sewell, to the scene. En route they stopped to pick up a further two gardaí, Ray Wimms and Eoin Griffin, who had been operating a checkpoint on the Galway road.

At Twomileditch, near Castlegar, some two miles from Galway, the crew of the Garda car saw a man pushing a bicycle. Sewell and Wimms approached the man and asked him for his name. He replied: 'I'm Nash. Stay away or I'll kill you.' He dropped the bicycle and pulled the hammer out of his pocket. He swung the hammer at the two gardaí, then turned and ran out onto the road, into the path of oncoming traffic, followed by the two gardaí. He threw himself in front of a van, then tried to pull the door open, but the quick-witted driver, on seeing him with the hammer and conscious of her two young children sitting beside her, attempted to accelerate away. Nash then smashed the windscreen with the hammer.

With the gardaí standing at the opposite side of the van, Nash turned and ran into the front garden of a nearby house. The owner of the house, Eileen O'Flynn, was standing in her open front door, having been alerted by all the noise coming from outside. When she saw the man with the hammer running into her front garden she turned to run into the house. Nash tried to push in after her and managed to get into the porch. Eileen's son Bert, who was inside the house, heard her cry of alarm and, on running out, saw her struggling at the door with a man who was carrying a hammer. Bert, fearing for his mother's life, heroically tackled Nash, knocking him to the ground and holding him down. He was quickly joined by the gardaí, and together they subdued Nash, who was roaring, screaming, biting and striking out at them. Garda Curtin told Nash, as they struggled on the ground, that he was arresting him for the assault on Sarah Jane Doyle. He was placed in the patrol car, which then headed for Mill Street Garda Station in Galway, with Nash continuing to struggle and to fight his captors throughout the journey.

————

Within minutes of the arrest, word had leaked out to the media, and the news was broadcast over local radio stations. The progress of the manhunt had occupied all the news and current affairs programmes throughout the day. There had been considerable speculation and concern over Nash's ability to avoid arrest, given both his distinctive appearance and his complete lack of knowledge of the area. He was known to have fled the scene on foot, and it was believed that he had no means of transport available to him. The Gardaí came in for a lot of criticism while Nash remained at large. By the time of his arrest he had travelled approximately seventy miles, either on foot or on the stolen bicycle.

However, I believe that this account of his movements clearly shows that Nash was not engaged in a panicked flight from the scene. From the time he ran from the Doyles' house I suggest he had calculated his every move. For instance, the hammer found in his possession had been stolen from a box on a tractor parked a short distance from the scene; this would show that even at that early stage he intended to resist being arrested. During that long day he had changed his clothes, changed his direction of travel by almost doubling back on his route, and stolen a bicycle. He was unfortunate in that one of the first people he met as he cycled through Castlerea happened to be familiar with both the bike and its owner.

Heading for Galway had been a carefully worked-out strategy. Had he succeeded in reaching the city he would have blended in with the students and tourists who flocked to the city. Equally—and of this there can be little doubt—had he met the 'right' person at any of the houses he called to on his journey he would have forced that person to allow him to hide out there.

Chapter 21 ~

ADMISSIONS MADE BY MARK NASH

Though Mark Nash had violently resisted arrest and had continued his struggle when being driven to the Garda station, his whole demeanour underwent a change once he was detained at the station, shortly after 8 p.m. He asked to be allowed to speak in private to the garda in charge of the station, Sergeant Kevin Duffy. Kevin readily agreed but insisted on administering the legal caution to him in order to preserve the integrity of any admissions or comments made to him by Nash.

In a subdued and relatively calm voice, Nash said: 'Things went crazy. I just killed two people.' He told Kevin that he knew that Sarah Jane was going to be all right, and that he had written two letters to her during that day, one of which he had addressed to her parents' address and the second to herself at Beaumont Hospital. (He must have picked up that bit of information somewhere along his escape route.) He said he had attempted to apologise to Sarah Jane and to explain what had driven him to commit the various assaults. He finished his conversation with Kevin by apologising to him for murdering both Catherine and Carl.

During a period of twenty-five minutes, between 8:25 and 8:50 p.m. that evening, Nash was interviewed by two local detectives, Tony Reidy and John C. O'Donnell. In a written statement he told the detectives that he had killed Carl by stabbing him in the chest. He went on to describe how he had taken the tool for the range with him and had followed Sarah Jane and Catherine upstairs. He casually described beating them both repeatedly with the tool. In addition, he said he had stabbed Catherine with a knife he had found downstairs and had also tried to strangle her.

The two detectives could only listen in amazement to the casual manner in which Nash talked about the murders of Catherine and Carl Doyle. It was almost as if he was bragging about his exploits.

But he did not finish there. He went on to tell them that on a previous occasion he had stabbed two women 'while they slept in their house in the Stonybatter area of Dublin.' He said that about three months previously he had been walking from the city centre towards his home and had broken into a house 'by the back window. I stabbed two women in their sleep. My mind was disturbed at the time. You have to understand that.'

It would be established from further information that Nash provided over the coming hours that this was a direct admission to the Grangegorman murders. Stonybatter lies adjacent to Lower Grangegorman and to the home of Sylvia Sheils and Mary Callinan. This admission was made at a time when Dean Lyons had already spent three weeks in custody for the murder of Mary Callinan.

Reidy and O'Donnell, as they prepared for their interview with Nash in the short time that was available to them, had probably expected their questioning to be met with either a wall of silence or some half-hearted attempt at justification. They could never have imagined that a man who only a few hours previously had stabbed two people to death and failed in an attempt to kill a third would almost casually sit with them and not only admit to those crimes but would almost throw in, by way of explanation, two other murders he had committed.

Tony and John, while certainly well informed about the Grangegorman murders, would not have been in a position to carry out a formal interview concerning them. They decided, at that early stage in Nash's detention and interview, not to seek elaboration or further admissions from him. In later years it would become both a source of pride and the subject of some canteen wit that while most gardaí throughout their service will never take an admission of murder, here were Tony and John, in the space of twenty-five minutes, obtaining admissions to four.

Whatever prompted Mark Nash, at such an early stage in his detention, to make admissions to two serious crimes that he was neither being questioned about nor even suspected of any involvement in has long been a source of much speculation. I am one of that school of thought that will never for a moment accept that he was driven to do so by any sense of remorse or guilt. I firmly believe that, to his twisted way of thinking, he was laying down a marker to the gardaí, as if saying to them: 'Do you know who I am? Do you know what I did, and what I'm capable of?' It is a common feature of the serial killer that he exhibits almost a sense of pride and achievement regarding his crimes. In the making of his admissions Nash was telling the gardaí and, by inference, the rest of the world that he was worthy of inclusion in that unique field.

Nash made a further two lengthy statements over the following hours, calmly describing, in graphic detail, his role in the murders of Catherine and Carl Doyle. During the making of one statement of admission he had been accompanied throughout by his solicitor.

Chief Superintendent Joe Kilgallon ordered that Nash be interviewed exclusively in relation to the Doyle murders, and that when those interviews were completed he should then be interviewed about the Grangegorman murders. This would be considered by most detectives to be a sensible investigative measure but in time would come in for severe criticism from those senior officers to whom it would always be Dean Lyons who murdered the women in Grangegorman. Joe Kilgallon was in fact accused by them of interfering with and jeopardising their investigation; their attitude was akin to telling him to investigate his own crimes and not be interfering in their separate investigations. This criticism was voiced at the highest levels. Joe should, instead, have been praised for the sensible and professional manner in which he approached the investigation of four very serious crimes, the potential fall-out from some of which could only be imagined at that stage.

———

On the morning of Sunday 17 August 1997, in a move that almost mirrors the events of the Sunday morning of 27 July, arrangements were made to bring Mark Nash before a special sitting of Galway

District Court to be charged with the murders of Catherine and Carl Doyle. The sitting was arranged for 3:30 p.m.

At 1:30 p.m. Chief Superintendent Kilgallon sent two of the most experienced detectives in the country, Detective-Sergeant Pat Lynagh and Detective-Garda Gerry Dillon, to the interview room to begin a formal interview with Nash about his admission to the Grangegorman murders. To comply with the regulations covering such a development, Nash was told that he was no longer being detained for questioning in connection with the deaths of Catherine and Carl Doyle and the assault on Sarah Jane Doyle but was now being detained for interview in relation to the murders of Sylvia Sheils and Mary Callinan. Nash acknowledged that he understood that and then dictated a lengthy statement, which the gardaí took down in writing. At the conclusion of the interview it was read over to him, and he readily agreed that the contents were correct and signed it.

He began the statement by saying that he wished to voluntarily provide information about a double murder he had committed some five months earlier in Dublin. He said that earlier that night he attended a fund-raising event at the GPO in Dublin, attended by a number of telesales company personnel, including four from his own company. The event concluded some time around 10:20 p.m., and he then went to a night-club in nearby Ormond Quay, where he drank two pints of beer. He left the club at about 11:30 p.m. and walked along Ormond Quay and then on to Ellis Quay, intending to return to his flat at 83 Prussia Street.

Somewhere on his journey home he took a wrong turning and found himself walking up through Grangegorman. As he passed the terrace of houses at Orchard View he completely lost control over himself and broke into the two-storey house at the end of the terrace. He was unable to state what was going through his mind or what his intentions were. Pulling a pair of stockings over his hands, he broke the bottom right-hand pane of glass in a four-paned window. He pulled himself in through this opening into a kitchen. As he did so he noticed a large swing-top litter bin just inside this window.

He armed himself with a red-handled bread knife with a serrated blade that he found in the kitchen and then walked out into the hallway. Two rooms led off this hallway, one of which appeared to be unoccupied while in the second room he noticed a black-coloured television set, the make of which might have been Osaki. This room was a sitting-room. He then went up the stairs, he said, and on turning at the top of it he walked along the landing.

He pushed open a bedroom door and on going into the room saw a large woman asleep in a single bed. The woman, he said, seemed to be about six feet tall, of heavy build and in her mid-fifties. She was lying flat on her back. He pulled down the duvet and stabbed her through the nightdress into the chest area. He said he also cut her throat. He described his attack on this woman as being 'frenzied' and added that it had lasted for some thirty seconds.

He then went into an adjoining bedroom, turning on the light as he entered. He saw a woman getting out of the double bed in this room. She walked as far as the foot of the bed, and he stabbed her while she was standing up. As with the other woman, he said he cut this victim's throat also. He described this woman as being in her late fifties and of slim build. She had grey hair. As she was getting out of the bed he noticed that she was wearing a nightdress.

After killing this second woman he walked out of her room and then opened a third bedroom door. In this room he found another woman sleeping in a single bed. He described this woman as wearing earphones, similar to those used to listen to personal cassette recorders. These earphones were black in colour. He stood over this woman for a few seconds as she lay sleeping. He still carried in his hand the knife he had used to murder the other two women.

Nash then told his interviewers, in a calm voice, that he had not assaulted this third woman. He had by now 'regained control of myself' and had run out of the room and down the stairs. He left the house through the front door, saying that, to the best of his memory, the key had been on the inside of the lock. As he ran downstairs he discarded at the foot of the stairs both the stockings he had been wearing on his hands and the knife. As he left the house he observed a man standing across the road near a gatepost.

After leaving the house he went back to his flat in Prussia Street, had a long shower, and then went to bed. His partner was still at work when he arrived home. He claimed to have lain awake in bed for the rest of the night, crying at the memory of the enormity of what he had done. He told the two detectives that he estimated that he had killed the two women some time between 12:30 and 1:30 a.m.

When he was asked what he had been wearing on the night of the murder Nash said that he had on black trousers, a white shirt, a black velvet jacket and brogue-type shoes. He had subsequently discarded all the clothing, with the exception of the velvet jacket, in a rubbish bin. The jacket, he said, was now hanging in the wardrobe in his new flat at 133 Clonliffe Road. This jacket would ultimately play a pivotal role in this whole investigation. Amazingly, that Sunday afternoon as Nash was being interviewed in Galway he told the gardaí that they had his permission to go into the flat and to take possession of the jacket. Not content with giving them permission orally to take it, he went on to give his consent in writing.

After the taking of this statement had finished, Nash was taken to the special sitting of Galway District Court, where at 3:30 p.m he appeared before District Justice Al O'Dea, charged with the murders of Catherine and Carl Doyle. He was remanded in custody to the same court on 19 August, and again the question of bail was not considered.

As he was being escorted back to the Garda station to await the issuing of the documents from the court that would authorise his detention in Mountjoy Prison, Gerry Dillon asked Nash if what he had been telling them about his involvement in the two murders at Grangegorman was the truth. Nash, to Gerry's amazement, said: 'Do you think I would admit to four murders if I only did two? Everything I said is the truth.'

When they arrived back at the station Nash asked the garda in charge if he could have a brief conversation with both Pat Lynagh and Gerry Dillon. This visit was permitted, on condition that there could be no discussion about the murders of Catherine and Carl Doyle, given that he was now before the court charged with their murders.

Detective-Superintendent John Gallagher of the NBCI would sit in for a portion of this interview. The previous day he been seconded with a team of detectives to assist in the investigation into the murders of the Doyles. The same officer had also played a central role in the investigation into the murders of Sylvia Sheils and Mary Callinan.

At the outset of this interview Nash asked the gardaí to supply him with a pen and paper. He then drew three separate sketches for them. These were:

(1) a map containing details he recalled of the interior of the house at 1 Orchard View;

(2)   a map showing the outside of the house;

(3)   a sketch of the type of shoe he was wearing on the night of the murders.

Later that evening Nash was taken under heavy escort to Mountjoy Prison in Dublin. Among the gardaí in the escort was Sergeant Kevin Duffy, to whom Nash had made the original admission when detained at Mill Street Station. Also in the escort party was Detective-Garda Tony Reidy, to whom within a period of twenty-five minutes Nash had admitted not two but four murders.

In a calm, conversational voice Nash asked them if they would like him to point out to them the house in Grangegorman where he had killed the two women. They responded that if he wished to do so he could, that as they were not based in Dublin they did not know either the area itself or the exact location of the murder scene. Nash told them not to worry, that he would direct them to the scene.

Amazingly, as the escort entered the outskirts of the city Nash began giving directions to the driver. He directed them to Lower Grangegorman, and outside number 1 Orchard View he told them to stop the car. Pointing at the house, he said to them: 'That's where I killed the two women.' Then, pointing at another house nearby, he said that when leaving the scene he had seen a man standing in the gateway who appeared to be watching him. He did not offer any further information, and the escort carried on to the gates of Mountjoy Prison, where Nash was handed into the custody of the prison governor.

––––

It was a strangely subdued team of gardaí who made the return journey to Galway that evening. On the one hand, they had just solved a double murder in their area, which was a cause for celebration in its own right; however, they had also heard a man admitting to a further two murders, the details of which were unknown both to themselves and to the rest of their colleagues in Galway. They could not have known, for instance, that entry to the house had been gained by breaking the bottom right-hand pane of a group of four panes in the window; that there was a large litter bin inside the window; that the first victim was the one who was found in her bed and the second had been standing at the foot of her bed; and that the murderer had left the house through the front door.

All this aside, however, the most chilling aspect of his admissions, and the one that would finally convince those of us who had always believed that Dean Lyons had not killed the two women that we had the right man in Mark Nash, was the statement that Ann Mernagh had been wearing black earphones as he stood over her sleeping form. I would wager that not alone was this fact unknown to anyone outside the investigation but that it was equally unknown to 90 per cent of the team involved in the Grangegorman investigation. This was one fact that we had always kept very close to our chests. I honestly think that the significance of that nugget of information was even lost on Pat and Gerry as they wrote down Nash's admissions.

Chapter 22 ∽

| LETTERS WRITTEN BY NASH

Before discussing the effect that this second set of admissions had—or, in some instances, didn't have—on the team investigating the Grangegorman murders I want to dwell for a moment on a number of letters that Mark Nash wrote to Sarah Jane Doyle after the murders of her sister and brother-in-law.

During his flight from the scene at Caran, Co. Roscommon, Nash had called in to Feeney's shop in Williamstown, where he bought a pen, paper and envelopes. Witnesses also told us about a strange man they had seen on the banks of the river outside Dunmore, writing a letter. Nash even told Sergeant Kevin Duffy that he had written two letters during the day to Sarah Jane, one addressed to her parents' house and the second to Beaumont Hospital, in which he had apologised to her for his actions.

The letter to Beaumont Hospital was in an envelope addressed *Miss Sarah Jane Doyle, (Patient, Head Injuries), Beaumont Hospital, Dublin.* Sarah Jane gave us permission to read the letter. In neat, precise handwriting Nash addressed the woman whom a few hours previously he had tried to kill. He told her he had written a second letter, which he had sent to her home, one that she 'must read.' He also mentioned the fact that he had enclosed £150 (about €180) with the letter. He ended this first, short letter: 'Goodbye, Mark.'

In the letter addressed to her house he described himself as not being able to explain his actions in Catherine and Carl's home. In his own words, he described himself as 'going from being a sane person to a madman,' and added that this was the second time this sort of thing had happened to him; he described that incident as 'leading to the same thing before.' He referred to himself as 'insane and not deserving to live' and said that by the time Sarah Jane came to read this letter he would be dead, that he intended killing himself, either by jumping under a train or by stealing a shotgun and shooting himself. Either way, he said, 'the world doesn't need people like me.'

He finished the letter by telling her how much he still loved her. He went on to tell her that he was praying to Holy God for her, hoping that she would soon heal, describing her as a 'strong little lady'.

Even now, some fifteen years after this letter was written, I have to ask myself what was going through Mark Nash's confused mind as he sat by the banks of the river on that warm summer afternoon and wrote this letter to the woman who, not twelve hours earlier, he had tried to beat to death and whose sister he had murdered in front of her. The tone and content of this letter would certainly match both his behaviour and his expectations when, as he stood in the doorway of the Doyles' house, he called out to her in a calm voice, asking her to come back, that everything would be all right.

While detained at Galway Garda Station, Nash had asked to be given pen and paper, as he wished to write a further letter to Sarah Jane. He began this lengthy letter by telling her that he had 'never made it to the tracks to carry out my intention'—a reference to his earlier threat to take his own life. He told her also that he had tried to commit suicide by jumping in front of a van while being arrested.

Nash described himself to her as having 'violent tendencies' followed by 'episodes' in which he would lose all self-control and turn into a 'madman'. He talked about a second personality he possessed, one that he 'normally buried beneath the surface and I don't know what the trigger is.' He said that this personality change had happened to him once before, in a place 'near Prussia Street.'

He went on to call her his 'princess' and said he would keep writing to her unless she preferred he should stop. It was his one great hope, he wrote, that one day she might bring herself to forgive him for what he had done. In the meantime he would continue to pray that her health would improve.

In a direct reference to his behaviour on the night he murdered Catherine and Carl Doyle he told Sarah Jane that he had lost all self-control, that 'all rational thought' had stopped and because of this he had turned into a 'monster'. Describing all these unnatural feelings and emotions as building up inside him, he wrote that he had 'exploded' in a 'blind fury'. He could recall, he said, every detail of the assaults he had carried out on her, and on Catherine and Carl. In his mind he could clearly see 'someone else doing those things, not me.' He believed he had a major personality problem, which, he hoped, would now be addressed by a psychiatrist whom he would be made to attend while in the prison.

———

While detained in prison on remand for the murders in Co. Roscommon, Mark Nash continued to write lengthy letters to Sarah Jane. As the weeks and months passed the letters became filled with protestations of his undying love for her and of the loneliness of prison life and continually begging her to forgive him. Page after page was filled with various attempts at excusing his behaviour and claims that, given his mental state, he should not be held responsible for his actions. He also wrote a letter to his former colleagues, telling them how lonely he was feeling and asking them to stay in touch with him. He also asked them if they could keep him updated on Sarah Jane's progress.

Chapter 23 ~

THE REACTION OF THE GRANGEGORMAN INQUIRY TEAM

Sunday 27 August 1997 was the seventy-fifth anniversary of a special day in the history of the Garda Síochána. On that day in 1922 Dublin Castle, the last bastion of British colonial power in the 26 Counties, was handed over to the recently formed government of 'Southern Ireland', later the Irish Free State. There followed the official lowering of the Union Jack for the last time on Dublin Castle and its replacement with the Tricolour. As the British soldiers marched out of the castle grounds to board their tenders to bring them to their waiting ships at the North Wall a company of the newly formed police force, the Civic Guard—shortly afterwards renamed An Garda Síochána— led by their new Commissioner, Michael Staines, marched in to take over from them. To mark the anniversary Commissioner Pat Byrne led a large contingent of gardaí in through the Lower Castle Gate and on into the Upper Castle Yard behind the Garda Band.

I attended the ceremony as a member of the committee of the Garda Historical Society. When the ceremonial part of the day was completed it was followed by the launch in the Castle grounds of a book by our colleague Jim Herlihy on the history of the Royal Irish Constabulary, the forerunners of the Garda Síochána. Sergeant Matt Mulhall remained on duty in the incident room at the Bridewell while I, as he put it, was wined and dined in style. As we celebrated in Dublin, however, developments in Galway would put a damper on our spirits that would take years to lift.

At the launch of Jim's book I was approached by a very senior officer who was also a friend with whom I had worked over the years. He was one of those who had marched through the gates a short time earlier. He asked me if anyone had been in touch with me from Galway. I said that no-one had but that I was aware from news reports that they had arrested Mark Nash for the double murders and that he was shortly to be brought to court by them.

He seemed to be taken aback by my response and asked me a second time if anyone from the Galway investigation team had been in contact with me. When I again told him that there had been no contact from anyone he said that he was going to tell me something that he believed I should know and, furthermore, that I should have been told about. He told me that when Mark Nash was arrested for the murder of Catherine and Carl Doyle he had made a number of admissions to those crimes. He had also made a number of admissions to the Grangegorman murders. Following this amazing development it was now the intention of the Commissioner to appoint a senior officer to carry out an internal Garda review of the whole matter, and further that, given his known friendship with me, he himself would not be considered for the role.

I have often been asked by colleagues how I felt at the moment I was given that news. I would reply that while on the one hand it was something I always expected, it nevertheless took my breath away. My mind raced through a range of emotions, which included vindication for the stance Matt and I had taken, concern for my own position, concern for Dean Lyons, who was still in custody for the murder, and of course the fear brought about by those dreaded words that no garda ever wants to hear, "internal inquiry"!

I immediately left the Castle grounds and ran back to the Bridewell. When I went into the incident room I was greeted by Matt Mulhall, who asked me what was wrong with me, telling me I looked as if I had seen a ghost. I asked him if anyone had rung the incident room from Galway, thinking that a call might have been received while I was away. He told me there had been one call from a member of the NBCI who was working in Galway on their murders. This officer, who had also worked for a brief period with us on the murders of Sylvia Sheils and Mary Callinan, had asked Matt if he would forward a copy of the charge sheet that we had used in charging Dean Lyons with the murder of Mary Callinan by fax to him at the Galway station. He said they were unsure about the new wording that was to be used in a murder charge and was aware that we had used the new formula.

Up to July that year a charge of murder simply read: 'That you, the said accused, did on .... at .... murder one .... contrary to common law.' Given the gravity of the offence alleged, it was, to say the least, a very understated form of words. Recent procedural changes would provide for a whole new formula. Given that the charge against Dean Lyons had been one of the first under the new system, the fact that we were requested to provide the information would not have come as any surprise.

Matt then looked me in the face and said: 'It's happened, hasn't it?' I knew that what he was referring to was what we had always thought might happen one day: someone else coming forward and admitting to the murders of Sylvia and Mary. I nodded and then described in detail what I had been told a short time earlier. However, I emphasised that I had been sworn to secrecy on the matter until such time as I was officially informed of the development. As a consequence, we were also unable to share this momentous news with the other members of our team.

Our immediate response was to put an end to the charade that building a case against Dean Lyons was more and more becoming as each day passed and to get down to proving the case against the real culprit. The rest of that Sunday is a blur, spent by us wondering how this news, when it got out, as it surely would, would affect ourselves personally, our families and our careers. Up to this point we had not been listened to when we voiced our concerns, and now we wondered if the coming weeks and months would be any different. We had always been aware when we voiced our opposition to Dean Lyons being charged that we were taking on some of the most powerful and influential officers in the job. We had no doubt, now that we were about to be the subject of an internal inquiry, that battle lines would be drawn. If the news about Mark Nash's admissions proved to be correct it would follow that our investigation was flawed, and therefore someone must be found responsible for having sent an innocent man to prison.

Late the following Monday afternoon Assistant Commissioner Jim McHugh arrived unannounced in the incident room. He was well known to both myself and Matt, having been a very active member of the Detective Branch over the years in the city. He asked us if we were aware of the purpose of his visit. I told him we had heard certain rumours but had not received any official notice of his visit. Unbelievable as it may now seem, we had not been contacted by any of the senior officers on our investigation and informed of this development up to the arrival of the assistant commissioner in our office. Our phone calls to them had all gone unreturned.

This failure by the senior officers on our team to inform either Matt or myself of the admissions to the crime that were made by Mark Nash has never been explained to me. At this point I am aware that at least one of our senior officers had been told about them late on the Sunday evening by a colleague, of equal standing, in a meeting they had at Lucan Garda Station. Equally it was well known that I was directly involved in attempting to put together a file for the law officers outlining the evidence we had established against Dean Lyons. The idea that someone somewhere had decided that I should not be told, or did not need to know, about a development that would have had such an effect on the case beggars belief.

The assistant commissioner formally put us on notice about his appointment by the Commissioner to investigate all the circumstances that had led up to the charging of Dean Lyons, together with the circumstances surrounding the admissions made by Mark Nash. He would evaluate the evidence established in both instances. He asked for an assurance from us that the members of his investigation team would receive our fullest co-operation in relation to any issues involved or any requirements they might make of us. I told him that he could expect our complete co-operation with anything they asked of us. I also said that both Matt and myself had consistently voiced our concerns about the charging of Dean Lyons, believing, as we did, that he was innocent. Matt added that we had brought these concerns to the attention of the senior officers on our investigation team a number of hours before Dean Lyons was charged with the murder.

We were informed by Jim McHugh that he would be assisted in his review by Chief Superintendent Martin Donnellan and Superintendent Derek Byrne. Again these were two officers who were well known and respected throughout the city as thorough, competent and professional investigators. In time both men would be promoted to the rank of assistant commissioner.

Knowing the calibre of the officers who were to be involved in the McHugh Inquiry, as it came to be called, made myself and Matt feel a lot more confident that nothing would be left undone by them in their work to establish the truth behind this whole sorry saga. Equally, and just as importantly, it meant that justice would be done for Dean Lyons.

———

It was some hours after the visit from Jim McHugh before any of the senior officers of the investigation arrived at the Bridewell. By that time we had informed as many of the inquiry team as we could contact of the development. We considered it important that they should know exactly what was going on. In addition, our phone had not stopped ringing with inquiries coming in from friends and colleagues to assure us of their support as we faced into this uncertain future.

It never ceases to amaze me just how difficult it can be to keep a secret in a police force. We must have one of the most finely tuned antennas for gossip imaginable. Of course it goes without saying that if the gardaí knew then it was only a matter of time before the media knew also. We received a number of phone calls from media people during that same afternoon. None of them mentioned Mark Nash by name, or even the development in Galway, but it was obvious from their line of questioning that they knew that something was going on. At that early stage they were engaged in nothing more than a fishing expedition. Someone somewhere outside the Garda family was beginning to smell blood in the water. Given the rules that govern cases that are before the courts, the media had to be cognisant at all times that Dean Lyons was in custody awaiting trial for the murder of Mary Callinan. They therefore had to be very circumspect in what they wrote or broadcast.

Chief Superintendent Kelly was one of the officers who would call to see us at the Bridewell. He asked us if we were aware of the admissions made by Mark Nash, and I told him that we had been visited earlier by Assistant Commissioner McHugh, who had asked us for our co-operation in his inquiry into the whole matter. Matt told him that it would have been far better all round if we had been given the news by our own officers.

I then asked the question uppermost in all our minds, and the one that each member of the team that we had contacted had wanted an answer to. Should we now abandon the lines of inquiry we were chasing in an attempt to firm up our case against Dean Lyons?—a task, I added, that was becoming daily more difficult to carry out. I suggested that we should now bring this new development to the attention of the law officers and ask them to withdraw the charge against Dean Lyons, at least until such time as this whole matter had been resolved. By taking this course we could also concentrate all our resources on building the case against Nash.

Matt further suggested appointing one of the gardaí centrally involved in the Galway murder as our liaison with the team down there, and that between the two teams the case against Nash for the murders of Catherine and Carl Doyle and, separately, for the murders of Sylvia Sheils and Mary Callinan could be prepared.

All our suggestions were summarily dismissed. Chief Superintendent Kelly directed that we continue with the job in hand, which was the preparation of a file for the law officers recommending that the charge against Dean Lyons for the murder of Mary Callinan should be proceeded with, and furthermore that a charge in relation to the murder of Sylvia Sheils should also be laid against him. He said that, as far as he was concerned, Dean Lyons had made clear and unambiguous admissions to the Grangegorman murders, some of which he had made while the interview was being electronically recorded. These admissions had been unsolicited, made freely and voluntarily, with no pressure and no promises made to him. He added that not alone had Dean Lyons admitted his crimes to the Gardaí but he had also made admissions to his mother and his father and to a number of other independent persons.

He said that through his own admissions Dean Lyons had placed himself 'fairly and squarely' both at the scene and in the killing of the two victims. We, as investigators, 'could not, should not and were not entitled to' ignore or ridicule the admissions, 'just because a few of us had issues with them.' It was never intended that our brief as police should be extended to sitting in judgement on evidence. The courts were the sole arbiters, and we must present our evidence fairly and impartially to them for their decision only, and not ours.

I remarked that we now had a second person making unsolicited admissions to the same murders, admissions that were far more believable than those made by Dean Lyons. Chief Superintendent Kelly responded by saying, once again, that we were not the arbiters: the decision would rest with the courts alone. The gardaí in Galway would be presenting their case to the law officers, and it was incumbent on us to do likewise. Matt responded by saying that were we to present our case against Dean Lyons and at the same time ignore what had taken place in Galway it would be akin to burying our heads in the sand.

We had decided between ourselves, before this meeting took place, that if we were ordered to complete the report into Dean's alleged involvement in the Grangegorman murders we would agree to do so only if we were permitted to incorporate all the details, including all admissions, established in the Catherine and Carl Doyle murder inquiry. Once again we were all too aware of the position we were placing ourselves in but felt it was the only way that the issue could be resolved. We also placed our faith in the McHugh Inquiry supporting our concerns about the reliability of Dean Lyons's admissions. Chief Superintendent Kelly told us he would accept our approach to completing the report and assured us that we would have all the relevant evidence available to us within the coming days.

I assured him that when the copies of the statements made by Nash were received by us I would introduce them into the report and impartially dissect and examine them, presenting this to the law officers in a 'what can and what cannot be proved' format, as I was already in the process of doing with Dean's admissions. Again he agreed with my suggested approach but insisted that I not let my opinion concerning the reliability of Dean's admissions colour my presentation of the facts. At the end of the day, he said, we now have two people admitting to the one crime, one, Dean Lyons, who had nothing to gain from admitting two murders and the second, Mark Nash, who had killed two other people and could be using a false admission to two other murders to prepare a defence of insanity. We should not lose sight of this possibility in our report. We accepted this compromise, believing, as we did, that we could better emphasise our concerns with Dean if we remained in control of compiling the report to the law officers.

As I have said already, the stance that Matt and I were taking could have had serious repercussions for our careers. To walk away from a continuing investigation would have been an unprecedented step that would for ever cast a doubt over our commitment to seeing an investigation through to its proper conclusion. The personal sacrifice, commitment and dedication required of a garda centrally involved in a protracted major investigation can never be properly quantified. It effectually rules your work, family and social life and dictates holidays and other external commitments. When it comes to the preparation of the final report you have both the pressure of the 42-day legal moratorium and the almost daily monitoring of your progress by your SIO. Lack of progress is constantly questioned.

Chapter 24 ∿

ESTABLISHED MOVEMENTS OF MARK NASH ON THE NIGHT OF 6 MARCH

The following day we received copies of the various admissions made by Mark Nash. Given the knock-on effect they were bound to have on Dean Lyons's case, they were carefully scrutinised by myself and Matt Mulhall. We set up a sub-team to concentrate exclusively on the actions we identified as arising from his statements.

At the outset I have to say that from reading his statements I was left in no doubt that in Nash we now had our real murderer. This point of view was equally shared by Matt. While the whole issue surrounding the arrest and charging of Dean Lyons remained to be resolved, we could at least rest assured that the man who had so brutally taken the lives of Sylvia Sheils and Mary Callinan was no longer free to roam the streets and re-offend.

It could be argued—and, I can assure you, was vigorously argued—that in Mark Nash and Dean Lyons we had two people whose only evidential link to the scene was their admissions, and that as a consequence we should not be favouring one over the other. The reality, however, was that when the contents of the two sets of admissions were compared, and when the backgrounds and known criminal behaviour of both were analysed, there could be no doubting the fact that Mark Nash was our man.

On the one hand we had Dean Lyons, who had even seemed unsure about how many women he had supposedly killed on the night.

Contrast him with Mark Nash, who, having killed two people, went on to tell gardaí he had broken the bottom right-hand pane in a four-pane window, that having climbed through the window he observed a large pedal bin, that there had been a black-coloured television in the sitting-room. His description of both victims was unerringly accurate, and he admitted to having murdered Sylvia first while she was still in bed and had then murdered Mary, who was standing up at the foot of her bed.

All these facts were indisputable; but the most telling admission Nash had made was when he talked about Ann Mernagh wearing earphones—and not just any earphones but black earphones—as she slept, even as he stood over her with her friends' blood on his hands. Ann's problems with sleep would certainly not have been common knowledge, much less the fact that she needed the sound of music to help her to sleep.

It is disconcerting, even to this day, to consider how close she came that night to being murdered and brutalised like Sylvia and Mary. We will probably never know what it was that stopped Nash in his killing spree. We know that in Caran the escape of Sarah Jane Doyle was probably what spared the children as they lay in their beds, but in Grangegorman there had been no such reason. Blood on the base of Ann's bed and on the door of her bedroom came from both Sylvia and Mary, and we can therefore say without contradiction that he had already killed two innocent and defenceless women before going into Ann's bedroom.

Our team would establish that Nash had indeed, as he said, attended a charity quiz night at the GPO with three of his colleagues. He had said he left the GPO at about 10:20 p.m. and walked to a club at Ormond Quay. We found that in fact he left at about 11:15 and went with his three colleagues to the nearby Eddie Rocket's fast-food restaurant, where his then partner, Lily Quinn (not her real name), was working. One of his colleagues told us that Nash was very drunk and that she was embarrassed by his behaviour at the quiz. When he turned up for work at eight o'clock the following morning she was surprised, as she thought he would have been too sick.

They left Eddie Rocket's at about midnight. Lily walked with them to the all-night Spar shop in Westmorland Street. Lily bought cigarettes and Nash walked her back to her work; the others all went their separate ways home. Nash stayed talking to Lily for a few minutes, then she went back to work and Nash walked away. This was at about 1 a.m.

He walked to the Temple of Sound Club at Ormond Quay, where he introduced himself to the doorman as a writer for a national music magazine. He was introduced to the manager and spoke about doing an article on the club. The manager, not being convinced that he was a genuine reporter, left after a few minutes. Nash drank two pints of beer and then left. It was now about 1:30 a.m.

All the people with whom Nash interacted through the course of the night were interviewed and asked about his demeanour and behaviour. All told us they saw no hint or suggestion of anger or violence in him. They agreed that he had had a lot of drink taken but insisted that he certainly gave no indication of the unimaginable savagery that he would visit on two defenceless women only a short time after leaving them.

It would have been some time around 2 a.m. when Nash reached Orchard View. To our way of thinking this might mean that he had selected this target beforehand. Given that Ann Mernagh would make her grim discovery at 6 a.m., this afforded him a very narrow window of opportunity, firstly to find a suitable house to target, then to case it and finally to enter the house, spend some time downstairs and then ascend to where he murdered both victims. The amount of time he spent interfering with both bodies lessened even further the time at his disposal. We were able to show, without any possibility of doubt, that he did not take a taxi either to the scene or to anywhere else in the area.

When Lily Quinn arrived back to the flat she shared with Mark Nash at 83 Prussia Street at about 6:30 a.m. she found him fast asleep in their bed. Their child had spent the night being cared for in a neighbour's flat. Nash got up at about 7:15 and dressed himself and went to work. Lily told us that the only difference she could see in his behaviour after that night was a big increase in the number of showers he took.

Given his behaviour in the immediate aftermath of his crimes it would be quite justified to describe Mark Nash as exhibiting a psychopathic personality. He showed a complete lack of remorse or shame, a complete disregard for normal standards of behaviour, used both his victims for sexual experimentation and displayed a complete lack of behavioural control. Within no more than three or four hours from committing his acts of savagery he was back at his place of work, sitting among his colleagues and reminiscing on the fun they had had at the quiz night.

The American psychiatrist Donald Lunde describes in his book *Murder and Madness* (1976) the arousal and gratification derived by a 'sexual sadist' from the killing and mutilation of his victim. The forensic pathologist and psychiatrist Robert Brittain in his paper "The Sadistic Murderer" (1970) found that such people were totally unconcerned with the moral implications of their brutality but are in fact aroused by the suffering and helplessness of their victims. Both descriptions could be attributed to Mark Nash.

Chapter 25 ～

| THE McHUGH INQUIRY

The remit of the McHugh Inquiry was to re-examine all the available evidence that had been established following upon the admissions by both Dean Lyons and Mark Nash to the Grangegorman murders. Any inquiry of this nature, no matter what attempts were made to keep it in house, attracted huge media interest. No press statement was issued at that point by the Garda authorities in relation to the matter, given that one person was still before the courts in connection with it.

Some of the daily papers published vague references to an internal Garda investigation into the Grangegorman case. The investigative journalist Jim Cusack, who had long questioned Dean Lyons's guilt, was the first to print the story about 'a second person' making admissions in relation to the murders. He also questioned the continued detention of Dean Lyons. I know that certain senior gardaí were highly critical of the stance that Jim Cusack continued to take on Dean's behalf, and that they continually questioned his integrity as a journalist. Undaunted, he continued to publicise the case.

McHugh's team, working night and day, had a preliminary report prepared within three weeks. They analysed and cross-referenced all the admissions made by both Lyons and Nash and, where it was available, provided supporting evidence. Where admissions or assertions were found to be inconsistent with the known or established facts they were highlighted and challenged by the team. Assistant Commissioner

McHugh asked that the question of the continuance of the charge against Dean be deferred until his full report was completed.

As part of the review process that led to the completion of his report, McHugh interviewed all those, including the senior officers, involved in both investigations. It quickly became clear to him that there was a serious conflict between certain of the gardaí on the Grangegorman investigation, centred on the thorny question whether certain members had expressed reservations about the veracity and reliability of Dean Lyons's admissions even before charges had been laid against him. It also became obvious that this divergence broke evenly between the senior officers on the investigation and the middle and lower-ranking gardaí.

At the outset we received assurances from McHugh's team that it was not his intention to allow his inquiry to degenerate into a witch hunt against any one person or group of people. Their sole brief was to establish the circumstances under which the two men had made their admissions and, more importantly, to decide which of them had probably committed the two murders. Given the calibre and reputation of all those on McHugh's team, Matt and myself, together with all the members of the investigation who had been involved in the arresting and interviewing of Dean Lyons, had no hesitation in affording them our fullest co-operation.

It became obvious to me while being interviewed that senior officers in the investigation were denying that any doubts or concerns in relation to Dean's admissions had been expressed to them. My statement that I had met a senior officer at about 8:30 p.m. on the Saturday night and had voiced my reservations to him was met by him with a blanket denial. This same officer also told the inquiry that he had no such meeting with either Sergeant Matt Mulhall or Detective-Garda Dominic Cox.

This really took me by surprise. The whole tenor of my interview with Dean was one of disbelief in his admissions, and this attitude had been reflected in his responses. I found it very difficult to accept that here we were, weeks later, with those to whom I had expressed my concerns denying that they had ever been voiced. I would have thought that as each day passed and we continued to be unable to corroborate any of Dean's admissions, some of those same officers might at least have conceded that I had expressed an alternative opinion to their own. I will say, however, that my suspicion that our concerns had been ignored was aroused when, as early as 31 July, we learnt that Commissioner Pat Byrne had formally sent his compliments on the successful outcome of our investigation. He wrote that we deserved acknowledgement for the success we had achieved in a case 'of significant importance to the most vulnerable in our society.' It appeared that he had not been briefed about any reservations about Dean's guilt having been expressed.

The divide within the investigation team became more and more apparent the further McHugh delved into the case. However, it was eventually established that, notwithstanding the assertions by the senior officers that no such reservations had been made known to them, a large number of other people would stand over what we were saying. Chief among these was Detective-Sergeant Robbie McNulty, the other member of the team who interviewed Dean with Dominic Cox. Robbie insisted that there had been a meeting during the break in the interview at which Dominic had voiced his doubts and had suggested that more time should be allocated to attempting to corroborate what Dean was saying. The significance of this statement of support from Robbie was that he would also claim that, in his opinion, Dean was telling the truth when he made his admissions. Equally, Garda Joe O'Connor, to whom Dean had made the original admissions, also insisted that reservations about them had been expressed.

Assistant Commissioner McHugh considered this matter to be so serious as to warrant further attention. He called all the senior officers together to a meeting in his office one Saturday morning and spent a considerable time describing in detail the evidence he had by then established. He asked that they would discuss the position among themselves and to afford them the privacy to do so left the office himself.

There ensued a lengthy conversation, at the conclusion of which they asked McHugh to return to meet them. They told him that their position remained unchanged, that no reservations about Dean Lyons's admissions had been expressed to them. In effect, this left McHugh back where he started.

Deputy Commissioner Noel Conroy, following a briefing from Jim McHugh, wrote directly to one of the senior officers and asked him formally whether doubts or concerns had been voiced, either to him personally or, to the best of his knowledge, to any of the other officers. This officer responded, in writing: 'There was no conflict between any of the members present in the Conference Room at the Bridewell on 26 July 1997.' He added that the Gardaí were in possession of admissions and statements made by Dean Lyons 'which contained compelling evidence.' It had been felt that the office of the DPP should be consulted, and 'this was done on 27 July.' McHugh openly expressed his dissatisfaction with this response.

Other gardaí who supported us in our contention that we had expressed concerns included

- Sergeant Eddie Corry, the sergeant in charge of the jail section when Dean was detained;
- Garda Laurence Luby, a uniformed garda on duty in the jail section during that time;
- Inspector Michael Burke, a uniformed inspector attached to the Bridewell;
- Garda Adrian Murray, who stated that the reservations that had been expressed by Dominic Cox were 'the talk of the station' on the Sunday morning;
- Garda Joe O'Connor, who named both myself and Matt Mulhall as two gardaí who had serious doubts;
- Detective-Garda Dave Lynch, my partner during the interview with Dean, who said that he was aware of my concerns because we had actually discussed them;
- Detective-Garda Ann Markey, whom Dominic had met in the station after midnight on the Saturday night and to whom he had expressed his concerns.

There was one other witness, independent of the Garda Síochána, who was in a position to verify what we were claiming. Within two or three days Dominic Cox, in his capacity as the garda with responsibility for delivering exhibits connected with the investigation, met Dr Louise McKenna at the Forensic Science Laboratory. She clearly recalled that, in discussion with Dominic about the development in the case with the charging of Dean Lyons, Dominic had told her he had 'worries' about Dean, whom he believed to be a 'Walter Mitty' type. Coming from a witness of Dr McKenna's calibre, and given her total independence, this was considered to be compelling evidence.

By the end of March 1998 Jim McHugh had completed his probative inquiry. In his report, addressed to both the law officers and his own authorities, he stated that he 'conscientiously' believed that Dean Lyons had not murdered Sylvia Sheils and Mary Callinan, and he recommended that the charge against Dean Lyons of murdering Mary Callinan should be dropped immediately.

Dean was due to appear at Dublin District Court on remand on 29 April. It was now an open secret that there was going to be a sensational development in the case against him. The crowd that gathered in court that day dwarfed the one that had been present on his first appearance.

Once again Dean was brought up the stairs leading from the cells under the courtroom, on this occasion flanked by two prison officers. In the period between being charged with the murder and 29 April he had pleaded guilty at Dublin Circuit Court to two charges of 'syringe robbery' and had been sentenced to six years' imprisonment. This meant that he was now in the custody of the Prison Service.

Matt and myself had arrived in the courtroom early via this same staircase to ensure that we would be present for this moment. The court clerk called the case of 'the Director of Public Prosecutions versus Dean Lyons.' An expectant hush fell on the crowd as counsel for the state rose to his feet and announced to the court that, on the instructions of the DPP, he was asking that the charge of murder against the accused, Dean Lyons, be struck out. Dean was told by the judge that the case against him was now withdrawn by the state. It had taken only moments to end the nightmare that, for Dean Lyons, had begun some nine months earlier.

The announcement by the judge brought uproar in the courtroom. Dean sat back in the dock with a bemused expression on his face. He then turned to the members of his family who had gathered in the courtroom and gave them a gentle wave. Given that they had waited nine months for this moment, together with the notoriety and hurt that this case had caused them, the dignified manner in which they behaved was a lesson to all those gathered in the courtroom on that fateful day.

The dropping of the charge against Dean Lyons meant that no person was now held accountable for the Grangegorman murders. It also meant that we at the Bridewell were effectually back where we started, with an unsolved double murder on our hands. The difference, however, was that we now had a viable suspect in Mark Nash, a man who had made believable and provable admissions to the crimes. The McHugh inquiry team now turned their attention to firming up a case against Nash, and we were directed to double our efforts in providing all the assistance and intelligence they requested.

There was one stumbling-block to be overcome before any such move could be made. If Nash ever stood trial for the murders, his defence counsel would apply to have his admissions struck out, on the grounds that another person existed who had made similar admissions and had in fact been charged with one of the murders. Nash, it could be argued, would be entitled to the same treatment. To address this issue it was decided to approach Dean, through his legal team, and ask him if he would be prepared to co-operate with the investigation and to give evidence at any forthcoming trial against Nash. If he was put in the witness box Dean would have the opportunity to deny any involvement in the murders, and to explain how he had come to make his admissions.

Following his appearance in the District Court on 29 April, Dean was granted temporary release from his prison sentence on humanitarian grounds. To allow his life to return to some kind of normality, it had been decided that, on his release, he would first complete a heroin treatment programme and then go to live in England for a few years. It was hoped that in time the media's interest and his notoriety would die down sufficiently to allow him to live some sort of normal life again back with his family. His address in the Manchester area would be shared only by his family, his legal team and the Department of Social Welfare.

Dean had met some of the McHugh team in his solicitor's office in Dublin that July and had made a short statement denying any involvement in the murders and claiming that he had made his various admissions because of his heroin addiction.

Throughout the early part of 1998, Chief Superintendent Martin Donnellan and Superintendent Derek Byrne twice travelled to Manchester to meet Dean. He assured them that he was prepared to come back to Ireland and come into court to give evidence. Armed with this information, Jim McHugh met the Director of Public Prosecutions, Éamonn Barnes. He asked Mr Barnes to consider the question of charging Nash with the Grangegorman murders.

Although no doubt conscious of the minefield any decision to charge Nash could create for his office, on 1 September 1999 Mr Barnes gave the go-ahead. The only proviso he insisted upon was that no charge should be laid against Nash until the full Garda report was on his desk and the case was ready to go ahead. This was considered a reasonable direction, given all the twists and turns this case had already thrown up.

All prisoners charged with a serious offence triable by a judge and jury must be supplied with a full copy of all the evidence that will be given against them during their trial. This is referred to as the 'book of evidence' and is prepared by the law officers from all the evidence submitted to them in the Garda report.

The granting of permission to charge Nash unfortunately threw up a huge problem in the investigation itself. Recent legislative changes had empowered the Gardaí to arrest a person serving a prison sentence for a crime for the purpose of interviewing them about a separate crime. Up to this time a person serving a sentence was out of bounds to any investigator. Permission to interview a prisoner could now be granted by the District Court on the application of a Garda superintendent. When the McHugh team told the law officers that they wanted to invoke this power and take Nash out of the prison to formally interview him they were told that, as the process of charging him with the Grangegorman murders had now begun, they could not do so.

All this would change again when, on 28 October 1999, following the retirement of Éamonn Barnes, his successor as DPP, James Hamilton, actually withdrew the consent that had been given to charge Nash; the question of charging him would only be considered when further evidence was established. Though this move was viewed as a body blow by all of us who had been waiting to see Nash charged, at the same time it opened the door to allowing Nash to be interviewed. It also provided additional time for furthering the case against him.

On 10 August 2000 Donnellan and Byrne again travelled to England to meet Dean. His solicitor was with them. At this point Dean was in custody in Strangeways Prison outside Manchester. He had been living in a residential unit in Rochdale but he had been arrested and sentenced for shoplifting.

He made a further lengthy statement. At the outset he denied any involvement in the Grangegorman murders; he claimed that it had only been when he was in the Garda car being taken to the Bridewell that morning that he was told they wanted to talk to him about the murders. When they mentioned them he had known straight away what they were talking about, as he had heard lots of stories 'around the Gorman' about them.

He claimed that from the beginning he had denied any involvement in the murders. He said he had been told by a copper that his social welfare card had been found near where the two women had been murdered. He described himself as having continued to deny the murders. Eventually he had become so sick from heroin withdrawal that he had admitted to the murders, thinking that he would then be let go. He said he had earlier in the morning given a friend a loan of £80 (about €100) to buy him heroin. He had an appointment after lunch to get the drugs from his friend and would have been able to make the appointment if the Gardaí had let him go then.

He described himself as feeling very sick: he had pains and aches and cramps in his stomach. His only wish had been to get out of the station. The Gardaí had sent a doctor in to see him; the doctor had examined him and prescribed methadone, which he was not given until much later in the day. He said he had believed when he admitted to the murders that he would have been let out of the Bridewell. He had described himself as being 'all messed up.' When asked why he had later told his father he had killed Sylvia and Mary, he said that 'I felt after admitting the murders to the Guards, I couldn't tell my father that I didn't do them.'

Derek Byrne again visited Dean at Strangeways Prison a few weeks later. He was formally asked if he was prepared to make himself available as a witness for the prosecution in any case taken against Mark Nash. He readily agreed to do so.

This formal consent was seen as the final step in the process, and Derek immediately returned to Ireland and conveyed the news to the law officers. It was, we believed, only a question now of waiting for Mr Hamilton to consider this development and then consent to court proceedings against Nash. This was on 7 September 2000, and it appeared that this long-drawn-out and draining investigation was finally coming to an end. How wrong we were!

Dean Lyons was released from prison on 11 September 2000, four days after this visit. He returned immediately to his rented accommodation and met the friends he had made since moving to England. His movements after this have never been established, but the following day, 12 September, he was found dead in his room. It appeared that he may have gone back to using drugs, and that whatever he had taken had contributed to his death. There was no suggestion of foul play.

The same evening I received a phone call at home from Martin Donnellan. I felt he was deeply shocked as he told me the tragic news. He told me also that Dean's family were devastated. Dean had appeared to be making considerable progress in his rehabilitation and also to have put the trauma of this whole incident behind him. It would also prove to be a huge source of regret to them that Dean had not lived to see himself completely exonerated when, in an unprecedented step, the Commissioner published a formal apology to Dean and his family on 24 February 2005. The apology categorically stated that Dean Lyons had no involvement in the Grangegorman murders.

This would bring a closure to the eight years of hell the Lyons family had suffered since July 1997, when Dean was arrested for the murders of Sylvia Sheils and Mary Callinan, during which time they campaigned tirelessly to see their son and brother finally vindicated.

Aside altogether from the human cost of Dean's death, there was another outcome. It threw the whole question of charging Mark Nash into turmoil. We feared that without Dean a gaping hole had again opened in the case. Our fears would prove to be correct.

A hastily convened case conference was arranged for 30 November 2000. The DPP, Mr Hamilton, accompanied by some of his most senior officials, attended, as did Jim McHugh and Martin Donnellan. Mr Hamilton opened the meeting by stating that the evidence available to him would not support a prosecution being brought against Mark Nash. Both Jim and Martin argued vehemently against this decision; however, Mr Hamilton said that all the legal advice available to him suggested that were we to proceed with Nash's statements of admission as our only evidence, any case against him was doomed to fail.

Some ten years later I would sit in the same conference room with Derek Byrne, now an assistant commissioner. This time, however, we would be given permission to charge Mark Nash with the murders of Sylvia Sheils and Mary Callinan.

Chapter 26

THE BACKGROUND OF MARK NASH

M ark Francis Andrew Nash was born in Huddersfield, Yorkshire, on 16 April 1973—four days before the birth of Dean Lyons. His mother was living at that time with her parents. His father, an Italian national, had moved to Australia some months before the birth, not realising that he had fathered a son in his brief liaison with Nash's mother.

In 1986 Nash and his mother moved out of the family home and into rented accommodation in the town of Bradley on the outskirts of Huddersfield. At this time his grandparents, whom he revered and who appeared to have been a stabilising influence in his life, moved back to their native Co. Mayo.

His mother secured part-time work locally, and Nash attended the English Martyrs' and All Saints' High School. At this time it appears that he became troublesome and disruptive. He left school at sixteen and drifted aimlessly for a while. No work record exists for him. His relationship with his mother deteriorated considerably, and in 1991, at the age of eighteen, he was put out of the family home after threatening to kill her. He then began a relationship with a woman some fifteen years his senior, which lasted a couple of months. At about this time also he began to come to the notice of the police.

By 1995 Nash had moved to Leeds, where he began a love affair with Lily Quinn, and they had a baby daughter. On 4 October 1996 he was arrested for a number of drug-related offences. By now he had built up a number of criminal convictions and he feared that this latest charge would result in his receiving a lengthy prison sentence. On being admitted to bail he fled to Ireland with Lily and their baby daughter. They presented themselves to the Eastern Health Board as a homeless couple and were housed in a flat at 83 Prussia Street.

Within days of arriving in Dublin, Nash secured employment in the telesales business. He was considered by all who knew him to be a smooth-talking confidence trickster. Lily would obtain work as a waitress.

Nash has a number of criminal convictions, which include burglary and larceny. On 6 November 1989, when he was sixteen, he was convicted of assault occasioning actual bodily harm and sexual assault on a girl, for which he received a sentence of eighteen weeks in a young offenders' institution. His fifteen-year-old victim told the police she had been approached by Nash as she walked home from a local dance. She had rejected the advances he had made towards her, whereupon, without any provocation, he had punched her in the face. He then kicked her in the stomach, and as she lay on the ground screaming for help he had attempted to pull down her underwear. She was rescued by passers-by. It is important to recall that Nash was only sixteen years of age when he committed this offence.

Chapter 27 ∾

NASH'S RETRACTION OF HIS CONFESSION TO THE GRANGEGORMAN MURDERS

While on remand in Mountjoy Prison for the murders of Catherine and Carl Doyle, Mark Nash seems to have spent some time considering his position. It has never been established whether at this point he had discussed his situation with some of the 'jailhouse lawyers' that abound in all prisons.

On 1 September 1997 Nash's solicitor handed Chief Superintendent Martin Donnellan a handwritten letter in which he retracted his admissions to the Grangegorman murders. He opened this letter by apologising to the police for wasting their time. He said that at the time he made the admissions in Galway he had been in 'serious mental anguish and distress,' and further that the interviewing police had prompted him and had given him certain details about the murders. He also described himself as being 'shocked' to discover that the police were taking his statement of admission seriously.

He attempted to explain how he had known so much about the murders. He referred to the widespread reporting of the crimes, the fact that he lived near the scene, and also that he had overheard two gardaí who were on duty at a checkpoint openly discussing details of the crime. His knowledge of the interior of the house had been gained when he was investigating similar houses to rent in the area. He said that when all this was put alongside the promptings he had received from the interviewing policemen it was easy to see where his statement came from. He finished by adding that his statement should be ignored as the 'babblings of a very unsteady man,' who would have 'taken the rap for killing the Pope.'

Jim McHugh and Martin Donnellan visited Nash in prison on 8 September and interviewed him in the presence of his solicitor. He repeated the various allegations about the police prompting him in making his confession.

Following this allegation by Nash, Jim McHugh's inquiry team turned their attention to the gardaí in Galway who had dealt with Nash. All of them emphatically denied asking him any leading questions or supplying him with any information. Every one of them said that they had never in fact been privy to the details that Nash supplied in his statement and his drawings. They had no knowledge of the physical layout of the scene or of the details that the Grangegorman investigation had established.

On 25 November 1997 Martin Donnellan and Derek Byrne visited Nash at the prison. Garda Dominic Cox, in his capacity as exhibits officer, was with them. They produced a pair of Caterpillar brand boots to him that had been found in the search of his flat at Clonliffe Road. Nash acknowledged that they were his property. During his examination of the murder scene Eugene Gilligan had identified a mark made by a Caterpillar boot in the blood of Mary Callinan. We had already established that Nash had bought a pair of such boots in Heather's shoe shop on the Quays.

On the day following this visit a suicide note was found by prison officers in a search of Nash's cell. It is full of self-pity for his present status, and he speaks at length of his loneliness. He again denies committing the crimes; however, what was most interesting from our point of view was that he now put himself at the scene of the murders.

He wrote that 'by chance I did see what had taken place in Grangegorman.' He said he had been passing the house at 3 a.m. and had seen a man running out, and he went in to 'investigate.' He said that what he saw inside haunted him. He suggested that the reader of his note 'after seeing what I saw would also go mad as I did.' He expressed the hope that after his death it would 'alleviate the grief' of those he had hurt and asked that all his property—bizarrely, including his hash pipe—be given to his partner, Lily Quinn. He revealed in the letter that he intended to stockpile enough of his medicine between then and the following January to allow him to take his own life. In the event, Nash did not make any suicide attempt.

Nash made a complaint to the Garda Complaints Board about being coerced by Pat Lynagh and Gerry Dillon into making a statement of admission to the Grangegorman murders as they interviewed him in Galway. Following an investigation by that independent body they would report back to the Commissioner that 'no offence or breach of discipline on their part has been disclosed.' Nash also made a complaint to the same board about Jim McHugh, who he described as being 'discourteous' to him in their meeting of 6 September. This complaint was also found to be without substance. He also complained that McHugh did not believe what he was saying to him.

On 18 December 1999, as part of the attempt to build a case against Nash, he was arrested by Superintendent Derek Byrne at Arbour Hill Prison, where he was serving two life sentences for the murder of Catherine and Carl Doyle and a ten-year sentence for the serious assault on Sarah Jane Doyle. He had been convicted on 12 October after a lengthy trial, during which he had pleaded not guilty. This arrest was on foot of a warrant issued by the District Court under the new Criminal Justice Act (1999). He was taken to the Bridewell and questioned there for a number of hours. He totally denied any involvement in the Grangegorman murders, and suggested that he had been coerced into making his statements. At 5 p.m. he was returned to the prison.

Chapter 28

THE INQUEST INTO THE DEATHS OF SYLVIA SHEILS AND MARY CALLINAN

The law of Ireland requires that an inquest be held in all instances of sudden, unexplained or violent death. If the cause of death cannot be explained, for example from a post-mortem examination, an inquest may be held. All inquests are presided over by the coroner for the area, who must have at least five years' experience in both the medical and the legal fields. The coroner is appointed by the local authority. An inquest cannot take place until at least six weeks after the death.

Juries must be used in the following cases: (*a*) murder, manslaughter or infanticide, (*b*) deaths in prison, (*c*) death due to accidental poisoning or disease where it is required that such deaths have to be reported, (*d*) road traffic accidents, (*e*) where the circumstances that caused the death might continue to endanger others, and (*f*) in any other case where the coroner considers it necessary. Deaths in any of these circumstances can be registered only after an inquest has been held and a verdict given. In cases where a jury sits at an inquest it is they and not the coroner who deliver the verdict. Selection for service on a jury is by summons, and if summoned one must attend. A decision by a jury is reached when a majority are in agreement.

In a Supreme Court judgement delivered in 1999 the public-interest duties of a coroner were set out. They include: to determine the medical cause of death and, by so doing, draw attention to circumstances that could lead to further deaths; to allay rumour or suspicion; to advance medical science; and to preserve the legal interests of all parties, including families.

It is important to remember that an inquest has no role in finding any person guilty or innocent in connection with the death of another: its role is confined to establishing the identity of the deceased and how, when and where the death occurred.

Before an inquest all witnesses are required to submit a written statement containing all the evidence they are in a position to give. This is then set out in the form of a deposition, which will be signed by the witness in the witness box. All depositions, post-mortem reports and verdict records are retained by the coroner's office. An inquest is a public forum, and members of the public are entitled to attend, and the records are available on request.

The range of verdicts available to a jury when deciding on a particular death include accidental death, death by misadventure (i.e. misfortune), suicide, natural causes, unlawful killing, and an open verdict (where the death is suspicious but the jury is unable to arrive at one of the other verdicts).

While the family of the deceased may of course attend, they are not legally bound to do so. Equally, they are entitled to avail of the services of a solicitor to represent their interests. Though jury service is obligatory once a person is summoned, an anomaly exists whereby attendance by any other person is not. A coroner can direct the attendance of any person at an inquest, but failure to attend only carries a nominal fine. As a result we regularly see situations where the last person to have been with a murder victim, particularly in the so-called gangland murders, is summoned to attend the inquest and refuses point-blank, though it is well known that they possess vital information.

Where a death is the subject of a continuing Garda investigation a coroner may open an inquest. The Gardaí may then apply for an adjournment pending the outcome of the investigation. Where a person has been charged and is before the courts it is important that an inquest not precede the trial, as it might influence the outcome.

——

Between 6 March 1997 and the mid-winter of 2002, a period of five-and-a-half years, a total of twenty adjournments had been granted in the cases of Sylvia Sheils and Mary Callinan. Understandably, this caused a lot of upset to Sylvia's family, who regularly attended at the adjourned inquests in the hope of finding out exactly what had happened to their sister. They firmly believed that an inquest would be their only hope of doing so.

The Supreme Court ruling of 1999 would strengthen their hand in this matter. The delay also caused widespread mistrust among the public and the media, who alleged that gardaí were engaged in a cover-up and wanted to avoid the information getting into the public domain. Considering the deafening silence from the Garda authorities that greeted any mention of this case, the reason for this mistrust was understandable. As investigators we were all too aware of the pitfalls that lay before us if some of the evidence we possessed was presented at an open inquest. We nevertheless had to acknowledge the right of the family to know what had happened to their sister.

In October 2002 the Dublin City Coroner, in response to the appeals from Sylvia's family, put the Garda authorities on notice that he had decided to hold an inquest into the deaths. The Commissioner appointed Superintendent Derek Byrne, Detective-Inspector John McMahon and myself to formally present the required evidence at the hearing. We would be represented by a barrister, whose function it would be to ensure that only the relevant evidence would be presented so as to avoid any problems in the future should the Nash case go to trial.

The Dublin City Coroner was, and is, Dr Brian Farrell, who is widely regarded as one of the leading experts in his field. He also has a reputation as a fair, reasonable and humane advocate whose treatment of the families and friends of the deceased is above reproach. In all the years I have attended his court I never once saw him fail to offer his sincere sympathy and condolences to the families who had to sit there as all the gory details of their loved one's death were aired in public.

Before the opening of the inquest proper, scheduled for 23 October, Dr Farrell ordered that Mark Nash be brought to court to give evidence, arguing that Nash, by his own admission, put himself at the scene of the crime and was therefore in effect the last person to see either of the victims alive.

This was a development that we had long foreseen. With the untimely death of Dean Lyons, Nash was the only person who claimed to possess the necessary information. In our opinion this was a ruling that it was incumbent on the coroner to make. We eagerly awaited seeing Nash either agree to or deny his involvement in a public forum. Also, given that he was now saying he had been coerced into making the admissions in the first place, it would give us a great opportunity to cross-examine him.

However, counsel for Nash objected vociferously to his attending the inquest and giving evidence. They held that his appearance could be extremely prejudicial to him, as it would only further fuel the widely held belief that he was the Grangegorman murderer. Dr Farrell decided not to issue an order compelling Nash to attend until he received further legal advice.

On Thursday 14 November, addressing a packed courtroom, Dr Farrell stated that, given the deficiencies in the existing law governing inquests, and despite his judicial role, he could not compel Nash to attend and give evidence. The inquest would therefore go ahead without the attendance of the main witness. Dr Farrell said he had considered taking a case to the Supreme Court on the issue but had found very little case law to support any such application. It is worth noting that in the ten years since Dr Farrell made this comment few if any changes have been made in this law.

The jury consisted of five men and three women drawn at random from among employees of local businesses and government offices. As they sat through the harrowing details of the injuries inflicted on the two victims, the effect on them was immediately apparent. Several times during the evidence from Prof. Harbison and the other experts who had attended at the scene of the murders Dr Farrell allowed them to take short breaks to give them, and the families and friends of the victims, some respite. One could only imagine what their feelings were on hearing the full extent of the injuries that had been inflicted. The jury would eventually deliver a verdict of death by misadventure.

One interesting nugget of information that emerged from the inquest came from Ann Mernagh's evidence. She told the coroner that before going to bed on that fateful night she had taken two sleeping tablets, as she was afraid that she might not be able to sleep. This was something she had never told us before, and accounted for her having slept through the attacks on her friends and for their assailant coming into her room and standing over her as she lay sleeping. On reflection, it seemed that those same two sleeping tablets may even have saved her life.

Chapter 29 ~

EXTERNAL REVIEWS

Given the notoriety that this case attracted and the ramifications that the charging of the wrong person with two murders could have, both within the Garda Síochána and within society as a whole, a number of inquiries, in addition to the probative inquiry by Assistant Commissioner Jim McHugh, were held into the matter.

In late 2001 a working group was set up within the Garda Síochána to set guidelines and standards for dealing with people perceived to have psychological vulnerabilities. It was also given the task of examining how people with known drug addiction problems were dealt with and to make recommendations in relation to their treatment. In a report to the Garda authorities in March 2002 the working group recommended that gardaí at all levels should be trained in the recognition of vulnerable persons. This was a recommendation that made perfect sense to all of us, given that there was no point in training gardaí in how to deal with vulnerable people if they did not first recognise them to be such. It also recommended certain safeguards to be used in dealing with such people. It was hoped that the adoption of such standards would prevent any recurrence of the events of the Dean Lyons case.

Following the apology given by the Gardaí to the Lyons family in 2005, the Government appointed Shane Murphy SC to examine all the relevant papers in the matter. Mr Murphy was an experienced practitioner and regularly appeared in serious cases before the courts. On more than one occasion he had successfully prosecuted cases in which I had a direct involvement, and one could not but be impressed by his thoroughness and professionalism. He was considered to be equally adept at prosecuting and defending. In time he would be appointed a member of the Criminal Law Codification Advisory Committee.

Mr Murphy's remit was to examine all the documents connected with the investigation and, while so doing, (1) to identify a means of establishing how Dean Lyons came to make his false confessions and (2) to make recommendations that could be used to ensure that such statements would never be made again.

His review began on 27 June 2005. He spent several days in the Bridewell, obtaining and examining all the available documents. In spite of the huge volume of work that faced him he had completed this mammoth task by the end of July and made his report to the Government. In it he recommended the establishment of a commission of investigation that would address the following questions:

1.   How did Dean Lyons come to make a false confession, and why did he persist in making admissions of guilt even after being charged?
2.   Was the Director of Public Prosecutions fully informed of all the available information on 27 July 1997?
3.   Did gardaí receive proper training that would ensure that there would not be a recurrence?
4.   What resources were required to allow gardaí to conduct an assessment of fitness to be interviewed for persons in custody?

On 30 November 2005 Dáil Éireann adopted a resolution providing for the establishment of a commission of investigation. The motion would be passed by Seanad Éireann the following day.

The news of this development filtered back to the Bridewell Station. At that stage only Garda Joe O'Connor and myself were left from the original team and still attached there. It amazed me to realise how little some of my present colleagues knew about the case, given that I had lived with it for more than eight years. A lot of them had not even by then been in the Gardaí when the murders were committed. By now I had been appointed detective-sergeant in charge at the Bridewell, Sergeant Matt Mulhall was retired (or, as someone said to me, supposed to be retired), Detective-Garda Dominic Cox had transferred to Mountjoy Station, and Detective-Sergeant Robbie McNulty had gone to Store Street.

The Government formally established the commission of investigation on 7 February 2006 under the Commissions of Investigation Act (2004). This act was designed specifically for the purpose of ensuring that any reviews or inquiries established under its jurisdiction would not turn into one of those long-drawn-out and expensive inquiries. George Birmingham SC, one of the most respected members of the legal profession, with an unsurpassed knowledge of the criminal law, was appointed sole member of the commission. The terms of reference of the commission would be clearly defined, and it would be required to report back to the Government within six months.

The first job of the commission was to obtain all the relevant material. It was no surprise that I was again, as with the McHugh Inquiry, directed to fully co-operate with the commission in relation to all documents and assistance it sought. At this time Superintendent Malachy Mulligan was in charge of the Bridewell Station. Malachy, for many years a detective-inspector in charge of the National Drug Squad, was a detectives' detective. He was no stranger to serious investigations and well knew the commitment that this appointment would take. He afforded me every facility and assistance in my new task.

The task of the commission was to assess

(1)   the circumstances surrounding the making of a confession by Dean Lyons (deceased) about the deaths of Ms Mary Callinan and Ms Sylvia Sheils;

(2)   the adequacy of the Garda assessment of the reliability of Mr Lyons's confession, both before and after he was charged with murder;

(3)   the adequacy of the information provided by the Garda Síochána on the morning of 27 July 1997 to the Director of Public Prosecutions and in particular whether any additional information should have been provided at that time.

On reading these grounds I thought that here, at last, was our opportunity for total vindication. The inclusion of the two terms of reference that referred to the assessment of the reliability of Dean's confessions and the adequacy of the information provided to the DPP meant that someone, somewhere, believed that we had, as we claimed all along, expressed our doubts about them.

The commission had Michael O'Higgins sc and Helen Boyle to act as its counsel. For the Garda side Detective-Superintendent Joe McHugh of the Garda Liaison and Protection Section would act as chief liaison officer.

Both formal and informal meetings were held over the coming months with members of Dean's family and with his friends and associates. His former schools were visited and his teachers interviewed. Reports prepared on Dean down through the years were made freely available. The crime scene and other places, which included certain areas in the Bridewell Garda Station, were physically inspected. Advertisements were placed in the newspapers inviting people with information about the case to come forward.

From their reading of the various reports and statements that we had taken during our investigation the commission selected and interviewed those it believed might have something to offer. All gardaí who had had any dealings with Dean were required to give evidence on oath. Each witness was cross-examined on the evidence they gave by counsel and by Mr Birmingham himself. We were entitled to have a solicitor present to represent us when giving our evidence. If it turned out that a subsequent witness gave contradictory evidence, we had the right to be recalled to answer it.

At the conclusion of the commission's work Mr Birmingham recommended to the Government that all the legal expenses incurred by Dean's family and friends should be paid for by the exchequer. He equally recommended that the legal expenses of the twelve middle-ranking gardaí who had given evidence to him should be paid by the Government. These included myself, Dominic Cox, Joe O'Connor, Billy Mullis and Dave Lynch—that is, all the gardaí who had been involved in the interviewing of Dean—and also Matt Mulhall.

It should be noted here that the combined legal costs incurred by the twelve Garda witnesses amounted to the princely sum of £76,000— about €90,000. When one compares this with the recently published legal costs in some of the other commissions and tribunals set up in recent years by the state it has to be acknowledged that the Birmingham Commission was good value for money!

When addressing the first term of reference in his report to the Government, Mr Birmingham described Dean Lyons variously as an 'exceptionally vulnerable interviewee' and a 'mildly mentally handicapped youth' with a 'huge drug dependency' and a 'history of attention seeking.' However, he admitted to having certain reservations about Dean's claim that he believed he would be released were he to admit to the murders. He likewise did not fully accept that Dean, at the time he made some of the admissions, was 'craving drugs.' After watching the video recording of Dean's first admissions when in custody the commission described Dean as being 'relaxed and at ease.' The comprehensive admissions made by Dean had been made in fact after he had taken the methadone prescribed by the visiting doctor. This would have alleviated any withdrawal stresses he may have been feeling. And, the commission pointed out, Dean continued to make further admissions even after being charged.

Mr Birmingham suggested that, because of his drug addiction, Dean was going through a 'confused and erratic mental process.' This tended to suggest that it was his desire for attention that had led him to make his confessions. He may even have begun to believe that he had been involved in the murders. Associates of Dean had stated in their evidence that he was finding life on the outside difficult, and he may actually have wanted to go to prison.

Therefore, according to Mr Birmingham, the question that remained to be addressed was how Dean had acquired all the knowledge of the murders that he appeared to have. He was satisfied that there was no evidence or suggestion that he had been abused or ill-treated by gardaí at any stage, and all requests made by him were fully complied with.

The commission and its advisers had viewed the videotaped interview in its entirety. Dean, in the recording, appears to be adept at acquiring information and details from the questions that were being put to him. In the subsequent written admissions it became clear that gardaí had actually corrected Dean in relation to the precise places where the assaults had taken place. In this manner, through being asked leading questions, he had been able to pick up certain details. Mr Birmingham described this communication to Dean as 'inadvertent'. He added that had the gardaí deliberately supplied information to Dean, in his opinion Detective-Garda Cox would never have expressed any reservations. When talking to Dr McKenna, Detective-Garda Cox had again expressed his concerns but equally had made reference to the knowledge of the crime that Dean appeared to possess.

Mr Birmingham criticised the failure of the Gardaí to keep comprehensive written records of those interviews that had not been electronically recorded. They had accepted that questions that might have provided information could have been put to Dean. This, in the opinion of the commission, might not have been an 'intentional wrongdoing' but was nevertheless regrettable and 'could have been viewed as a miscarriage of justice' had Dean stood trial solely on the strength of the admissions.

According to Mr Birmingham, the various comments about the admissions made by Dean led to one important question, which quite simply was, Had he stood trial, solely on the strength of these admissions, would he have been convicted? Mr Birmingham described himself as being 'absolutely convinced' that any such trial would have been 'doomed to fail.' The vagueness and inaccuracies of the videotaped admissions would have been contrasted with the detail contained in the written interviews. For example, in the taped interview Dean is unable to get the sequence of the murders right, but in the written interview he can be seen to be able to recall even that there had been white clips on the blades of the knife. He expressed the opinion that had Prof. Gudjónsson given evidence at a trial the judge would almost certainly not have permitted the admissions even to be given in evidence.

Mr Birmingham then addressed the issue of the Garda assessment of the admissions. He described himself as not being able to sense that the persons in positions of authority in the investigation had subjected the admissions to critical analysis. While on the one hand it appeared that the admissions were being investigated, equally it appeared to him that they had been accepted at face value.

Before the DPP was consulted that Sunday morning the investigators had attempted to corroborate three points that, in the commission's opinion, were important. These were:

(1) to find the prostitute whom Dean had mentioned;
(2) to recover the bloodstained gloves;
(3) to find the burnt clothing in the derelict building.

Despite intensive inquiries and investigations it had not been possible to prove any of these points. This meant that at the time the

DPP was consulted there was no corroboration available for any of these points.

The Gardaí, in Mr Birmingham's opinion, would appear to have been 'lulled into a false sense of security' by the circumstances of the admissions. To him it appeared that they were concentrating on substantiating the admissions, as opposed to questioning their reliability.

The electronically recorded interviews proved that the admissions had been free and voluntary. In this regard the separate admissions made by Dean to both his parents were also significant. Mr Birmingham suggested that the 'false sense of security' held by the Gardaí was understandable. It would have appeared unlikely, he added, that Dean would make the admissions to his parents if he had not in fact committed the crimes. Detective-Sergeant Robbie McNulty, in his evidence to the commission, described the admissions made to Dean's parents as 'the most significant moment of the entire day.'

In addition, it appeared to Mr Birmingham from the evidence given to him that some of the management team were influenced by the way in which Dean seemed to fit the profile that had been supplied to the Gardaí. One of the officers had in fact described this fit to him as 'significant'.

According to Mr Birmingham, in the period after Dean was charged there had been diligent and determined efforts to corroborate or support his statements. The statements had been dissected, with every admission extracted and every effort made to confirm them. A total of 160 'actions' had been activated by the staff in the incident room, some of which would prove to be very demanding and time-consuming. Huge resources had been channelled into tracing all Dean's friends and associates. However, in his opinion there appeared to have been no assessment of the significance of the admissions that had been made and disproved. An example of this was that when the woman that Dean had alleged was carrying his child was interviewed she vehemently denied having had any relationship whatsoever with him.

It appeared that when the investigation team learnt that Dean had been lying about having an affair, rather than this lie leading to their questioning the reliability of his admissions they actually drew comfort from it. To some of them this absence of an affair would appear to have been viewed as having brought him even nearer to fitting the profile, which suggested that our culprit would probably be socially isolated and sexually inexperienced. In fact, he said, the lie should have raised serious doubts about the reliability of any of the admissions.

Despite strenuous further efforts, the bloody gloves Dean claimed to have given to his friend in the hostel to mind for him had not been found. When the area in the derelict house where he claimed to have burned his clothing was searched it did not yield any evidence whatsoever. The prostitute he alleged he had met after the murders had never been found. A young woman of the same name had been found living near his home. She, however, had never engaged in prostitution and had certainly not been in the Benburb Street area on the night of the murders.

Mr Birmingham also found that a continuous assessment of Dean's admissions had not been maintained. Normally in such cases there would have been an initial assessment when the prisoner is charged, with the next assessment taking place when the report is being submitted to the law officers. In this case, however, where indications of unease or doubt about the strength of the case had been made there was an obligation to carry out continuous assessment. Mr Birmingham accepted that indications of unease or doubt had been made.

The report stated that even at the stage when no corroboration had been established and another person who was making admissions to the same murder had emerged, the leadership of the inquiry had continued to believe that Dean Lyons was the culprit. This mentality was evident in the reports that they had submitted to their own Garda authorities and to the law officers. The fact that they were still recommending that the charges against Dean Lyons should be proceeded with was 'suggestive of a fixed view having being formed and minds that were not open to the significance of what was emerging.' This was at a time when the failure to corroborate Dean's admissions meant that the major element of the case was collapsing.

Mr Birmingham then addressed the final issue for consideration, namely the adequacy of the information provided to the law officers. It was established that contact had been made by telephone with Niall Lombard of the DPP's office at about 9 a.m. on the Sunday morning at his home. Though no contemporaneous notes of the call had been maintained, Mr Birmingham was satisfied that there had been a 'reasonably full and balanced presentation' of the evidence given by Detective-Superintendent Gordon, who had been accompanied by Detective Chief Superintendent Camon. This included the fact that certain of the admissions had not then been corroborated. Mr Birmingham stressed that there was no evidence to support any suggestion that either of the two senior officers attempted to deceive Mr Lombard. For his part, Mr Lombard would say that he did not feel that any attempt was made to pressure him into giving his consent to charging Dean Lyons.

The desire of the Garda officers to contact the DPP was 'entirely understandable.' Faced with a case of this gravity, with a culprit making repeated admissions, they were at all times conscious of the warning they had been given that the culprit was likely to re-offend. Dean's statement that he had contemplated suicide would, in Mr Birmingham's opinion, have added a further pressure on them. To the leaders of the investigation, who believed they had the right man, their support for the decision to grant permission to charge Dean was an understandable position.

Given this situation, it now fell to Mr Birmingham to consider whether or not the law officers should have been informed that certain members of the investigation team had expressed doubts about the reliability of the admissions. Niall Lombard stated in his evidence to the commission that he could not recall exactly what had been said to him. The main problem with his recollection, he said, was that, given his involvement in the case, he had read a significant number of documents in relation to it. He believed that he may have been made aware of 'certain difficulties', which included Dean having made a mistake in relation to the sequence of the murders.

Detective-Superintendent Gordon told the commission that he had informed Mr Lombard that they had been unable to find the prostitute who had been named, and also that Dean had pointed out the wrong window when he was at the scene.

After receiving the phone call, Mr Lombard had in turn rung the Director of Public Prosecutions, Éamonn Barnes. Mr Barnes said that he had no recollection of having received the call. He added, however, that while his decision might not have been swayed by the failures that Detective-Superintendent Gordon had outlined, nevertheless had he been told that experienced members of the investigation team had doubts about the strength of the case he would have deferred any decision to lay charges.

It is an accepted general rule that before consent is given by the DPP to the laying of certain charges the Gardaí must first submit a written report. However, there are certain exceptions to this rule. These include where (*a*) the amount and quality of the evidence are sufficient to make it appear that the laying of charges is inevitable and (*b*) where the public interest necessitates an immediate decision.

It is normal procedure that in serious cases contact will be made by phone with the representative of the DPP who is on call, and that consent to laying a charge is given where the evidence is substantial. Such consent would not be given by Mr Barnes if he was aware of reservations about the evidence. Mr Birmingham stated in his report that he accepted that had the DPP's office been notified on the morning of 27 July about the existence of reservations, no charges would have been laid against Dean Lyons.

This situation, he stated, then raised the question whether or not the DPP should have been so informed when contacted by the Gardaí. In the normal course of events, he said, it is unlikely that the DPP would have any interest in the opinions of either large numbers or individual members of the Garda Síochána. However, there are cases and occasions when the DPP will be assisted in making their decision by receiving the views of the investigators. One instance of this is when the reliability of the suspect is an issue.

In the case of Dean Lyons, any prosecution would have been almost entirely dependent on his uncorroborated admissions. Given the degree to which, over the course of that Saturday, his admissions had changed, when one of the gardaí who were interviewing him expressed doubts it had to be 'highly significant'. At the very least, if told about this the official in the DPP's office would have wanted to read all the admissions. Mr Birmingham stated that he himself was satisfied that Detective-Garda Dominic Cox's doubts should have been brought to the attention of the DPP's officer. He should also have been furnished with all the statements.

In summation, Mr Birmingham stated: 'One has to conclude that had the office of the DPP been made aware of the fact that there were differences of opinion within the investigation team, then Dean Lyons would not have been charged on 27 July 1997.'

―――

Before the formal publication of the report, all the principal people who had given evidence to the commission were supplied with a copy, as the legislation directs. The last paragraph of the report, which I have quoted in its entirety above, was to me a vindication, after a long, hard struggle, of the stance we had taken in expressing our doubts about the reliability of Dean's admissions. It made all we had gone through in the preceding nine years worth while. I wish to stress that what I felt was not triumphalism or superiority: it was, purely and simply, vindication. Had our expressed concerns only been acknowledged, then, to quote the commission, 'all the consequences that arise from that [the charging of Dean], and this commission of investigation, would never have been established.'

Mr Birmingham held that the misgivings felt by Dominic Cox and expressed by him on two occasions before Dean had been charged were 'not recognised and acted upon by those present, including the senior officers leading the investigation.' He further commented that 'two other significant figures' on the investigation team, the 'Incident Room manager, Detective Garda Alan Bailey, and the Station Collator, Sergeant Matt Mulhall also expressed reservations and expressed them about that time.'

This was an issue that had been totally denied throughout nine long years by the senior officers leading the investigation, and would even be denied to the commission itself. However, the commission described itself as being 'quite satisfied' that concerns had been expressed throughout the night of 26 July.

From a personal viewpoint, I had been anxious to find out what the commission would rule in connection with my interview with Dean on the Sunday morning. I found that Mr Birmingham described it as 'quite unusual' and said in fact that it supported my claim that even when Dave Lynch and myself were going in to interview Dean that Sunday morning we had reservations about his reliability. Remarks by us to the effect that we were not satisfied that Dean was telling us the truth and that it might not have been him who committed the murders would only have been made, he said, if we had doubts.

However, to my amazement, and annoyance, I read in the commission's report that some of the senior officers had described my expressing doubts to Dean as being no more than an 'interview tactic', used to provoke the interviewee into providing further details. In response to this, Mr Birmingham suggested that were this to be the case it had worked, in that Dean had responded angrily and reiterated his involvement in the murders. Mr Birmingham went on, however, to dismiss this suggestion totally. The reality of the situation, he said, was that this remark had been put to Dean at the close of his period of detention, a time when, had he retracted his admissions, the Gardaí would not have been able to make up the lost ground. Equally, he said, any defence counsel would have been delighted to be able to point out to a jury that the investigating gardaí had both openly and in writing expressed doubts about the reliability of Dean's admissions. It would, he said, have caused serious doubts in the minds of the jury.

This support for our stance by a member of the legal profession with the status of George Birmingham made vindication all the sweeter. It is with some disappointment that I have to add that the Garda Síochána, in which I served to the best of my ability for thirty-nine years, has never acknowledged our role in this matter. Certainly the majority of our senior officers and colleagues were fulsome in their praise of our brave stance, but it was never reflected in any official medium.

While the acknowledgement of my role by Mr Birmingham was particularly sweet, given all that had preceded it, one final phone call arising from the report went a long way in helping me to deal with the whole matter. Shortly after the publication of the Birmingham Report I was contacted at the Bridewell by Rourke Sheils, the brother of Sylvia. He congratulated me on my being exonerated by the commission and for my efforts in attempting to bring the killer of his sister to justice.

Chapter 30

THE LEAKING OF THE COMMISSION'S REPORT

On 10 July 2006 the Birmingham Commission, before publication and in accordance with the relevant legislation, gave each of the central witnesses a draft copy of what was to be its report to the Government, together with its conclusions. Each recipient was asked to study the report insofar as it referred to any finding or ruling that was specific to them. If they found any reference that might cause them any personal concern they were to contact the commission without delay. Each recipient was also advised that disclosure of the report or its contents was a criminal offence, punishable by a term of imprisonment of up to five years or a substantial fine, or both. The five-year sentence is important, in that it allows the detention of a suspect for the purpose of interview as part of the investigation.

In total, fifteen members of the Garda Síochána received copies. This included the various senior management personnel on the investigation, all those of us who had dealt, in one form or another with Dean Lyons, and Sergeant Matt Mulhall, because of his role in the incident room.

On the afternoon of 10 August 2006 a colleague rang me at home to tell me that he was sitting in traffic at the rear of Christ Church Cathedral when he spotted one of the newsvendors selling the early edition of the *Evening Herald*. There appeared to be a mention of the Birmingham Report in it and a claim to have exclusive details from that report. I ran across to my local shop and bought a copy. As I stood outside the shop reading the paper I remember thinking that this is surely going to bring a bucketful of trouble down on those of us who had received a copy of the report. Reading on, I quickly realised that the journalist, Mick McCaffrey, was quoting directly from the commission's draft report.

The story on the front page described how senior gardaí had ignored concerns raised about the innocence of Dean Lyons and had not informed the DPP about the doubts being expressed. On pages 2, 3, 4 and 5 the article continued in the same vein. Given that I realised what the outcome of this leak would be, it was small comfort to see myself being named as one of the two gardaí who had expressed our doubts to senior officers. Further revelations would appear in the *Evening Herald* the following day.

The reaction from the Department of Justice was swift. A senior Garda investigator was appointed with a special team to investigate the leak and to identify the source. It was obvious that retribution was going to be fast and all-encompassing. All sorts of motives were attributed from within the force to whoever was the source of the leak. These included suggestions about efforts to sabotage the commission's work and a disgruntled witness to the commission seeking revenge.

The team that was set up to investigate the matter interviewed each of us individually. Our telephone traffic was checked and analysed to establish whether we had had any contact with McCaffrey. For many of us, this was the last straw. We had suffered through internal inquiries, probative inquiries, complaint procedures and, ultimately, a full commission of investigation. We now had to suffer the ignominy of again being investigated by our colleagues. Given that the article preceded the date of publication of the official report by only a few weeks, this intrusion into our lives and careers was both unwelcome and, we felt, unnecessary.

Those of us who throughout had attempted to persuade our superiors that charging Dean Lyons was a mistake really felt aggrieved when, as part of the investigation, we were asked to hand back the copy of the draft report we had been given, for the purpose of having it technically examined. Our problem was that here at last was official recognition that we had acted only in the interests of Dean Lyons and, ultimately, of justice, and we now had to hand it over. We had waited almost ten years for this moment. Matt Mulhall, to his credit, told the officer who asked him to hand over his copy to get a direction in writing for him from George Birmingham first. So far he has not received this notice, nor has he handed over his copy.

The copies of the draft report that were handed over, including my own, were submitted to the Fingerprint Section for testing. Page after page was put into a special oven and, through the use of a chemical called ninhydrin, latent fingermarks were developed. The majority of the developed fingermarks were quickly identified as those of the original recipients. On one copy, however, the one given to Detective-Sergeant Robbie McNulty, Mick McCaffrey's fingerprints were identified. Robbie's phone would also reveal traffic between himself and Mick McCaffrey. At the time of Dean's arrest Robbie was a detective-sergeant attached to the Bridewell Station. He had previously served in the Central Detective Unit for many years and had been involved in a large number of serious investigations.

It should be recalled that Robbie had been with Dominic Cox throughout the taking of the lengthy statement from Dean on the Saturday evening. He would later say that he never doubted the reliability of Dean's admissions but had been distinctly aware that Dominic had grave reservations. He had also given evidence of having heard Dominic voice his concerns. Mr Birmingham had in fact referred to Robbie's evidence as further proof, if this were needed, of Dominic's concern.

Armed with this evidence, the investigation team arrested him on Saturday 21 February 2007 for the purpose of interviewing him about the leak. Mick McCaffrey met the gardaí at Harcourt Terrace Station the same day by appointment and was also arrested. Throughout his period of detention McCaffrey gave the stock answer employed by all journalists at such times and claimed privilege on the source of his information. This defence has come to be accepted by the courts over the years. Journalists employ a strict code in relation to the non-disclosure of details about informants, except when a person's innocence is at stake. It is recognised as a distinct category of privilege.

Robbie freely admitted to having shown McCaffrey his copy of the report. By way of a defence he strongly argued that for the previous nine years he had lived under the shadow cast by Dean's arrest and his being charged for a crime he had not committed. He claimed that at all times he had acted in a fair and humane manner in all his dealings with Dean. The admissions had been made to him, and he had taken them down in writing, as was his duty. In the years since then he had suffered innuendo and rumour that he had been involved in alleged ill-treatment of an innocent man. When he had finally received the report, which clearly and unequivocally showed that neither he nor any of his colleagues had been guilty of any wrongdoing, he felt he had waited long enough. Anxious to get the story out to the public and to clear his name, he had passed the report on.

Both men were released from custody later that day. We all hoped that, now that the source of the leak, together with the motive for doing so, was known, this would be the end of the matter, especially given that in the meantime the report had been published without any alteration. Unfortunately for Robbie, however, the matter did not end there. The law officers decided that he had a case to answer; it was also decided that Mick McCaffrey had not. On 15 October 2007 Robbie was arrested and charged in relation to his disclosure of the report. He appeared in the District Court the same day and was remanded on bail. On 23 November he was sent forward for trial to the Circuit Court.

The case was finally listed for hearing some two years later, on 7 July 2009, twelve years almost to the day from when Dean Lyons had stood in the dock charged with the murder of Mary Callinan. Had Robbie pleaded not guilty now, the prosecutors would have been faced with the daunting decision of having to put George Birmingham, now a High Court judge, into the witness box and to face the possibility of cross-examination. In the event, Robbie pleaded guilty to the offence. His defence counsel, Pádraig Dwyer, claimed in mitigation that he was a man 'obsessed with vindicating his reputation.' His actions during the investigation, he said, had been vindicated, both in the leaked draft and in the final report. However, this plea fell on deaf ears. Robbie was given a prison sentence of twelve months, which was suspended, and fined €5,000. The presiding judge, Judge Hogan, described Robbie's actions as 'a serious breach of his obligations as a garda.' On top of this conviction, Robbie, a 28-year veteran of the Garda Síochána, was summarily dismissed, having been suspended from duty since being charged some two years earlier.

This whole incident was a devastating blow to a career detective and father of a young family. We, his former colleagues, found it very difficult to accept the rationale that Robbie, who had leaked the document to one person, should face such a high price while Mick McCaffrey, who had released the contents to the entire nation, should face no censure. While not for one moment condoning the leaking of the document, I have to say that personally I could fully empathise with the motive for so doing. The legislation under which Robbie was sentenced had been introduced by Michael McDowell, himself a senior barrister, during his tenure as Minister for Justice. During that period it would be alleged that the minister himself had leaked a confidential document to a particular journalist, concerning a bogus application form for a passport made by an associate of the 'Colombia Three'. As far as I am aware, this matter was never investigated, and there certainly was never any censure imposed.

Furthermore, the *Irish Times* in September 2006, within weeks of Mick McCaffrey's article, published an article about a continuing inquiry being conducted by the Mahon Tribunal into financial donations made to the Taoiseach, Bertie Ahern. No censure ever followed that leak, despite the fact that this same tribunal would go on to sit for another six years.

The consensus among many members of the original team was that in many ways we had all suffered more than enough over the preceding years, and that an internal censure by way of demotion or unwanted transfer would have been ample punishment, given all the circumstances. When he was dismissed Robbie had less than twelve months to serve to obtain his full pension.

On that fateful morning in March 1997, as I stood in the front bedroom of 1 Orchard View and tried to come to terms with the reality of what one human being is capable of inflicting on another, little did I think that it would be twelve years before anyone was convicted of any offence in relation to the murders; and it certainly would never have occurred to me that that person would be a colleague also involved in the investigation.

Chapter 31 ~

FURTHER COURT PROCEEDINGS ARISING FROM THE COMMISSION'S REPORT

Mick McCaffrey's articles in the *Evening Herald* appeared over 10 and 11 August 2006. They occupied more than six pages of newsprint, a considerable journalistic feat. The article on 10 August referred by name to all six gardaí who had been involved in the interviewing of Dean Lyons, adding that we had been 'exonerated of any wrongdoing.' The following day's article made reference to two gardaí, Detective-Garda Dominic Cox and Detective-Garda Alan Bailey, having 'expressed doubts to senior Garda Management.'

Although one might question both the wisdom and the legality of publishing the article, it has to be said that, in the minds of anyone outside the job, far from casting any suspicion of wrongdoing on the part of those of us who had interviewed Dean, it absolved us of all suspicion. It even showed that Dominic and myself had tried to stop the whole process before it went any further. To my mind, this was a public vindication of my role.

It is hard to believe then what was to follow. On 20 August 2006, less than two weeks after the articles were published, RTE Radio's Sunday lunchtime programme 'This Week' broadcast an interview with the then leader of the Labour Party, Pat Rabbitte TD. The programme was, as usual, presented by Ray Colgan and Gerald Barry.

The interview was concerned with revelations arising from the inquiry held by Mr Justice Morris into the allegations of wrongdoing by certain members of the Garda Síochána in the Donegal Division. Mr Rabbitte at various times during this interview described the findings of the report as 'shocking' and added that 'it's not just particular behaviour as it relates to Donegal but it is the fear that this is countrywide.' He stated that 'it is a matter of concern that you have this scale of dereliction in normal policing and that it is, as I say, not restricted to Donegal.' He went on to make the comment that 'there's a whole question of culture and standards and discipline.'

By any standards this must surely rank as one of the most sweeping statements ever made by one of our politicians in describing a particular group or organisation. However, this intrepid supporter of fairness, impartiality and justice for all was not finished there. He went on, in a voice filled with mock concern and self-righteous indignation, to state that 'to be framed, for example, for a murder when there was no murder in the first place, I can scarcely think of anything more serious than that—to have a constituent of my own, for example in the case of Dean Lyons, fitted up to confess in great detail to a murder, the details of which could only be known to the actual murderer and to the Garda Síochána, when it was manifest and now established that he didn't commit that murder.'

I have to admit that I did not hear this statement myself, but within moments of it being broadcast my phone was hopping, with colleagues ringing to ask if I had heard it. The following day, Monday, I obtained a recording of the programme. I listened incredulously to the words over and over again. I could not help but think, What exactly do people want? Is it not enough that the commission has found no wrongdoing in our dealings with Dean, and further that I was personally exonerated from any blame in it? From listening to his statement I had no doubt that Mr Rabbitte must have read either the report or the newspaper articles, as he makes a reference to the fact that Dean's innocence has been 'now established.'

I immediately consulted my solicitor, Seán Costello. Seán had been with me throughout the many weeks and months of the various investigations, inquiries and commission and was well aware of the role I had played throughout. I believe that, on a personal level, he realised just how hurtful I found this broadcast. We sent a letter to RTE on 18 October 2006, complaining about the remarks that had been broadcast and asking for an unqualified retraction and apology.

All I wanted was an acknowledgement that I had done nothing wrong. I honestly believe that this was not an unreasonable request. Unfortunately, this would not be forthcoming.

Thus began the usual lengthy and protracted legal battle that can accompany issues of this nature. It quickly became obvious that if I wanted an apology I was left with no option but to take the matter to court. One senior counsel I consulted gave me dire warnings about the dangers of taking the case and 'risking losing my life savings and little pension'—strong words of encouragement indeed.

However, with the support of my wife and family, I decided to pursue it. The case eventually came up for trial on 2 May 2012, some six years after the offensive broadcast and a full fifteen years after the murders of Sylvia Sheils and Mary Callinan. In the meantime Pat Rabbitte had become a Government minister—not any Government minister either but Minister for Communications, in charge of RTE itself. Also during the same week he would be embroiled in serious discussions with the RTE Authority about their standards in broadcasting, arising from the Father Kevin Reynolds libel action against the station.

We spent three days in court waiting to get our case called. On the third day I was asked what it would take to settle the case without it proceeding to trial. I stated that all I had ever wanted was for it to be acknowledged that I personally had done no wrong and furthermore had voiced my objections to Dean Lyons being charged. Such a letter, I was informed, could form the basis of a settlement. A short while later we reached agreement on the main points. I was delighted. It would have taken six years, endless letters between solicitors and an expensive legal action before I could, once again, walk away with my head held high.

Chapter 32 ∽

PROGRESSING THE CASE AGAINST MARK NASH

The decision of the Director of Public Prosecutions not to proceed with charging Mark Nash following the death of Dean Lyons effectually meant that without some startling new evidence Nash would never be held accountable for the murders of Sylvia Sheils and Mary Callinan. Through his legal team, within a couple of years of being convicted of the murders of Catherine and Carl Doyle he began canvassing the Minister for Justice to be repatriated to England to serve out his sentence in an English prison. A reciprocal arrangement exists between Ireland and England whereby a native of one jurisdiction serving a lengthy sentence in the other jurisdiction can apply to transfer to a prison in their own country.

Of course the news of this application was greeted with horror by those of us still involved in the investigation. After all that had happened it must be remembered that we in the Bridewell were left with two unsolved murders on our books. The case file remained open and was regularly updated by myself. The notion that Nash's application might be granted caused us great concern, and we vigorously opposed it, believing, as we did, that if he were to be allowed to transfer he would never stand trial if we ever established any further evidence against him. Although he had attempted to withdraw his admissions, the fact remained that they were considered by the law officers to be significant and of great evidential value. All that was required was some other, independent evidence to back up these admissions and push the case across the line.

We supported our objections on the grounds that Nash remained the principal suspect in the double murders and that our attempts to further link him were continuing. We also referred to the constant improvements in the field of forensic science and in particular to the growing use of DNA evidence and its potential in our case. We still retained all the exhibits collected during the various technical examinations that had been carried out in the case. The applications by Nash continued to be lodged in the Department of Justice, and we continued to voice our opposition to them.

On 3 March 2004 Tony Hickey, who a short time previously had been appointed assistant commissioner in charge of the Dublin Metropolitan Area, convened a meeting at his office of all the parties involved in the Grangegorman murder inquiry. Tony had spent almost all his service in the Detective Branch and had been involved in some of the most important investigations in the country: he had led, for example, the investigations into the murder of Veronica Guerin and the arrest of Malcolm MacArthur for a double murder while MacArthur was hiding out in the home of the then Attorney-General. Tony's reputation as an investigator was without parallel within the force. He was the quintessential detective and was familiar with the various paths that the investigation had taken. Also, given that he was a former detective of D District, including the Bridewell and Mountjoy Stations, he was well aware of the effect that having two unsolved murders would have on the morale of the gardaí there.

The meeting was attended by Malachy Mulligan, then superintendent in charge at the Bridewell, Detective-Inspector John McMahon, the new SIO, and myself, who would continue as IRC. Detective-Superintendent Liam Coen attended as head of the Technical Bureau, while Dr Maureen Smyth and Dr Bríd McBride attended from the Forensic Science Laboratory. Hickey directed that a 'root and branch' appraisal be made of all the items technically examined so far with a view to establishing whether they should be submitted for further testing, given the advances in DNA identification in the intervening seven years. Both the scientists present enthusiastically embraced the task and offered to provide the necessary expertise as it became available. Liam Coen—another former D District man—again offered to provide whatever personnel and facilities were required. I was directed to obtain and to secure all exhibits from whatever areas they were stored in for testing. Once the exhibits were all accounted for and available, testing would begin. Regular meetings were convened to update all of us on the progress of this cold-case scientific review, one of the first such full reviews ever carried out in Ireland.

To ensure the safety of all exhibits, and to maintain a chain of continuity, more than half the secure storage area in the Bridewell Station had been cordoned off a number of years earlier to facilitate the storage of the Grangegorman exhibits. A former cell in the jail section had been fitted out with storage bins and, in addition to the fireproof door, also boasted a set of steel gates. After exhibits from the investigation had been examined over the intervening years they were returned to the station and secured. Gardaí requiring exhibits or evidence from other cases were always accompanied by myself when going in and out of the storage area. There was only one key for the door, and that remained throughout in my possession. When I left the Bridewell on permanent transfer in 2007, after serving there almost continuously since 1972, a successor was appointed to take over the custody of the exhibits.

I sincerely believe that we always knew that at the end of the day something of significance would turn on these exhibits, and their safety and continuity were always considered paramount. How right we would be proved!

The group involved in the scientific review regularly convened informally to assess what progress, if any, was taking place. Nash would continue to make his applications for repatriation, and we would continue to vigorously oppose them.

From the outset of the original investigation Dr Louise McKenna, one of the most experienced of our forensic scientists, had been involved in the examination of the various exhibits. She had been assisted throughout by Dr Fiona Thornton. Both scientists had attended at the murder scene and also at the post-mortem examinations. During these latter examinations Prof. Harbison, in the presence of Dr McKenna, had taken a number of internal and external swabs from both bodies. He also took a total of seven separate blood samples from the body of Sylvia Sheils and six from that of Mary Callinan. All these samples were subsequently handed to Dr McKenna. The blood and body samples were profiled for DNA comparison.

In lay person's terms, a blood profile resembles a bar-code of the kind we see on every item we purchase in shops and supermarkets. Each characteristic in the make-up of the sample is itemised individually. When this profile is compared with a profile created from a suspect, there must be at least thirteen exact matches between the various characteristics before the scientist can say that they have a 'hit'.

Almost daily throughout that summer of 1997 Dr McKenna received blood samples from the various people of interest to the investigation. They would eventually total over two hundred blood samples alone. Given their dedication and commitment, the forensic science team ensured that each such item was carefully screened to establish if any transfer of evidence either to or from the scene were present in them. At times the sheer volume of the work threatened to swamp Dr McKenna and her colleagues.

On 28 July, Dr McKenna received the various body samples taken over the weekend from Dean Lyons at the Bridewell. It was at this point that she had the conversation with Dominic Cox during which he expressed his concerns to her. Blood and saliva taken from Dean were grouped and profiled and then compared, without success, with samples from the crime scene. The clothing that Dean had been wearing, together with items found during the search of the skipper in Grangegorman and from his friend Helen in Haven House, were examined under laboratory conditions, and nothing of evidential value was established.

From 18 August onwards exhibits connected with Mark Nash began arriving at the Forensic Science Laboratory. Given that, by his own admissions, Nash was now considered a suspect in a total of four murders, it was considered imperative that exhibits that might have a bearing solely on the murders of Sylvia and Mary were designated as such and isolated from those connected purely with the murders of Catherine and Carl Doyle.

On 18 August, Detective-Sergeant Dominic Hayes met Dr Fiona Thornton at the laboratory. He handed her four individually sealed packages that he told her he had taken earlier from Mark Nash's flat at 133 Clonliffe Road. The bags were labelled DH1 to DH4. The initials used in such cases are those of the garda who finds an exhibit, and the number ensures that they are treated as separate exhibits. In this manner it is very simple to establish the provenance of each item. The bag labelled DH2 contained a pair of Caterpillar boots, while DH3 contained a black velvet pinstripe jacket.

When Nash was being interviewed by Pat Lynagh and Gerry Dillon at Galway Garda Station on Sunday 17 August he had described, in detail, the clothes he had been wearing when he killed Sylvia and Mary: he said he was wearing black trousers, a white shirt, a black velvet jacket and brogue-type shoes. After the murders he claimed he had discarded all the clothing, with the exception of the black velvet jacket. This jacket, he said, was hanging in the wardrobe of his flat at Clonliffe Road. He had then given his permission to the gardaí to take possession of that jacket, even going so far as to give this permission to them in writing.

The admissions made by Nash were relayed to Dr McKenna, and as a consequence any items connected with him were treated as part of the Grangegorman investigation. On 3 September her colleague Dr Thornton handed her a number of items. These included the bags labelled DH2 and DH3; she added her own exhibit numbers, 113 and 114, to them.

Preliminary testing of the jacket revealed the presence of a tiny bloodstain on the lowest button on the right-hand cuff. This stain was so small that at that time our Forensic Science Laboratory did not have the facilities to carry out any further tests on it. Louise McKenna then carefully removed this button and placed it in a self-seal plastic evidence bag. Not content with this, she then removed the threads that held the button in place and sealed them in a separate bag. This attention to detail by Louise would ultimately lead to Mark Nash standing trial for the murders. The other two buttons on the cuff were also removed and bagged.

On 17 September, Louise handed the bags containing the buttons and threads to Detective-Sergeant Brendan McArdle, who personally brought them to the Cellmark Diagnostic Laboratory at Birmingham, England, for analysis. This laboratory, considered the most advanced in Britain, was used at that time on contract by our Forensic Science Laboratory for all DNA work. Within weeks, however, we would be informed that the amount of blood on the button was too small for them to be able to group it and that it could only produce a partial profile, which was of no evidential value. The items were collected and returned to the Forensic Science Laboratory, where Louise put them into secure storage and where they would be retained. She believed the possibility always existed that, given the advances in DNA analysis, some day she might submit them for further analysis, which could yield further evidence.

As the years passed, our objections to Mark Nash being repatriated to England would continue. For his part, his new legal team began to push for a formal ruling on his application. Finally, they had formal proceedings listed in the High Court for 15 October 2009. This was seen now as make-or-break time. While we could continue to argue that his application should not be acceded to, we equally feared that it would be granted, given our failure to establish any further linking evidence to the murders. It certainly would not be enough for us to go into court and say that in our opinion he should not be let go, because we believed that somewhere there was a vital piece of evidence just waiting to be found.

By now Derek Byrne, who had been on the original McHugh team, had been appointed assistant commissioner in charge of National Support Services. This was an all-encompassing role, given that it included all major crime investigation sections. Derek was also now my direct boss, as I had been appointed sergeant in charge of the Cold Case Unit in 2007, which also came under his command. Throughout the years Derek had always maintained an interest in the Grangegorman case and maintained a hands-on approach in any development in the case.

In May 2009 Derek decided that a full audit of all the exhibits connected with the case should be carried out for the purpose of ensuring that any and all items that were considered to have the potential to yield results should be re-examined. This was to include items that might already have been tested as far as they could, given the limitations of testing at the time they were first done. In this way we would be able to ensure that no stone had been left unturned should the courts decide to grant his application to Mark Nash.

With the co-operation of Dr Maureen Smyth of the Forensic Science Laboratory, this painstaking task was performed by Dr Bríd McBride and Dr Linda Williams. Bríd was also our liaison between the Cold Case Unit and the laboratory and was considered one of our foremost experts on DNA comparison. By now we had developed our own DNA laboratory, and all our work was now being done 'in house'.

———

I realise now that I should have suspected something when, a few weeks into the review, Bríd requested that the velvet jacket, then in storage at the Bridewell, should be returned immediately to the laboratory. However, we had had so many false dawns in this case that the jacket was just handed over without question.

On 1 October 2009, a little over a fortnight before Nash's application was due to be heard by the courts, I received a phone call from Derek Byrne. I was then involved in the cold-case review of an unsolved murder in the west of Ireland. Derek told me to be at the Forensic Science Laboratory at nine o'clock the following morning. When I told him we had a conference organised for that time, he instructed me to cancel it. When I asked what the conference was about I was told that it would be explained to me when I arrived.

I spent that night wondering and worrying what this was all about. It was with some trepidation that I entered the book-lined conference room at the laboratory the following morning. Nicky McGrath, who was now the detective-inspector at the Bridewell, was also there. We exchanged pleasantries and then tried to guess what this was all about. When Derek came into the room he remained tight-lipped and just nodded in greeting. He was followed by Dr Sheila Willis, Dr Maureen Smyth, Dr Bríd McBride and Dr Linda Williams, all of whom looked suitably solemn.

The meeting began, and Bríd McBride announced to us that arising from the audit of the exhibits in the Mark Nash case they had decided to re-examine the button on which Louise McKenna, all those years earlier, had found bloodstaining. In addition, they had also decided to examine the threads that had held the button in place. They had found a full DNA profile on the threads that exactly matched the blood sample taken from Sylvia Sheils. It was at this point, she added, that they had then asked for the velvet jacket to be returned to them. Under laboratory conditions, they had opened the seam in the sleeve of the jacket, and inside, where the button had been, they found a further minute trace of dried blood. When profiled, it was found to be an exact match for Mary Callinan. So, she said, we now have samples linking Mark Nash to the murder of Sylvia Sheils and Mary Callinan.

I could not believe what I had just heard. I sat back in my chair (in the process knocking everything off the table in front of me) and said, 'Thank God, at last!' I looked across the table, and Maureen Smyth was grinning across at me. She said she had been waiting to see the look on my face when I heard this news, and that she certainly had not been disappointed.

It was pointed out to us that only those present at this meeting were aware of this development, and that we were not to discuss it with anyone. Derek ordered that, as a priority, I was to return to the Bridewell and ensure that all documents and exhibits connected with this investigation would be available if required. I was not to discuss with anyone the purpose of my visit, and if asked what I was doing by my friends and former colleagues I was to tell them that it was connected with a totally separate investigation. I was also directed by him to work out of his office over the coming days, in order that we could put a file together for the information of the DPP.

I worked day and night over the next few days with Derek Byrne, preparing a report that, we hoped, we could present to the law officers for their consideration and that would allow them to arrive at the decision that we now had enough evidence to charge Mark Nash.

At 5 p.m. on the evening of 9 October I went with Derek Byrne to the office of the Director of Public Prosecutions. We met the Deputy Director, Barry Donoghue, and presented our case to him. While he said he agreed, in principle, that we now had a case, he would first have to discuss it with the DPP before any final decision could be reached. Unfortunately, as we spoke the DPP was on a flight to Paris, so his conversation with him would have to wait until after he had landed. We returned to Derek's office and spent an anxious few hours waiting for some word back from Barry.

At about 7 p.m. that evening Barry rang Derek and told him that the DPP was now satisfied that we had sufficient evidence to warrant the laying of charges against Mark Nash for the murders of Sylvia Sheils and Mary Callinan. Although never having given up hope of this development, I have to say that as the years went by I had begun to despair of ever seeing it. Here now, after all this time, was the moment we had been waiting for.

That night passed in a flurry of activity. Arrangements were made with the prison authorities to have Mark Nash produced at the District Court the following morning. It was decided that he would not be told until the last moment, to avoid any scene at the prison. The Garda Press Office was informed and agreed to ensure that there was no leak to the morning papers. The superintendent in the Bridewell was asked to ensure that sufficient personnel would be available to police the courts that morning. We were well aware of the interest that the case would, once again, generate. It was further decided that Detective Chief Superintendent Pádraig Kennedy, head of the NBCI, should be the formal arresting officer, given the importance of the case.

There remained two final chores to be performed that night. I first called to the home of Rourke Sheils and told him that a man was due to appear in court the following morning charged with his sister's murder. His one question to me was if it was Mark Nash who was to be charged. When I replied that it was, he said simply, 'Thank God!' I then went to the home of Sarah Jane Doyle's parents in Blanchardstown. In an emotion-filled meeting I told them that the killer of their daughter Catherine would be appearing in court the following morning. Sarah Jane was not at home when I called, but they immediately relayed the news to her.

Shortly after 10 a.m. the following Saturday morning I went with Pádraig Kennedy to the jail section in the Bridewell Station. In an interview room there we met Mark Nash, who was accompanied by two prison officers. Chief Superintendent Kennedy introduced the two of us to Nash, who just sat there and made no reply; nor could I perceive any physical reaction from him. Pádraig then told him that, on the instructions of the Director of Public Prosecutions, he now intended charging him with the murders of Sylvia Sheils and Mary Callinan, and that he would then be brought to court.

I don't know what reaction I expected from Nash on hearing this news. Would he, I wondered, protest his innocence, attempt to escape, or attempt to disrupt the process? He did none of these things, just sat there staring at us. Pádraig read out Bridewell charge sheets 9548999 and 9549004, and in response, after being cautioned, Nash simply replied 'No' to each charge.

We then brought him through the underground tunnel into the District Court. I preceded him as we mounted the stairs from the cells into the courtroom. I could hear the excited babble from the crowds gathered there, many of whom had been on this journey with me from the beginning. I could not help having a feeling of déjà vu, having twice been here with Dean Lyons, the first time to charge him and the second time to withdraw the charges.

Standing in the courtroom watching Mark Nash in the dock and hearing the judge remand him in custody for the Grangegorman murders, I felt a great sense of pride, coupled with regret at the journey it had taken to get here. I thought of Sylvia Sheils and Mary Callinan, who had suffered a death no human being should ever have to endure. Perhaps now, I thought, they could rest easy.

I thought of Dean Lyons, also no longer with us. I thought of all that he and his family had to endure and how proud they must have felt to receive a formal apology from the Gardaí. That same pride, however, was accompanied by sadness, as he was not here himself to accept it.

I thought of my friends and colleagues and what we had endured throughout the same period. I know that indulging in 'If only' or 'What if' is a total waste of time, but I nevertheless felt that at last the burden of this investigation had been lifted from my shoulders.

———

As I left the packed courtroom on that bright October morning I was joined by Matt Mulhall. We spoke briefly, commenting on the length of time we believed it would take to, at last, bring this long-running saga to a finality. Our estimations ranged between six months to a year. We could not have foreseen that this part of our journey had only just begun, and that it would take a further four and a half years to finally close the door on the Grangegorman murders investigation.

Nash's legal team immediately instigated High Court proceedings. An application was made to restrain the Director of Public Prosecutions from proceeding with the charges. Various delays and applications meant that it would be August of 2012 before Mr Justice Moriarty would deliver his judgment on the defence application.

The various grounds upon which the application had been made included adverse publicity, prosecutorial delay, possible prejudice due to the unavailability of certain witnesses (a number of prominent witnesses had died or were medically unfit to give evidence), and systematic failures in the proper preservation of exhibits.

James McGuill, solicitor for Mark Nash, had argued that the media publicity surrounding Nash's alleged involvement in the murders would make it impossible to empanel an unbiased jury.

All of the objections were rejected outright by Mr Justice Moriarty. In his ruling he referred to the crime scene as 'horrific', adding that the victims had received 'multiple injuries' to their upper bodies and genital areas. He also commented on the choice of weapons used by the assailant.

His ruling was immediately appealed to the Supreme Court, which would deliver its judgment in early January 2015. It held with the findings of Mr Justice Moriarty, ruling that despite all legal argument to the contrary there had been no prosecutorial delay in bringing Nash to justice.

This was to be the final stumbling block; the case against Nash could now proceed. In the intervening period following his arrest, Nash's trial date had been set on a number of occasions. Unfortunately, as each date approached the trial had to be adjourned until all legal steps had been completed.

The trial of Mark Nash for the murders of Sylvia Sheils and Mary Callinan began on 12 January 2015 before Judge Carroll Moran at the Central Criminal Court complex at Parkgate Street. Judge Moran is considered to be one of the most experienced trial judges in the state. The prosecution was represented by two senior counsel, Brendan Grehan and Úna Ní Raifeartaigh, while the defence team consisted of Hugh Hartnett and Patrick McGrath. A jury of seven men and five women were sworn in to try the case, but the actual presenting of evidence to the jury did not begin until 19 January.

Almost immediately the trial became bogged down in legal argument. I found myself in the witness box on the very first day being cross-examined about the existence of this very book. I refused to hand over the manuscript to the defence who, for some reason, felt that their defence of Mark Nash would be dealt a fatal blow if they did not receive it. However, the trial judge directed that I comply with their request. This would be the first of four separate visits by me to the witness box.

A team of young detectives from the Bridewell Station were tasked with the day-to-day running of the case, ensuring the availability of exhibits, witnesses and so on. Given that none of them were in the job at the time of the murders, I must pay a special tribute to Detectives Kevin Moran, Stephen Mullins and Colm Kelly on a thoroughly professional and competent job—the future is in safe hands.

Almost four weeks into the trial, over half of which had been spent in legal argument in the absence of the jury, an issue arose that some of us feared might have serious repercussions for the continuation of the trial. During the hearing of 17 February, a jury member requested that he be excused for a day on the following Wednesday. The trial judge innocently asked why the day off was needed, but he could not have anticipated the response. The juror required the day off to complete various aptitude tests connected with his application to join An Garda Síochána.

Given that the credibility of the various Garda witnesses formed a huge part of the defence case, this knowledge presented a dilemma for the trial judge. On the one hand, Judge Moran did not want to give the impression that he believed the juror might be biased towards the Garda witnesses, but he equally realised that to allow this juror to continue to serve might form grounds to appeal against the outcome of the trial.

The judge told the hapless juror that he had to preclude him from service. Whilst all of us gathered there considered it to be the lesser of two evils—the alternative possibly being a retrial—it now meant that we were left with just eleven jurors, given that no arrangement for substitute jurors exists in this jurisdiction in criminal cases. Although all juries are instructed at the outset of their deliberations that they must return a unanimous decision, as the days progress the judge usually tells them that he will accept a majority decision. Unfortunately, there must be at least ten in agreement with the decision, which meant that we could only afford to have one dissenting juror.

After almost 50 days of evidence, argument and counter argument, innuendo, veiled insults and expert evidence, the trial arrived at closing speeches. By that stage the jury had heard from a total of 71 witnesses from the prosecution and just two from the defence, whose evidence was directed at undermining the DNA evidence. Thirty-nine witnesses had given evidence during the course of the various legal arguments held in the absence of the jury.

By tradition, counsel for the prosecution lead the closing speeches process, providing a synopsis of the evidence presented throughout the trial. It then turns to the defence to present their rebuttal evidence and argue that the defendant is innocent. The final phase falls to the trial judge, who will advise the jury on the law in the various issues that have been raised. He will instruct the jury to decide if the accused is guilty beyond all reasonable doubt, and that any doubts they may have about the evidence must be for the benefit of the accused.

At 2:23 p.m. on Thursday 17 April, the jury left the witness box to begin their deliberations with the cautionary admonitions of Judge Moran still ringing in their ears. They would be sent home at 4 p.m. Almost all of Friday would, once again, be spent in various legal argument and the trial would eventually be adjourned until Monday 20 April.

Shortly before 3 p.m. that Monday, the jury returned to the courtroom and asked to be allowed view certain physical exhibits that they had been shown during the course of the trial. Among the exhibits they sought to review was the piece of lino bearing the imprint made in blood found in the front bedroom, together with the pair of Caterpillar boots removed from Nash's home at Clonliffe Road. I viewed this as a positive for the prosecution and felt that the jury were about to find him guilty.

For all of those engaged in the trial process, this waiting around for the jury to deliver a verdict can be a harrowing time. Prior to a jury returning to the court room, word will be filtered down through the jury minder to the court clerk that they were about to return for one reason or another. As a consequence, all the various parties would be in place when a jury re-enters the courtroom.

Less than 30 minutes after the jury had once again retired, bringing with them the various exhibits they had requested, word was passed down that they were about to return and that they had reached a verdict. At that stage they had been deliberating for slightly less than five hours. The foreman of the jury handed the court clerk the verdict sheet. Turning towards the hushed courtroom, he began to read the verdict aloud. They found Mark Nash guilty on both counts of the murders of Sylvia Sheils and Mary Callinan.

I watched Mark Nash as the verdict was delivered and his reaction to the news was minimal. Throughout the entirety of the trial, Nash sat impassively in the dock, never making eye contact with anyone. He maintained notes as the evidence of the various witnesses was being delivered, but otherwise occupied his time by reading a book that bore the prison library stamp. Even as the gruesome injuries inflicted on both the deceased were itemised to the court there was no visible reaction from him. The only time he looked up from his notes and his book was when being spoken to by his defence team in the absence of the jury.

Given that convictions for murder carry a mandatory life sentence, Judge Moran stated that there would be no lengthy sentencing hearing. He adjourned the court for half an hour to permit all parties to prepare their submissions.

When the court returned, the members of the jury heard for the first time about the circumstances surrounding Nash's conviction for the murders of Catherine and Carl Doyle. Great pains had been taken throughout the Grangegorman trial to ensure that the fact that Nash was actually in custody wasn't made obvious. He would always be seated in the courtroom when the jury arrived into court, his prison officer escort seated some distance from him and they never saw him handcuffed. Again he displayed no emotion as he listened to the details of the deaths of Catherine and Carl Doyle. The jury would also hear details of a very serious assault carried out on a young female in England by a 17-year-old Nash.

A victim impact statement was then read out to the court by Suzanne Nolan, a niece of Sylvia Sheils. In an emotionally charged voice, she told us that her family had found Sylvia's death very difficult and that they had waited 18 years for justice. The effects of the murder, she added, 'never goes away' and that for her mother 'there is no joy only sadness and loss'.

Rejecting all the various pleas by Nash's defence team, Judge Moran refused to backdate his sentence and Mark Nash was led away to begin a new life sentence, having already served 17 years for previous murders.

His conviction has made Mark Nash the most prolific serial killer in this state.

In one of those strange little coincidences that life throws at us, the date of his conviction for the murders of Sylvia Sheils and Mary Callinan also marked what would have been Dean Lyons' 42nd birthday.

Sylvia, Mary and Dean can now rest easily. In their cases justice delayed was not justice denied.

Ar dheis Dé go raibh a n-anamacha.

SOME TECHNICAL AND SLANG TERMS

actions (also called 'jobs'): the various inquiries and investigative leads created during the course of an investigation and distributed from the incident room

Adam and Eve's: a drop-in centre catering almost exclusively for drug users at the rear of the Church of the Immaculate Conception (popularly called Adam and Eve's Church), Merchants' Quay, Dublin

Army Hostel: a common name for the emergency sheltered accommodation for homeless people provided by Dublin City Council in a pre-fab building in the grounds of the derelict St Brendan's Hospital, Grangegorman

buckshee: a uniformed garda temporarily involved in detective duties in plain clothes and receiving no extra payment (British military slang, meaning 'free' or 'gratuitous', derived from service in India, from Hindi 'baksheesh,' a gratuity)

Compusketch: a computer sketching program that generates an image of the probable appearance of a person from the descriptions supplied

District Detective Unit (DDU): those gardaí attached to the Detective Branch in a particular Garda district

DNA (deoxyribonucleic acid): the hereditary material in human cells, unique to each person (except for identical twins), making it possible to identify a person through 'genetic fingerprinting'

fingermark: the latent mark of a finger left by a person at the scene of a crime, normally developed using specialist equipment

fingerprint: an inked impression taken from the tips of the fingers, showing the arrangement of ridges and whorls unique to each person and therefore used as a means of identification

Forensic Science Laboratory: a state agency (not part of the Garda Síochána) responsible for the examination of evidence obtained from crime scenes

forensic suit: overalls that completely cover a person investigating a crime scene so as not to accidentally contaminate the scene or the evidence

Garda Complaints Board: an independent board for investigating complaints against gardaí, replaced by the Garda Ombudsman's Office

gear: a term used by drug users for drugs

high: a term used by drug users for the feeling of euphoria after taking drugs

incident room: an office or room used solely by the 'bookman' during the investigation of a serious crime

incident room co-ordinator (IRC): familiarly called the 'bookman', the member of the investigation team responsible for ensuring that all leads are identified and investigated

jobs book: a journal that contains the original copy of each separate action or job, retained in the incident room and continuously referred to

Judges' Rules: rules developed over the years in the English courts, codified and published in 1913, commonly used for regulating the conduct of police investigations and the nature of evidence that can be admitted in trials

locus in quo (Latin, 'the place in which'): a legal term for the place where the cause of an action arose and hence used for the scene at which a crime was committed

methadone: an anti-addictive and painkilling drug used in heroin withdrawal treatment

National Bureau of Criminal Investigation (NBCI): a specialist branch of the Garda Síochána available for assisting in the investigation of serious crime anywhere in the country

scoring: a term used by drug users for buying their drugs

senior investigation officer (SIO): the garda in charge of a particular investigation

shooting up: a term used by drug users for injecting themselves with heroin or other drugs

skipper: a term used by homeless people for their personal sleeping area

Technical Bureau: the branch of the Garda Síochána that supplies fingerprint, photographic, ballistic and other technical expertise at crime scenes

TIE ('trace, implicate, or eliminate'): a term used by gardaí for describing people of interest in an investigation

works: a term used by drug users for a syringe and other drug-taking equipment

BIBLIOGRAPHY

Alison, Laurence, and Eyre, Marie, *Killer in the Shadows: The Monstrous Crimes of Robert Napper*, London: Pennant Books, 2009.

Brittain, Robert P., 'The sadistic murderer,' *Medicine, Science and the Law*, 10 (1970), p. 198–207.

Britton, Paul, *The Jigsaw Man*, London: Corgi, 1998.

Canter, David V., *Mapping Murder: Walking in Killers' Footsteps*, London: Virgin Books, 2003.

Conlon, Gerry, *Proved Innocent: The Story of Gerry Conlon of the Guildford Four*, London: Penguin, 1991.

Courtney, John, *It Was Murder!* Dublin: Blackwater Press, 1996.

Cummins, Barry, *Missing: Missing Without Trace in Ireland*, Dublin: Gill & Macmillan, 2003.

Dowson, Jonathan H., and Grounds, Adrian T., *Personality Disorders: Recognition and Clinical Management*, Cambridge: Cambridge University Press, 1995.

Kassin, Saul M., et al., 'Police-induced confessions: Risk factors and recommendations,' *Law and Human Behavior*, vol. 34 (2010), p. 3–38.

Lunde, Donald T., *Murder and Madness*, San Francisco: San Francisco Book Company, 1976.

Mullin, Chris, *Error of Judgement: The Truth about the Birmingham Bombings*, London: Chatto & Windus, 1986.

Rae, Stephen, *Guilty: Violent Crimes in Ireland*, Dublin: Blackwater Press, 2002.

Report of the Commission of Investigation (Dean Lyons Case), Dublin: Stationery Office [2006].

Wyre, Ray, and Tate, Tim, *The Murder of Childhood*, London: Penguin, 1995.